Robert Mark Wenley

Socrates and Christ

A Study in the Philosophy of Religion

Robert Mark Wenley

Socrates and Christ
A Study in the Philosophy of Religion

ISBN/EAN: 9783337077495

Printed in Europe, USA, Canada, Australia, Japan

Cover: Foto ©ninafisch / pixelio.de

More available books at **www.hansebooks.com**

SOCRATES AND CHRIST

" Subsists no law of Life outside of Life.

. . . .

The Christ himself had been no Lawgiver,
Unless he had given the *life*, too, with the Law."
—*Aurora Leigh.*

" He led him, step by step, through the noble resolve by which Socrates
—at frightful odds, and with all ordinary experience against him—main-
tains the advantage to be derived from truth ; . . . and he showed him
how . . . it was expedient that a nobler than Socrates should die for the
people,—-nobler, that is, in that he did what Socrates failed in doing, and
carried the lowest of the people with him to the ethereal gates."
—*John Inglesant.*

" There is no word of life in Socrates. This little period of life . . . is
an infinite arena, where infinite issues are played out. . . . This truth we
must recognise in Christianity and its belief independent of all theories."
—CARLYLE.

SOCRATES AND CHRIST

A STUDY IN THE PHILOSOPHY OF RELIGION

BY

R. M. WENLEY, M.A.

LECTURER ON MENTAL AND MORAL PHILOSOPHY IN QUEEN MARGARET
COLLEGE, GLASGOW; EXAMINER IN PHILOSOPHY IN
THE UNIVERSITY OF GLASGOW

WILLIAM BLACKWOOD AND SONS
EDINBURGH AND LONDON
MDCCCLXXXIX

1 8

PREFACE.

THIS brief study, covering as it does a wide and pre-eminently important period of human history, is not in any way exhaustive. Of its shortcomings in many directions I am deeply sensible. Throughout, the design has been to group afresh ascertained facts, to exhibit their inter-connection, and to emphasise their essential differences, rather than to bring forward evidence which had been neglected or even unnoted hitherto. An attempt has been made to show that the development of Greek thought and the peculiar character of Judaism necessarily rendered Christ's work different from that of Socrates. While dogmatic theology undoubtedly contains very many elements derived from Greek philosophy, Christianity at its source is in no wise Greek. Philosophy partly prepared the way for it, and originated not a few doctrines which afterwards became incorporated in Christian dogma. This, however, was only a secondary relationship.

It has been my endeavour to eliminate doctrinal considerations as far as possible, and to lay stress on what is inherent in the Christian religion. As a study in the Philosophy of Religion,—which "seeks to ascertain how much of the content of religion may be discovered, proved, or at least confirmed, agreeably to reason,"—the book aims at being constructive and not controversial. No pretence is made to trench upon disputed points of creed.

I am indebted to many sources of information, and I have tried to indicate my main obligations in the notes. It need scarcely be said that without the venerable Zeller's monumental work this study could not have been undertaken. I should like to add that, in their various departments, the books of Drs Jowett, James Drummond, Kuenen, Wellhausen, and Keim, have been of the utmost assistance. But these writers are in no way to be held responsible for the errors into which I may have fallen.

It may be of interest to state that direction was first given to this review by the preparation of an essay to which the Rae-Wilson Medal at Glasgow University was awarded in 1883. But no part of that dissertation has been reproduced here.

R. M. W.

QUEEN MARGARET COLLEGE,
GLASGOW, *May* 1889.

CONTENTS.

SOCRATES AND CHRIST.

CHAPTER I.

INTRODUCTORY—SOCRATES AND CHRIST.

SINCE the time of Bossuet's 'Histoire Universelle,' as Burnouf points out,[1] many have supposed the various forms of religion to be but corruptions of an original revelation. The Platonic doctrine of reminiscence was resuscitated after a fashion, and employed to explain the apparently inexplicable. If the Greek philosopher thought that man's sublimer moments were simply faint memories of a former pure state, the earlier modern investigators of the "science of religion" believed, similarly, that faith and worship were adaptations of a "primordial revelation." On this theory it would not be difficult to form a comparative estimate of any given religious system. For, if at the outset of the inquiry a *deus ex machinâ* be assumed, it is easy to deal with even the most formidable problems. But, unfortun-

---

[1] Cf. La Science des Religions, p. 81.

A

ately, the opinion of Bossuet and those who think with
him is no longer tenable. Religion is progressing towards a pure manifestation rather than looking back
with more or less distorted vision. Had a specific
revelation been planted on this earth at the first, and
left to take its chance, so to speak, then of the "Three
Reverences"[1] the first alone would have been possible.
The fear of the Lord is only the beginning of wisdom,
and reverence for what is above us is only the beginning of religion. "The Second Religion," as Goethe
has it, "founds itself on reverence for what is around
us. . . . The Third Religion is grounded on reverence
for what is beneath us. . . . And this being now attained, the human species cannot retrograde." For,
"out of those three Reverences springs the highest
reverence, reverence for one's self, and those again un-
fold themselves from this; so that man attains the
highest elevation of which he is capable, that of being
justified in reckoning himself the best that God and
Nature have produced: nay, of being able to continue
on this lofty eminence, without being again by self-
conceit and presumption drawn down from it into the
vulgar level."[2] In other words, each one has his own
place in the spiritual order of the world, and his work
cannot be done for him by any other person. His
value is absolute because he is unique. If this
doctrine be true universally, its significance in special
cases is supreme. Those who have given shape to
the ideals of entire nations and ages achieve a fuller
immortality. Sacredness diffuses itself over all who
have toiled amidst difficulty, or suffered for con-

---

[1] Cf. Wilhelm Meister's Wanderjahre, chaps. x., xi.
[2] The translation is Carlyle's.

science' sake, but of some few a double portion remains the peculiar possession.

> " Such souls
> Whose sudden visitations daze the world,
> Vanish like lightning, but they leave behind
> A voice that in the distance far away
> Wakens the slumbering ages."

From this point of view, the old opposition between
the so-called sacred and the secular is not only hurtful
but impossible. The two spheres overlap, or the one
is complementary to the other. The recognition that
everyday existence possesses a depth usually associated
with religion, and that spiritual life has a usefulness
reserved, as some are apt to suppose, for profession or
occupation, is sure to lend added significance to individual effort. When, in some such way, the secular is
transformed by the sacred, when the finer perceptions
are permitted to qualify the grosser continually, and
not at stated times only, then the growing identification of creed with conduct is an undeniable benefit.

Sometimes, however, this higher aspect seems to be
forgotten; and of late years a false direction has on
several occasions been given to the doctrine of spiritual
continuity. It is not impossible to find a reputation
for liberality in questions of faith based on a species
of special pleading. Ingenious parallels between Greek
and barbarian, striking coincidences in the lives of
great teachers, learned disquisitions on Christianity
before Christ, and the like, serve to invest their in-
ventors or authors with a superiority based on their
presumed freedom from dogmatic prejudice. Now it
is possible to be wholly in sympathy with those who
desire to see in all religion a uniform manifestation of

the higher life, and in all sincere searching after God a pathetic confession of finitude that cannot be too tenderly treated, and at the same time to pervert their views by an undue identification of ideas or individuals seemingly alike. The truth that *natura non facit saltus* has, as its reverse side, the fact that nature never stands still. The life of the Greek protomartyr invites compassion, misleading in its completeness, with that of Christ. Yet there is no immediate connection between the two. History and the ascertained course of religious development are arrayed against the parallelism. Nevertheless, some who take their stand upon these very principles—who well know how to use the historical and comparative methods—are prone to forget that a due sense of perspective is the one faculty with which their favourite study is unable to dispense. Wherein do we detract from the sublimity of Socrates' life and death when we say that he only originated, or perhaps only gave new direction to a growth which more than four centuries of half-hidden progress, and the influence of several civilisations, were at length to make perfect in weakness ? There is little essential similarity between Socrates and Christ, for the simple reason that the work which was given them to do has value in that it was different for each.

It need hardly be said that one by no means intends to dispute the many literary and other references to the likeness between Socrates and Christ. When, for example, Justin Martyr claims inspiration for Socrates, and almost classes him as a Christian ;[1] when Shelley calls him "the Jesus Christ of Greece"; when, in the preface to Lamartine's 'La Mort de Socrate,' it

[1] Cf. Apol., ii. 8, 12, 13.

is written, "Il avait combattu toute sa vie cet empire des sens que le Christ venait renverser; sa philosophie était toute religieuse;" when Hugo exclaims—

"Dieu que cherchait Socrate, et que Jésus trouva,"

or cries—

"Oui, c'est un prêtre que Socrate!"—

no one need question the appropriateness of the parallel. Nor, again, is it possible to complain when Professor Mayor[1] and Mr Benn, following Schleiermacher,—who speaks of "the too prosaic Xenophon, and the idealising Plato,"—write that "there is, curiously enough, much the same inner discrepancy between Xenophon's 'Memorabilia' and those Platonic dialogues where Socrates is the principal spokesman, as that which distinguishes the Synoptic from the Johannine Gospels."[2] Rhetorical licence and legitimate illustration lend little aid in the creation of illegitimate identities.

But another and widely different kind of comparison merits attention, even if it do not excite immediate opposition. In the introduction to his large work on 'Le Christianisme et ses Origines,' M. Ernest Havet, writing of the general relation between Greek philosophy and Christianity, makes the following remarkable statement: "J'étudie le Christianisme dans ses origines, non pas seulement dans ses origines immédiates, c'est-à-dire la prédication de celui qu'on nomme le Christ et de ses apôtres, mais dans ses sources premières et plus profondes, celles de l'antiquité hellénique, *dont il est sorti presque tout entier;*"[3] and again, "C'est précisé-

---

[1] Cf. Sketch of Ancient Philosophy, pp. 31, 32.
[2] The Greek Philosophers, A. W. Benn, vol. i. pp. 110, 111.
[3] Vol. I., Introduction, p. v.

ment ce que je me propose d'établir, que le Christianisme est beaucoup plus hellénique *qu'il n'est juif.*"[1]
Further, coming now more particularly to the connection between Socrates and Christ, another author has
committed himself to a somewhat extreme opinion.
" The Christian movement was, in many respects, analogous to the philosophic movement begun with Socrates.
. . . Ideal righteousness, the search for divine perfection, the endeavour to be 'as good and wise as possible,'
these were the true and only means of 'escape,' or salvation contemplated both by Socrates and Jesus. *To
the truths already uttered in the Athenian prison, Christianity added little or nothing*, except a few symbols,
which, though perhaps well calculated for popular
acceptance, are more likely to perplex than to instruct,
and offer the best opportunity for priestly mystifica-
tion."[2]   Comparisons of this sort are doubtless instituted sincerely in the name of scientific inquiry.   Yet,
although they have an element of truth, they are in
many ways misleading.   For, having assumed the fact
of development in religion, their authors proceed to forget its chief characteristic.[3]   In religious as in other
progress, growth is from the less to the greater, from
the half to the whole truth.[4]   Christianity is a historical
religion in the strictest sense only because, as Novalis
said, " the spirit leads an eternal self-demonstration."
It may possibly be profitable to consider some of the
phases of this " self-demonstration " now in question.

---

[1] Vol. I., Introduction, p. vi.   (The italics are mine.)

[2] The Rise and Progress of Christianity, R. W. Mackay, pp. 19, 20.
(The italics are mine.)

[3] Cf. Bruno Bauer's 'Christus und die Cæsaren,' see below, p. 204, n. 2.

[4] I willingly acknowledge the value of M. Havet's work as a study
of Greek monotheism.

At the outset, it must be admitted with F. C. Baur that "the well-known parallel drawn by so many writers between Socrates and Christ . . . is certainly not without justice."[1] Yet, as we hope to see in the sequel, for the very reason that "Christianity closes a movement which arose upon the soil of pagan religion and philosophy, and the seed of which was sown by Socrates," that "each of the principal forms assumed by Greek philosophy during this interval must have been a step in the preparation for Christianity,"[2] the comparison is, in what may fairly be termed essentials, of external interest only. It is easy to show that the life of Socrates, like that of Christ, was remarkable for its consistency. Neither the one nor the other found a kingdom in this world; gain and loss were not meted out to them in terms of drachma or shekel, notwithstanding the mina of silver and the reward of Judas. We know, again, that the personality of each was endowed with a wonderful magnetic charm, a faculty of drawing men to it. Both were inspired, not only in their ability to rise superior to their age, but because they were quite conscious of this power. An unseen spiritual force,—the Dæmon of Socrates, the Father in heaven of Christ,— ruled them alike. Both were faithful unto death that they might in no wise deviate from their obedience to this strange self-consciousness. For this reason, if for none other, " Christians deem it no irreverence to compare " Socrates "with the Founder of their religion." Continuing the parallel, one might further show that the aims of both were not unlike. Socrates continually insisted upon man's ignorance of himself, and pled for

[1] Church History of the First Three Centuries, vol. i. pp. 11, 12.
[2] Ibid., p. 12.

self-knowledge,—for the recognition that his moral nature makes man half divine. Christ came preaching repentance, calling upon men to recognise their own sinfulness, and bidding them render satisfaction by striving to be at one with God as of old.

The methods employed in the furtherance of those aims also present a certain likeness. Mixing with all sorts and conditions of people, both teachers strove, by cross-examination, and by a species of enigmatic exhortation, to impress upon their hearers the illusiveness of this present life. Once more, Socrates before the Dicastery, and Christ before the Sanhedrim, were alike accused of endangering public morals. They came not to send peace on earth, but a sword. Christ openly proclaimed that the good tidings would cause division; Socrates was condemned because the judges considered that his message had separated the children from their fathers. In short, the Socratic method, and the parabolic discourse, both served to reveal a new order of existence. Finally, it might even be allowed that a " Passion " was common to Socrates and to Christ. Be this as it may, there is no question that one so disposed could easily institute a satisfactory comparison between the two " apologies." " Socrates, this time we will let you go, but on one condition, that you cease from carrying on this search, and from philosophy. . . . Athenians, I hold you in the highest regard and love; but I shall obey the God rather than you: and so long as I have life and strength I shall not cease from philosophy, exhorting any one whom I meet after my manner, and setting forth the truth, saying : O my friend, you are a citizen of Athens, a city very great and very famous for wisdom and power of mind; are you not ashamed of caring so much for the making of money, and for reputation and honour? Will you not spend thought or care on wisdom and truth, and the perfecting of your soul? . . . And therefore, Athenians, . . . either acquit me, or do not acquit me; but be sure that I shall never alter my life, not even if I have to die many times."[1] "Jesus answered him, I spake openly to the world; I ever taught in the synagogue, and in the temple, whither the Jews always resort; and in secret have I said nothing. . . . My kingdom is not of this world: if my kingdom were of this world, then would my servants fight, that I should not be delivered to the Jews: but now is my kingdom not from hence. Pilate therefore said unto Him, Art thou a king then? Jesus answered, Thou sayest that I am a king. To this end was I born, and for this cause came I into the world, that I should bear witness unto the truth."[2] Socrates died because he was a philosopher, Christ because He was the founder of a new religion. But, notwithstanding this difference with its wealth of significance, later ages owe the poison-cup and the cross a debt which can never be estimated. The doctrines of the dead were transfigured, their followers touched, and transformed into living epistles. This no other cause could have wrought. Out of death came life. The Athenian prison gave Plato to humanity, Golgotha gifted Paul.

Yet, even allowing all this, the parallel holds of externals rather than of essentials. Although it refers to certain personal traits, it tells nothing of the genesis of character, or of the surroundings in relation to which life came to be what it was. Consider the mutual interaction of individual and environment, com-

---

[1] Plato's Apology, 29, 30.   [2] St John, xviii. 20, 36, 37.

pare the varied conditions out of which Greek philosophy and Christianity respectively grew, and it must become abundantly plain that, saving the external resemblances already noted, there is no more parallelism between Socrates and Christ than between Plato and Paul. Nay, sometimes the undeniable similarity serves only to confuse. The familiar puzzle about the pound of lead and the pound of feathers is, in a sense, more fully solved when wrongly answered. External points of contact for the most part obscure internal differences.

As a rule exceptional standards are applied to great men. Perhaps those whom "the great man condemns to the task of explaining him" have no other convenient means of revenge. But in practice this is so far disadvantageous that two errors often occur. The tendency is either to magnify the hero overmuch or to belittle him unfairly. Hegel and Emerson estimate Plato somewhat differently from De Quincey, to make no mention of the *naïve* utilitarian Bentham.[1] One living writer, again, regards the 'Critique of Pure Reason' as the key to modern philosophy, another rests satisfied when he has reduced it to its lowest terms. Such variations serve to hint that genius is paradoxical in nature. And so it is. The individual is never greater than his age. Yet, if he have any sort of inspiration, he is always greater than his age. His work is wrought out of elements which he finds lying ready to hand; these are given to him. No *man*

---

[1] Cf. Deontology, vol. i. p. 39, where Bentham, with original genius, says: "While Xenophon was writing history, and Euclid giving instructions in geometry, Socrates and Plato were talking nonsense, under pretence of teaching wisdom."

ever created anything out of nothing. But, on the other side, the unity of purpose which pervades all, the faculty that sets all the endless parts in fresh relations to one another and to the whole, those are his own. Genius cannot indeed destroy, but it can build up. What is history but a series of biographies? When "the power of the man and the power of the moment concur,"[1] the present is thereby rendered the sure foundation of the future. Even Mill, with his tinkering "permanent possibilities of sensation," is constrained to put aside his baneful "acuteness," and to admit that "the volitions of exceptional persons . . . may be indispensable links in the chain of causation by which even the general causes produce their effects. . . . Philosophy and religion are abundantly amenable to general causes; yet few will doubt, that had there been no Socrates, no Plato, and no Aristotle, there would have been no philosophy for the next two thousand years, nor in all probability then; and that if there had been no Christ, and no St Paul, there would have been no Christianity."[2] A man cannot rise superior to his environment, except as he is able to fertilise what he receives from it, and thus to fill it with the promise of new life.

Goethe was right when, in reply to Eckermann's suggestion,—that every line of 'Faust' bore marks of a careful study of life and the world,—he said, "Perhaps so; yet, had I not the world already in my soul through anticipation, I should have remained blind with seeing eyes, and all experience and observation would have been dead, unproductive labour."[3]

[1] Essays in Criticism, Matthew Arnold, p. 5.
[2] Logic, vol. ii. pp. 538, 539.   [3] Conversations, p. 70.

He knew there was that within him which no study could give. In like manner, it may be affirmed of every master-spirit, that "the more you take from it the greater it appears." The secret source of its significance is an inalienable property. Nor can Socrates be deprived of this. What is indestructible in him does not pertain to this or that aspect of his life, as others saw it; his relation to the entire movement of Greek thought, and, very specially, the new direction which he gave to the search for self-knowledge, these constitute his own contribution to universal history. In a degree rarely paralleled he was both product and producer. Free, under certain conditions, those very limitations rendered his freedom worth the name.

Attention thus divides itself naturally between the character of Greek life, especially as influencing Socrates, and Socrates' interpretation of that life, with its results.

CHAPTER II.

THE ANTECEDENTS OF SOCRATES.

DESPITE the long age of laborious scholarship, with
all its subtle reconstruction and minute explanation
of the ancient world, Greek thought must ever remain
remote from us. Some, no doubt, like Landor, or
Winckelmann, or Hegel in his early period, are richer
than others in pagan affinities. Still, even for them, a
great gulf is fixed between the Greek and the modern
mind. It is no more possible to set aside completely
the achievements of the Christian centuries than to be
unaffected by the law of gravitation. And, in proportion to this inability, is the past, or any given part
of it, mysterious. "We know little indeed of the ways
our own thoughts take; still less of those of our best
friends. What, then, can we know of the thoughts
of men whom we never saw, who lived centuries before
us? What of the intellectual current which prevailed
when they lived? For each age has its peculiar atmosphere, through which it must be viewed if we are to
understand it clearly. . . . Shakespeare describes
Cæsar as fighting with cannon; of course, we all know
better. But how his battles were carried on no one can

say; for, were his own accounts of them twice as clear and exact as they are, there would still be so much omitted that was familiar to his contemporaries, that we should need the Roman public of his day to interpret Cæsar's words precisely in the sense in which he uses them, to enable us to obtain a distinct picture of his manner of action."[1]

But, on the other hand, there had been no progress in civilisation did not all, unconsciously perhaps, share the legacy of the past. Nor would any knowledge of olden time be possible did not a select mind, once and again, put forth "an infinite and electrical power of combination, bringing together from the four winds, like the angel of the resurrection, what else were dust from dead men's bones, into the unity of breathing life." Greek thought was *sui generis;* as such it has become an integral portion of later culture. Yet, in so far as it can be disentangled from this highly complex growth, it presents certain peculiar qualities which the abundant records of history, art, religion, and social life mirror with tolerable vividness even at so late a day.

Athens during the life of Socrates,—B.C. 469-399,—was the most marvellous microcosm that the world has ever witnessed. In later times whole empires must be laid under contribution to furnish a galaxy of talent at all comparable with that which once graced a single city. Yet even thus, traces of that mysterious oft-repeated writing on the wall,—"Thou art weighed in the balances, and art found wanting,"—were not absent. The Greek religion is not altogether "the religion of the beautiful,"[2] as is frequently supposed. And, even amid

---

[1] Essays, H. Grimm, pp. 132-134.   [2] Hegel.

the glory of the Periclean era, the ideal of the beautiful had experienced several rude shocks.

Greek mythology, rooted as it was in the nature-worship common to the Indo-German peoples,[1] originally possessed few of the elements indispensable to religion. Gradually, however, as anthropomorphism progressed, man's ethical qualities came to be associated more and more intimately with the objects of worship. No doubt, in comparatively early stages, when the animistic phase was ended, and when the new-found humanity of the gods was coalescing with the other accessories of naturalism, the maxim that what is natural is not wonderful acquired surprising importance. The varied peccadilloes of the Pantheon only proved that its members were very near to their devotees. The freedom of a joyous light-hearted existence was characteristic of the gods as of men. The purely pagan sentiment, which finds no place for spirit save in body, never received illustration so perfect as in the days of the heroes before Agamemnon, and in the epic of the Trojan war. Certainly, in one aspect, Hellenic religion is the religion of the beautiful. But just where this is most true is it also least true. The more of the beautiful, the less of religion; the deeper really religious life, the more marked the departure from the artistically conceived deities. Originally it was not an ethical, but an imaginative faith that Phidias and the rest served. "The national games, the religious pageants, the theatrical shows, and the gymnastic exercises of the Greeks were sculpturesque. The conditions of their speculative thought in the first dawn of civilised self-consciousness, when spiritual

[1] Cf. Outlines of the History of Religion, C. P. Tiele, p. 202 *sq.*

energy was still conceived as incarnate only in a
form of flesh, and the soul was inseparable from the
body except by an unfamiliar process of analysis,
harmonised with the art which interprets the mind
in all its movements by the features and the limbs."[1]
It is true, further, that the Greeks ever remained the
children of their own deeds.   For, although Zeus
and Apollo, Athene and Aphrodite, stood at the last
outside of religious life, the æsthetic sense, in answer
to which they were of old embodied in perfect plastic
forms, was not dulled.   The art of the tragedians, and
no less the skill of the Platonic dialogue—witness the
' Apology ' itself—the Aristotelian theory of virtue, nay,
even the far-off "harmony with self" of the later
Roman Stoics, owe dignity and repose to that antique
lore, happy in its innocence of reflection, which found
heaven enough in contemplating the perfection of bodily
grace or strength.

A mythology like the Greek, lacking conspicuously
the internals of religion, and, at the same time, so
intimately connected with human life, must at some
period be either thoroughly modified or cast aside
altogether.   Man's ethical nature is fated to develop
in spite of every obstruction.   The Greeks, as has been
hinted, were not a religious people, in the usual accep-
tation of the term, but their affinity for things moral
amounted to genius.   The strange division between
religion, as delineated say in Homer, and the deeper
tendencies of life, as expressed by the dramatists, by
Xenophanes, and by Socrates, precipitated a crisis disastrous enough for Greece, but of the last importance to
the world at large.   The moment at which the Hellenic

[1] Studies of the Greek Poets (second series), J. A. Symonds, p. 376.

mythology became anthropomorphic was the hour of its strength and weakness alike. For, as Aristotle declares, the Greeks made the gods in their own image. To equal the perfection of this humanised form has been the despair of later artists. Nevertheless, the men who made the gods thus, were as yet unconscious of their own real nature. The holiness of beauty is no sufficient creed for one who has had a glimpse of the beauty of holiness. The individual is not enriched by appearance, but by character. But great poets, artists, and men of action so consecrated this holiness of beauty by their shining words, choice works, and high deeds,[1] that it became an integral portion of the national mind. As civilisation advanced and morality grew more definite, the ancient religion of external form was less and less able to express current ideas of the spiritual. The mythology, which is sometimes taken to be the whole of Hellenic religion, remained; nay, long after literary and philosophical activity had ended, sacrifice and adoration were rendered to the old gods. But it remained stationary. The reflective side of Greek life, disguise it as one may, was the more truly religious. It came into existence beside, and, in a sense, away from, the older belief. Finding no place for an ever-deepening ethical consciousness even in the gratification of a strongly marked æsthetic sympathy, the dramatists and philosophers turned from the material to the spiritual. Æschylus and Sophocles, Socrates and Plato were, in their day, the true representatives of what was essential in Greek religion. It no longer suffices to picture the gods sipping ambrosia on Olympus under the presidency of Zeus, but

---

[1] Cf. Preller, Griech. Myth., vol. i. p. 155.

B

the god is found within,—Socrates knows that he has a
Dæmon.   As everywhere, so in Greece, mythology may
serve the purpose of religion.   But when man begins to
realise that the earth is not his sole possession, he is
done with mythology.   It remains maybe, as it did in
Greece, shrined in " a magnificent ritualistic system,
and a cycle of poetical conceptions,"[1] but it no longer
plays the part of religion.   The glory of Greek art, in
its relation to this mythology, is that it was adequate to
what it expressed.   Yet this very adequacy caused its
office in religion to be fleeting.   Art can no more completely represent Sophocles' Nemesis, Socrates' Dæmon,
Plato's Idea of the Good, or even the Stoic wise man,
than it can sum in picture or *pieta* the agonised " Eloi,
Eloi, lama sabachthani ? "

While the Greek religion thus passed through a perfectly natural development, the coexistence of the early
mythology with the later ethical religion of the poets and
philosophers rendered it peculiarly interesting.   When
Socrates began his exhortations, the inevitable rupture
between old and new had already taken place.   Not, certainly, that the people as a whole had lost touch with
the Homeric gods.   Their attitude towards Æschylus,
Euripides, Anaxagoras, and Socrates, tells another tale.
Yet, in what proved to be of moment to the advance
of civilisation, a transformation had occurred.   The
now full-grown drama opened up the sphere of the
moral consciousness, and gave the first articulate expression to ideas which the plastic arts could not embody.
" Tragedy is better suited than any other kind of poetry
to arouse ethical reflection, to portray the moral consciousness of a people, and to express the highest senti-

[1] The Renaissance, Walter Pater, p. 189.

ments of which an age, or at least individual prominent
spirits in an age, are capable.   Every deeper tragic
plot rests on the conflicting calls of duty and interest." [1]
Man, struggling with himself, could find no sort of
satisfaction in the external representations of deity.
The individual is free, yet he finds himself overcome
by the stress of outer necessity.   Some power, impersonal and changeless, rules men and gods alike.   The
semi-monotheism of Æschylus and Sophocles points
to a supreme being, but a being whose very supremacy
precludes the definite revelation inseparable from personality.   Nemesis is not a subject, but rather a principle everywhere visible yet nowhere accessible.   It is
sublime in both the Kantian senses.   For, while the
imagination can form no definite representation of it,
Greek heroism, in pride of hopelessness, accepts it as a
fact.   The dramatists thus grafted one species of poetry
on to another, as Schlegel remarks.   They rose superior
to the physical godhead of the popular mythology, but
their ideal of deity was largely abstract.   Advance in
ethical life had become a necessity; the direction in
which to seek the commentary on human nature incident
to that advance was not yet clear.   Socrates was the first
to realise this defect, and to indicate how it might be
made good.   Æschylus and Sophocles could no more cast
away the past, than they could add one cubit to their
stature by going beyond their set task.   Even if they
would not, the poetry of ancestral nature-worship held
them ever in its spell.   With them, no less than with
all the Greeks, "beauty was the tongue on the balance
of expression."   It was reserved for Socrates not only

---

[1] Socrates and the Socratic School, Zeller, pp. 4, 5.

to furnish the first intelligent utterance, but also to speak the truth.

Greek philosophy, in its initial period, was a semi-scientific counterpart of that satisfaction with the world which the old mythology evidenced. As a race the Greeks were long preoccupied with things seen and temporal. Eminently at home in their lovely sur-roundings, they found the attraction of visible nature irresistible. Accordingly, the early thinkers concern themselves to discover the origins and properties of matter. They, more than any pre-Christian philoso-phers, warrant the common generalisation that ancient speculation, as contrasted with modern, addresses itself to the problem of being rather than of knowing. No theory of self-consciousness was necessary, for the fact of self-consciousness had been little, if at all, realised. The universe of mind was as yet outside the range of philosophical experiment. Man, the thinker, and his immediate knowledge of the objects about which he thinks, were taken for granted. Investigation confined its efforts to the explanation of the material world. The tendency of pre-Socratic speculation is thus entirely in consonance with the character of Hellenic naturalism. Slightly as poetry and science seem to be connected, they were even thus early intimately related. The free-dom from dogmatic restraint which enabled the Greeks to deify all nature, was also the essential condition of the fearless inquiries conducted by the first physicists. "This objectivity was no doubt far more easily attain-able for Greek philosophy than for our own ; thought, having then before it neither a previous scientific de-velopment nor a fixed religious system, could grapple with scientific problems from their very commencement with complete freedom. Such objectivity, furthermore, constitutes not only the strength, but also the weakness of this philosophy; for it is essentially conditional on man's not having yet become mistrustful of his thought, on his being but partially conscious of the subjective activity through which his presentations are formed, and therefore of the share which this activity has in their content; in a word, on his not having arrived at self-criticism." [1] . . . "The intuition of nature is thus the starting-point of the earliest philosophy, and even when immaterial principles are admitted, it is evident that they have been attained through reflection on the data furnished by the senses, not through observation of spiritual life." [2] Moreover, this philosophy was a genuine outgrowth of the mind of a specially gifted people, as the circumstances of its wide diffusion yet invariable Hellenic origin prove. Thales, Pythagoras, Parmenides, Zeno, Empedocles, and Anaxagoras were all, with one doubtful exception,[3] sprung from the Greek stock scattered among the widespread colonies of Hellas. The subtle intensiveness of philosophy, due to the contact of mind with mind, may account to some extent for the gathering of later and more subjective thinkers into one city. This question, though full of interest, is beyond our present inquiry. Whatever be the explanation, certain it is that, to the fifth century B.C., Greek philosophy, from Agrigentum in the West to Colophon in the East, confined itself to theories respecting the constitution of the physical world. The Ionians, the Pythagoreans, and the Eleatics alike in-

---

[1] Pre-Socratic Philosophy, Zeller, vol. i. pp. 145, 146.

[2] Ibid., pp. 197, 198.

[3] Thales was said to have been of Phœnician descent.

vestigate the origin of material things.   For Thales
"water is the one original substance;" Pythagoras
systematises the universe by means of number; Xenophanes, in a tone of polemic, and Parmenides, with
some regard for detail, formulate a doctrine not without
analogy to the theory of the conservation of energy.
For, according to the Eleatics, change is an illusion,
the permanent sum-total of Being is the only reality.
These, then, were all so-called "positive" thinkers in
the strictest sense of the term.

But, as Greek religion had undergone a change ere
the time of Socrates, so the philosophy of external
phenomena began to present new features.   Pythagoreanism was less concrete then the Ionian physics,
and the Eleatic metaphysic was in turn more abstract
than either.   Finally, with the appearance of Heracleitus
reflection entered upon a new stage.   The customary
classification of Parmenides with Xenophanes and the
Eleatics is so far unfortunate that it obscures or leaves
out of account his relation to Heracleitus.   Whether
these thinkers were thoroughly conscious of the antagonism or not, there can be no question that "the
clearly marked opposition between the Ionic and the
Eleatic views of nature, as shown in Heracleitus and
Parmenides, had a powerful influence on the subsequent
course of philosophy."[1]   Previously the schools had
been content to assume the facts of Being and change;
but the conflict between Parmenides and Heracleitus
rendered the explanation of these terms necessary.
Thus philosophy was diverted from the investigation of
external phenomena to the discussion of universal prin-

[1] Ancient Philosophy, J. B. Mayor, p. 17.

ciples.[1] In this respect the antagonism brought about
a twofold result. On the one hand, both thinkers
denied the ordinary conception of phenomena, yet the
theories substituted by them were mutually contradic-
tory. And when doctors differ, who shall decide? In
this difficulty the Sophists appeared teaching philosophical despair, and advising every individual to consider
his own prejudices paramount. On the other hand, the
opposition between the doctrines of changeless Being
and of ever-changing Becoming caused later philosophy
to reconsider these concepts. This reconsideration was
the work of a school which still flourished in the latest
days of the pre-Christian world. While the physicists
of the fifth century thus altered the direction of Greek
speculation, it cannot be said that their influence was
directly formative of Socrates. At the same time, the
two radical changes which overtook philosophy before
the outbreak of the Peloponnesian war were largely due
to them. Parmenides and Heracleitus, in short, determined Socrates through the medium of Anaxagoras and
the Sophists.

It may therefore be maintained that, just as the
dramatists denote the advance in religious and ethical
ideas, of which Socrates was an heir, so Anaxagoras
and the Sophists are the representatives of speculative
progress. The Atomists, who in a manner attempted
to unify the contradictions of Parmenides and Heracleitus, formulated a mechanical theory of the universe.
Like Parmenides they held the unchangeableness of
Being, like Heracleitus they taught the plurality of
phenomena. They were thus at a disadvantage in
their explanation of the world. For, on the supposi-

[1] Cf. Pre-Socratic Philosophy, Zeller, p. 19 *sq.*

tion that atoms,—the original Being of Parmenides,—
were fixed quantities alike as single units and as members of a universe, the whole question of phenomenal
difference presented much difficulty.   Plainly, one
course alone was possible for the solution of this
problem.   The world could only be regarded as a
series of conjoined particles, united so externally that
the interconnection produced no alteration in their
ultimate nature.   This, the last of the purely physical
philosophies, was so far identical with the earliest, that
troubles occasioned by the separation between subjective and objective were unknown to it.   Knowledge
seemed to be taken as a fact, its processes and their
conditions were still left unconsidered.

The first great change which pointed directly to the
Socratic philosophy was effected by Anaxagoras.   In
some respects his importance for the history of Greek
thought is apt to be underestimated.   No doubt he may
be classed with the other physicists, yet his distinctive
contribution to the progress of philosophy entitles him
to more pointed recognition.   For he was the first to
throw any light upon the absolute difference between
spirit and matter.   The intimate of Pericles and Aspasia,
he also made philosophy the prominent social force
which it afterwards remained.   Moreover, if there be
solid truth in the remark of Xenophon,[1]—that Socrates sat at the feet of Aspasia as a learner in love,—
it may be inferred that the discussions at the house
of Pericles, in which Anaxagoras figured prominently,[2]

[1] Cf. Memorabilia, ii. 6, 36.

[2] It seems possible that Socrates never met Anaxagoras, but this
does not affect the fact that such discussions did take place, as
Aristophanes very well knew.   Cf. History of Philosophy, Ueberweg,
vol. i. p. 87.

were among the earliest illustrations of the Socratic method. Anaxagoras is to be linked with Socrates in that his "reflection was directed to subjective processes and phenomena." [1] Like the Atomists, Anaxagoras held that there were a number of original substances. But these differed from the atoms because they might be divided, they were not simple. Various qualities were supposed to pertain to each of the combining parts, and the character of the resultant whole was determined by the qualities of the predominating elements. Thus, whilst denying real qualitative change, Anaxagoras leaves room for apparent variation. This is the purely physical side of his philosophy, and it results in a chaos. For, obviously, a world composed of substances which are in turn compounded of fortuitous elements, is a mere aggregate in which no definite differentiation can be manifested. Therefore Reason, which is one in itself, and has no admixture of natures, must be the power which reduces this chaos to order. "All things were in chaos, Reason came and arranged them." Spirit is thus at last distinguished from matter, and the dualism, of which all later philosophy is the history, receives half-conscious recognition. Anaxagoras is the true forerunner of Socrates because he introduced a new object of thought. Nature is no longer alone, but is controlled by a higher power, which must also be investigated. This, then, is the first conscious glimpse of that inner spirit which Socrates was to emphasise so strongly. But Anaxagoras, like many reformers, did not appreciate his discovery to the full. His conception of Reason was elementary, and was formulated almost entirely by means of physical analogies. Mind

[1] Cf. Phædo, 97.

is not a presupposition of the world, the two are coeternal. Personality is not among its attributes. Indeed Anaxagoras' conception and use of Reason point rather to a principle of motion than to a spirit which arranges phenomena in rational order. Aristotle's criticism [1] is quite to the point, for mind is only employed because matter avails not. That is to say, it does what mechanism cannot do, but, as far as possible, it is kept down to the mechanical level. Reason is set by itself, and made the cause of motion, but how it performs the characteristic functions of spirit Anaxagoras does not explain.[2] It remained for Socrates to show the nature of knowledge, although the direction in which the explanation was to be sought had been indicated. Like the Nemesis of the dramatists, the Nous of Anaxagoras was something more than the old Greek mythology had thought of,—men were now desirous of seeing beyond the material world to its conditions.

If, then, it may be fairly held that the speculations of Anaxagoras gave direction to Socrates' investigations, the immediate cause of his activity must now be sought.

The philosophy of Socrates was developed in opposition to the teaching of the Sophists. These often maligned men were characteristic products of their age. The success which they achieved, whether merited or not, corresponded to the need which they supplied. Three main circumstances, none of them without influence on Socrates also, may be said to have brought forth Protagoras, Gorgias, and the host of their less known fellows. Two of these have already received

[1] Cf. Metaphysics, i. 3, 4.   [2] Cf. De Animâ, Bk. i. ii., 13, 22.

some attention. First, the break between the old religion and the recent drama had become very marked. If Æschylus and Sophocles went beyond the traditional conception of the gods, they never gave rein to any undue irreverence. But the inevitable trend of "the dialectic of moral relations and duties" could not fail to result in a more pronounced scepticism. Discounting entirely the influence of the Sophists, Euripides was, from the nature of the case, the exponent of defection from the ancient faith in its less pleasing aspects. His attitude in this matter exhibits most clearly the state of the religious atmosphere in which Socrates moved. Secondly, in spite of Anaxagoras' affirmative tendency, he, in common with Parmenides and Heracleitus, had administered a rude shock to the complacency of ordinary opinion. Parmenides had asserted that the customary conviction of the senses with regard to the endless differentiation of phenomena was unjustifiable. Heracleitus, on the contrary, had as confidently declared that the senses deceive themselves when they attribute permanence and stability to material things. And now Anaxagoras denied that the ordinary perceptions of sense were able to furnish any adequate knowledge of the real in phenomenal nature. This universal doubt concerning matters of which doubt is usually thought impossible was, in a way, the starting-point of the Sophistic dialectic. But, in addition to the failing strength of traditional religion, and the growing boldness of philosophical speculation, a third and most important influence was at work. Athens, from being a city among cities, had suddenly become the first power of the civilised world. Like a victorious leader in a momentous struggle, she had reaped a reward out of all proportion to that bestowed on the rank and file who fought with her. Her citizens, as partakers in the new-found dignity, came to regard themselves with peculiar satisfaction. The sovereign people acquired unexpected importance, and those who could sway the democracy by art or by ability were assured of surpassing success in life. Till Socrates taught a more excellent way, it was altogether forgotten that " where rhetorical skill is regarded as paramount, the higher ends of education are apt to be overlooked, for readiness and fluency of speech may proceed out of emptiness, no less than out of fulness, of mind."[1] In response to some such combination of influences the Sophists appeared. Many of them were, no doubt, sincere and able men. But for others, and those were perhaps the majority, it was as certainly true that skill to prove the worse the better reason stood in place of higher wisdom. The delightful contrast between Gorgias' theory and his practice may serve to illustrate their general *morale.* He was able to show metaphysically "that nothing could exist, that what did exist could not be known by us, and that what was known could not be imparted"[2] to any one. Yet we are aware that he amassed wealth, and was held in much repute as a teacher. Surely the apotheosis of eristic—to teach that teaching is impossible! The inevitable result was, that "to expose fallacy or inconsistency was found to be both an easier process, and a more appreciable display of ingenuity, than the discovery and establishment of truth in such a manner as to command assent."[3] Cultivated criticism, secured

[1] Ferrier's Greek Philosophy, p. 188.
[2] Outlines of Greek Philosophy, Zeller, p. 93.
[3] Plato, Grote, vol. i. p. 106 (ed. 1885).

from defeat by a recognised dogmatic appeal to self, took the place of the older positive philosophy. Matter and mind, no less than physics and ethics, were forgotten for the moment amid the parade of a wisdom which recommended itself by a certain ease of attainment. Opinion celebrated its triumph in obliteration of the distinction between right and wrong, or in convenient disregard of the evidence of sense-perception.

Socrates thus appeared at a turning-point in the history of Greek thought. Religion could not be expanded so as to include man's growing ethical consciousness within its purely mythological and naturalistic conceptions. Philosophy, while discrediting the objectivity of truth, had failed to furnish any homogeneous account of the world or of human life. The subordination of the individual to the state had resulted in such splendid achievement, that each citizen now sought his own share of the general good, *plus* as much more as superior education or cunning enabled him to filch. Disregard for customs once venerated, degradation if not despair of philosophy, and belief only in self were not a little characteristic of the Athenians towards the close of the Periclean era. But the crisis was not merely subjective. When Socrates began to teach, it was aggravated by certain objective relationships. After Pericles' death the glory slowly departed from Athens. The exhausting and disastrous course of the Peloponnesian war was but the prelude to a continuous and almost unparalleled decline. Socrates did his best work during the years of this war. While Athens and Lacedæmon were ruining Greece by their bootless rivalry, he was providing his countrymen with a more lasting kingdom than that built up at the expense of Xerxes. The city-state, for which every one had hitherto been spent, was already in process of passing away. Yet the individual, at least so far as concerned his moral and spiritual value, was scarcely discovered. For Socrates the years had reserved the appreciation of this new factor in philosophy and in life. His it was to react on his conditions, to transform them, and so to render them organic factors in the development not only of Greek, but also of all civilisation. He was "an exceptional person" who came to deliver man from an exceptional difficulty, and, as a consequence, the interaction between his personality and the circumstances of the time was unusually intense. To this attention must now be given.

CHAPTER III.

THE MISSION AND PHILOSOPHY OF SOCRATES.

AT the outset it is to be remembered that Socrates is known to us only as an elderly man. The period of his life with which we are directly acquainted does not begin before his forty-fifth year, and the principal records relate to the last decade of his life. In short, the historical Socrates is neither a youth suffering the pangs of *welt-schmerz*, nor a young man striving, like Goetz von Berlichingen, to subdue the world by force. He has cast away the illusions and hopes of early life, and has consciously set himself to realise more serious aims. What, then, was his peculiar work, and how came it to be forced upon him?

Socrates is, in a sense, the first of the Greeks who was not entirely Greek. "The Grecian state," Emerson said, "is the era of the bodily nature, the perfection of the senses—of the spiritual nature unfolded in strict unity with the body."[1] In Socrates this characteristic unconsciousness passed away never to be regained. The personal nature of man, with its implications of intellectual and practical activity, asserted itself. Great

[1] Essay on History.

questions regarding knowledge and conduct were now
for the first time consciously put. Metaphysical difficulties vaguely indicated by Socrates still engage
thinkers, while his ethical problem, with which, as we
shall see, no Greek could be fully acquainted, was to
find solution not in any theory, but in a unique life.

It is a commonplace to say that the atmosphere in
which Socrates found himself was eminently favourable
to the decisive change which he was to inaugurate. The
serious events which marked the struggle for the hege-
mony of Greece could not fail to turn some away from
the barren irreflective scepticism of the Sophists and
the educated class. If knowledge were valueless save
to the individual in possession of it, if religious belief
existed only to draw down insult, and if, after all sacrifices, the greatness of his city were not eternally assured,
what resource had the Athenian but in his own human
nature ? As strong manhood ripened into vigorous age,
Socrates appears to have appreciated more and more
the necessity of his time. It is easy to contrast his
lack of customary philosophical formalism with the
importance assigned to him in the progress of Greek
thought,[1] and to cavil at " his excellent qualities, which,
yet, are not such as fit a man to play a brilliant part in
history." But this has about as much integral bearing on the state of the case as has Heine's typical
comment,—"that Xanthippe's husband should have
become so great a philosopher, is remarkable. Amid
all the scolding, to be able to think ! But he could
not write ; that was impossible." The very fact that
Socrates revealed a theory through the medium of his

[1] Cf. Schleiermacher, The Worth of Socrates as a Philosopher, pp.
129, 141.

common life and conversation is the cause of his re-markable influence. When scepticism is rife, fine words avail little, if unaccompanied by fine works, which prove that the spoken gospel has a real and applicable mean-ing. The merest glance at the 'Memorabilia' brings home an irresistible conviction that Socrates was an "epoch-making" thinker more because he was a living person than because he discovered an abstract principle. No doubt there was such a principle present in his life, yet it appealed to Xenophon, Plato, and the others, not as an abstraction, but as the pervading secret of the moral power which prevailed in the deeds of Socrates the man. Was his admonition to Aristippus,[1] concern-ing the necessity of temperance as a statesman's virtue, a bare dogma founded on some preconceived Greek idea of a ruler? Certainly not. "He disciplined his mind and body by such a course of life," Xenophon tells us,[2] "that he who should adopt a similar one would, if no supernatural influence prevented, live in good spirits and uninterrupted health; nor would he ever be in want of the necessary expenses for it. So frugal was he, that I do not know whether any one could earn so little by the labour of his hands, as not to procure sufficient food to have satisfied Socrates." The difficulty of estimating Socrates' work with any approach to fair-ness, is chiefly occasioned by this intimate connection between doctrine and life. The theory that "virtue is knowledge," for example, loses much significance if divorced from the circumstances in which Socrates himself gave practical illustration to the maxim. The spirit of his interpretation of Circe and the swine is also that in which his life must be viewed. The

---

[1] Cf. Memorabilia, ii. 1, 1-7. [2] Ibid., i. 3, 5.

sorceress did not transform men into swine, but provided opportunities which inevitably issued in acts
of self-brutalisation. Socrates, too, had his opportunities, and his life was the embodiment of the doctrines which he considered suitable to the occasion.
He was, in fact, the first moral philosopher who
understood that intellect and will are but different
revelations of the same spirit. His insistence upon
self-knowledge lends an apparent truth to Hegel's view
of his position in Greek philosophy.[1] But, notwithstanding, Hegel forgets that, even if Socrates were
subjective as regards his theorising about the external
universe, he was also objective because he considered individual life in relation to its social surroundings. In
other words, so far as his really important achievement,
—that is, his ethical work,—was concerned, Socrates
was not more subjective than objective. Contemporary
events, political and social, had filled him with a deep
sense of the grave defect in the conditions of man's
moral wellbeing, and his scheme of regeneration was exemplified in his life. Action based on self-knowledge
formed the remedy he had to offer. His own personality was the medium through which this remedy
found application. The former is subjective, if such
you choose to term it; the latter, surely as essential,
is objective. It concerned others as much as, nay, as
the result proved, far more than, it did Socrates himself.

The mission of Socrates was the natural outgrowth
of the entire past course of Greek thought. It could
not have been other than it was, and without it his
freedom would have proved an empty name. His own
contribution to the burden of history lay in his con-

[1] Cf. Gesch. d. Phil., vol. ii. p. 40 *sq.*

ception of his office, and in the methods which he employed to realise its demands. The various ideas which were dominant in Athens, at the time say of Anaxagoras (434 B.C.), all tended in one direction. Reconstruction of opinion concerning the deep things of life had become an absolute necessity. The accusation of Anaxagoras was, in part, a result of the desire to rehabilitate traditional religion. But Greece formed no exception to the general rule, and reconstruction by way of harking back on the course of development was impossible. Although a new basis for religion might not be at once discoverable, the assumptions of Sophistic teachers might at least be subjected to searching scrutiny. From this point of view, then, the mission which waited Socrates' coming was to probe the commonly accepted dogmas of philosophy, and thus to show how far scepticism was capable of justification, or to what extent it was unwarrantable. Intensiveness is one of the most prominent characteristics of philosophical inquiry. Friction among men seems to be a condition of that quick perception which observes things under new aspects, and so, produces fresh ideas to correct or transform the old. Given such circumstances, progress only needs a Socrates to fix the form which these ideas ought to take. It was for Socrates to fall into line with his age, in order to lead it eventually. His skill in the Sophists' special art, although put to very different use, cost him his life. Yet, without dialectic deftness, he had been unable to transcend the frivolous jugglery in which eristic ended. His life-work, as prepared for him by historical progress, was to turn investigation from nature to man, and, by a refutation of ordinary Sophistic assumption, to reconstruct the theory of conduct on a totally new basis. To the successful accomplishment of this task his individuality lent incalculable weight. For his conflict was not merely with subjective ideas, but also with the whole practice of those who imparted wisdom in consideration of personal gain.

Of the slow steps by which Socrates gradually arrived at an understanding of his mission no record remains. During the period of his life sketched by Xenophon and Plato he was quite conscious of it. He knew that his office was to reform philosophy rather than to purify religion. With regard to the latter he seems to have maintained an attitude of reserve, and to have pronounced no very definite opinions. He unquestionably rebuked scepticism for the sake of scepticism in religious matters,[1] and appeared in no wise averse to accept established customs[2] when they did not interfere with free self-examination. If the early physical philosophies were objectionable in that they attempted secrets beyond human ken, so, Socrates apparently argued, the teaching of the Sophists was hurtful because, although assuming the activity of mind, it sought to deprive thought of all value. He therefore proceeded to examine the implications of the Sophistic dialectic.

The extraordinary interest which his personality excited, as well as the influence which he is known to have had, prove that he was aware of the difference between himself and other teachers. In many ways he was by no means unlike the Sophists. The same spirit of free and fearless inquiry was evinced by them. Like Socrates, they were accustomed to converse in market-place and in social gathering, and all, equally, discussed

---

[1] Cf. Memorabilia, iv. 7.

[2] Cf. Phædo, 118; and Memorabilia, i. 1, 2.

common subjects. But Socrates, being in his own estimation only a learner, had no pupils; he talked with
intimates and acquaintances. The result of his arguments, the simplicity of his ways, and his refusal to receive money, indicated that he was conscious of a new
mission. For example, he entices into conversation one
Euthydemus, " who had collected many writings of the
most celebrated poets and Sophists, and imagined that
by that means he was outstripping his contemporaries
in accomplishments."[1] But the Sophist, who is at first
represented as having " never learned anything from
any person,"[2] and yet is " willing to offer such advice
as may occur to him without premeditation,"[3] finds himself forced to declare after a little discussion: " I no
longer put confidence in the answers which I give; for
all that I said before appears to me now to be quite
different from what I then thought."[4] After this
confession Socrates goes on to point out positively the
value of self-knowledge. Euthydemus in the end
admits his ignorance, and departs holding himself in
contempt. But, thereafter, he associates constantly
with Socrates; and, as Xenophon adds, " when Socrates
saw that he was thus disposed, he no longer puzzled
him with questions, but explained to him, in the
simplest and clearest manner, what he thought that
he ought to know, and what it would be best for him
to study."[5] Throughout there is not only an obvious
purpose, but also a method of pursuing it. This purpose was Socrates' mission as he conceived it. His
aim was to arrive at clear notions respecting life and
self. The assurance that he was able to reach such
certainty, and the belief that serious personal convic-

---

[1] Memorabilia, iv. 2, 1. [2] Ibid., iv. 2, 4. [3] Ibid.
[4] Ibid., iv. 2, 19. [5] Ibid., iv. 2, 40.

tion was the sole hope at the moment for the elevating of the Greek citizen, were chief among the elements in what is termed his *Daimonion*. He had discerned the signs of the times. The necessity for a reformation of knowledge respecting ethico-religious questions pressed upon him as it did upon a later teacher. His consciousness that he must needs be the organ of this reconstruction—his Dæmon—guided him throughout life, and nerved him to meet a death which, in his refusal to permit the easy removal of a misunderstanding which he considered final, came very near to sublime suicide.

The methods by which Socrates sought to carry out his work have been variously classed and analysed. Probably Cicero's famous statement implies more than most commentaries: "Socrates called philosophy down from the heavens to earth, and introduced it into the cities and houses of men, compelling men to inquire concerning life and morals, and things good and evil."[1] A philosophy, taught objectively in social intercourse with all sorts and conditions of men, could not have been the "cut and dried" theoretical system to which the term is now apt to be applied. It was rather a species of reflection upon common things, with a view to the discovery of underlying conceptions. The sophistic disputations concerning knowledge and morals resulted only in the discrediting of philosophy. The individual was so exalted, that no authority save his own formed an ultimate court of appeal in matters of thought. One man's ideas were as good as his neighbour's, and so truth and falsehood were such to the person for whom they seemed truth or falsehood.

[1] Tusc., v. 4, 10.

But, although eristic was thus negative, it had a certain positive aspect also. "Man is the measure of all things, of the existence of things that are, and of the non-existence of things that are not."[1] Absolute within his own sphere, the individual might well consider that *he*, and not the external physical world, should be the object of philosophical investigation. This was, by implication, the teaching of the Sophists, but they never carried it out. On the other hand, Socrates, perceiving the real tendency, proceeded to develop and to improve upon it. He adopted the sophistical dialectic, not for the purpose of exalting the individual, but in the hope of finding a principle to which all acts of reason, both in knowledge and life, might be referred. His dialogues "were essentially a negative discussion of the great questions of philosophy and life, directed with consummate skill to the purpose of convincing any one who had merely adopted the commonplaces of received opinion, that he did not understand the subject—that he as yet attached no definite meaning to the doctrines he professed—in order that, becoming aware of his ignorance, he might be put in the way to obtain a stable belief, resting on a clear apprehension both of the meaning of the doctrines and of their evidence."[2] Socrates, in short, accepted the abstract subjective individual as presupposed by the Sophists, and, by bringing him to confess his obligations, made him objective—related him to other minds in thought, and to other persons in society. This was what Aristotle meant when he said that Socrates discovered the

---

[1] Theætetus, 152.

[2] On Liberty, J. S. Mill, p. 26 (people's edition). Cf. Zeller's Socrates, p. 113 *sq.*

inductive mode of inquiry, and introduced the practice
of seeking general definitions."[1] By this, however,
the modern conceptions of general definition and of
the induction to which it is subordinate, must not be
understood. For Socrates excluded physical speculations from his philosophy, and concerned himself solely
with man's intellectual and moral nature. He gained
Aristotle's approbation, not on account of discoveries
such as those for which Bacon, Newton, or Mill might
be praised, but because he sought the essence of truth
outside of the isolated individual, yet not apart from
reason. Man was no longer the measure of all things,
but thoughts and acts were to be judged by their agreement with what is universally acknowledged true or
right. Thus the general definitions of Socrates related
to mind as it diffused itself throughout society, and
thereby afforded a basis for the regulation of life. His
aim was to bring about the recognition of reason viewed
in this way. Time was not yet for a completed theory
of knowledge, and so the Socratic method cannot be
treated like the customary organon of philosophy.
Insisting, as he did, upon the importance of mind,
Socrates tried to impress this upon others. And
surely the most obvious method was that which he
adopted; he tried to induce others to use their own
rational faculties. For this purpose the sophistical
dialectic was an excellent instrument. When Theodorus said to Socrates, "You will not allow any one
who approaches you to depart until you have stripped
him, and he has tried a fall with you in argument," he
received the frank enough avowal, "I am always at
this rough game, which inspires me like a passion."[2]

[1] Metaph., xiii. 4.   [2] Theætetus, 169.

Accordingly, we do not find Socrates *teaching* the art of wisdom, but preaching the virtue of knowledge. He put his associates to the question, and, by skill in interrogation, gradually induced them to draw conclusions of which they had no conscious idea at the outset. He thereby showed that a certain mental nature was common to men, if they but knew how to seek for it. " As part, therefore, of the Socratic dialectic, it was quite indispensable to show that thought was an indigenous endowment, a quality of human nature no less than sensation, appetite, and desire. This proof, accordingly, was the main part of the business which Socrates was called upon to perform."[1] Yet he did not rest satisfied even here. Not only do men possess certain ideas in common, but they also act together. Knowledge manifests itself in specific concepts upon the import of which all are agreed. The numerous acts of life, both as they proceed from one will and as they concern many, are therefore referable to certain general conceptions. Socrates thus " brought into conscious review the *method* of philosophising, which was afterwards still further considered and illustrated by Plato. General and abstract terms and their meaning stood out as the capital problems of philosophical research, and as the governing agents of the human mind during the process."[2] Out of apparent conflict he aimed thus to bring consistency. Consequently, his method, taken as a whole, is at once analytic and synthetic. It seeks, first, to prove the unity of experience for all men, and then to trace the result of this agreement in special ideas according to a common

[1] Ferrier's Greek Philosophy, p. 217.
[2] Grote's Plato, vol. i. p. 92.

understanding of which both individuals and com-
munities act. The object is "to doubt men's doubts
away," to rehabilitate the testimony of the senses by
showing that multifarious perceptions originate certain
conceptions which all men alike possess. Derived from
the Sophists, the use of the method in Socrates' hands
was entirely original, and its results unexampled. A
far greater exemplar than any Sophist of the truth
that every individual has his own "personal equation,"
his life yet served to prove that the unique character is peculiar in development but not in natural constitution.

The general effect of the Socratic method, then, was
to bring about a reconstruction of knowledge concerning the isolated individual of whom the Sophists had
made so much. Each one has a *proprium* only in that,
as a condition, he shares in a community of mental
goods. In knowledge, just as in life, debt is the source
of wealth. Socrates probably did not see that the "soli-
tary man is either a god or a beast," but of the non-
existence of such an one he was perfectly aware. Self-
knowledge is thus the panacea for the evils of scepticism
and of intellectual pride. But, what is its content, to
what does it amount? The interpretations of Socrates'
maxim, "Know thyself," have generally been in number
according to the interpreters. Some have thought that
it implied an analytic self-reflection, such as that in
which introspective psychology deals; others have
supposed that, in opposition to the assurance of the
Sophists, it was the enunciation of human frailty;
while, again, it has been taken as the starting-point of
a search for the unity of contradictories—which cannot
be unified. But to force any such meaning upon the

phrase is more than unfair. Socrates has no system, and although his maxim may *post facto* be turned to the defence of modern theory, it is to be remembered that such was not its original object. Rather let it be read in its own light. The true meaning is negatively put in 'The Apology,'[1] thus—"If I tell you that no better thing can happen to a man than to converse every day about virtue, and the other matters on which you have heard me conversing, and examining myself and others, and that *an unexamined life is not worth living*, then you will believe me still less. But that is the truth, my friends, though it is not easy to convince you of it." Yes, "an unexamined life is not worth living,"—it is not a life at all in the Socratic sense. It is because this was the manner in which Socrates understood his maxim that he is worthy of comparison with Christ. Virtue is its own reward; and Socrates' whole philosophy, both in its theoretical and practical aspects, was there only for the sake of its ethical conclusion. Self-knowledge was a means, but not an end. Admirable because it led to a better life, it was in no way valued except as it found practical application in raising its possessors above the ordinary complacencies of the day. "This examination was not a mere discipline ending in itself, but a preparation to qualify a man for receiving culture and improvement, for attaining correctness of knowledge and rational method in action, and for doing the best by himself and the state."[2] Socratic self-knowledge, then, means primarily a search for convictions,—for generally admitted truths,—and results in an application of these convictions to life. So too, in practice, the individual is only able to live

[1] 38.   [2] The Apology (Riddell's edition), p. 90, note 1.

consistently when he is acquainted with the ideas which are operative there. He cannot be a good citizen, for example, unless he is familiar with the implicit but recognisable relationship between fellow-countrymen. The solidarity of knowledge and action, apprehended by an understanding of universally diffused concepts, is thus the import of the Socratic maxim.

This, in turn, naturally led to some very important deductions, which may fairly be taken as indicative of Socrates' creative activity, and which furnish his contribution to his age, as indeed to all time. Virtue and knowledge, if not absolutely identical, are in any case inseparable. Hence the immediate value of self-knowledge lies in its intimate connection with life. This, then, indicates the two points in Socratic theory. Virtue and knowledge have one bearing on the individual life taken by itself, another on social relationship. If virtue and knowledge be inseparable, it is necessary that the individual should know himself. In other words, the presupposition of a moral life is a certain intellectual activity. Mind, on this view, is a *causa sui*, because it contains something ultimate which must be made matter of discovery. A *quasi*-knowledge is not to be forced into it, as the Sophists would have had men believe; truth is there already, and requires only judicious search for its revelation. Possibly this may have been the germ of the Platonic doctrine of recollection; it certainly bears witness to the intuitiveness of the individual mind. Just as a person in buying a horse seeks to ascertain if it be serviceable,—strong or weak, swift or slow,—so man must discover with regard to himself what he is fitted to do in this world.[1] Ac-

---

[1] Cf. Memorabilia, iv. 2, 25.

cording to Socrates, this search is conducted by an analysis of the knowledge which the individual already possesses. In ordinary affairs the majority are able enough to explain what they mean. Socrates would have them give a reason for the faith that is in them. Opinion may be wrong, or it may be unconsciously right —right, yet unable to defend itself. The first result of this inquiry is negative. It issues in a consciousness of one's own ignorance—that is, in a lower estimate of the knowledge that one has. This, again, brings about a positive result in the reconstruction of knowledge upon a reasoned basis. Conviction of ignorance is the prelude to rebuilding thought "to one's own soul."

Socrates himself was in the habit of making a profession of ignorance; he was not a teacher, nor did he call his associates pupils. They all shared the search for truth in common. What is usually known as the irony of Socrates is connected with this feature in his career. No doubt it was real irony in one way, but in another it was not. His profession of ignorance was insincere in so far as he was consciously at an advantage. He had a mission and a conviction of it, and to this extent knew what he desired; his associates did not. Hence his irony in "its proper nature consists rather herein, that without any positive knowledge, and prompted only by a desire for knowledge, Socrates addresses himself to others, in the hope of learning from them what they know, but that in the attempt to discover it, upon a critical analysis of their notions, even their supposed knowledge vanishes."[1] Socrates is thus ironical because he has the advantage of his fellows in knowing his own ignorance. But, on the other hand,

[1] Zeller's Socrates, p. 127.

there is a sense in which this knowledge of ignorance is not ironical. Socrates himself possessed no system, and in many ways the problem of life was a dark enigma to him. He might trap Euthydemus and the rest into unguarded statements by his apparent anxiety to obtain information, but he could not supply an infallible test of knowledge or rule of conduct. Socrates was ironical, therefore, in that he appreciated the necessity for distinguishing the known from the unknown. He saw that ordinary opinion stood in need of sifting. Perception of personal ignorance prompted a search for truth, not at the expense, but through the co-operation of others. Appealing to his friend in conversation, Socrates found that after a certain amount of mutual explanation, discussion could be reduced to a common measure. Certain ideas were discovered to be admitted by all. Thus opinion, which was often unwarrantably taken for truth, was corrected by means of its own interaction with the opinions of others. People call the man mad who errs in matters understood by all, not him who is at fault in things little known.[1] Hence it is, that in searching for truth, aid is derivable from one's fellows. Commonly received ideas are made the basis of an advance in true attainment.

This, then, leads us at once to the essentially ethical import of the Socratic philosophy. If virtue and knowledge be inseparable, the very fact that knowledge is obtained largely through intercourse with men gives rise to another proposition. The individual and society are inseparable. Consequently all this virtue—which is knowledge — while theoretically applicable to the individual, is social in practice. It is ethical in the

---

[1] Cf. Memorabilia, iii. 9, 6.

highest sense. "For· himself," as Xenophon tells us, " he would hold discourse, from time to time, on what concerned mankind, considering . . . what was just, what unjust ; . . . what a state was, and what the character of a statesman ; what was the nature of government over men, and the qualities of one skilled in governing them ; and touching on other subjects, with which he thought that those who were acquainted were men of worth and estimation, but that those who were ignorant of them might justly be deemed no better than slaves."[1] Man's knowledge of his own true nature enables him to put that nature to its proper use in human life. Granted that the individual is acquainted with himself, he is then and thereby able to live morally —able to rule his acts according to the principles upon which society is founded, and, according to the measure of his fitness, able to strengthen the state. The moral being is in fact progressing to an end as he has opportunity. Although Anaxagoras may have failed to apply his theory of mind, knowledge of thought appeared to Socrates at once the starting-point and the efficient cause of ethics. " Man, therefore, has only to consider what is best for himself, or for other things, and then it follows necessarily that he will know what is the worse ; for both are included in the same science."[2] All life is moral life. It begins in the individual, but it grows in him only in so far as he has opportunity of allying himself with others. ˙

If all knowledge thus exist for the sake of virtue, what, one naturally inquires, is virtue itself ? It is knowledge, as we know, but knowledge of what ? To begin with, it is knowledge of self, *plus* the application

[1] Memorabilia, i. 1, 16.　　　　[2] Phædo, 97.

of that knowledge in practice. Or, to put it otherwise, it has reference to the development of the individual nature in society, and this is simply the wise use of life. The knowledge which implies virtue is therefore a knowledge of what is good. Man, if he be acquainted with his inherent morality, will pursue it. He will cut and carve the passions, for example, so that they may be duly fitted into their proper position as parts of a perfect character. To know the good is thus the motive force of an ethical being, as well as the end which he seeks to attain. Not by any means that the intellectual life is the only worthy one, as Aristotle appeared to teach; but rather, mind is the pervading power which compels all acts into a harmonious whole. Through it the individual knows his nature, and so, through it he finds himself able to gauge his own worth, and his consequent place in relation to his fellows. Every one who is bad is evil by a kind of ignorance. He does not know himself, is unaware of the good, and so fails to practise that virtue, which his very nature preaches, were he but acquainted with it. The principle which pervades moral life and welds it into a unity, does not begin to act, if Socrates be right, until it has received recognition.

When, however, this principle is recognised, it leads to " well-doing." But the well-doing is that of a living being, and therefore it cannot stand still. To what then does it tend? At this point the Socratic philosophy appears to waver, and the want of a definite system makes itself plainly felt. At the same time, Socrates' general idea is, that the virtuous life tends more and more to a knowledge of the good—it grows towards the highest good. A certain ideal dominates it. And it is

here that we see how completely relative to his time
Socrates was. Although he placed life upon a reasoned
basis, he could only depict its final cause as he had
light. His highest good, so far as any notion of it can
be gleaned, is typically Greek. Partly artistic, partly
eudæmonistic, partly utilitarian, it is the highest good,
yet only one among other goods. For the individual
himself the highest good is artistic, because he is to
mould a perfect life out of the materials with which
nature has gifted him. Mind is to subdue the passions,
the passions are to call forth the ordering power of mind,
and a flawless man is to result. Again, the highest
good is also eudæmonistic for the individual. Only he
who knows himself will attain true happiness. Permanent satisfaction will accrue to the temperate man
who is master of himself, and therefore cultivator of his
best nature. On the other hand, when individuals
come into contact with each other,—and this, as we
have seen, is Socrates' prevailing view,—the highest
good is utilitarian. This, indeed, is but an extension of
the eudæmonism just noticed. But the highest good
now ceases to be absolute. Socrates felt that, were his
maxim to be regardlessly applied by every man everywhere, it could only result in a great system of casuistry.
Hence, for each man, the highest good comes to be the
subject of limitation according as he may live in one or
another set of circumstances. It thus gains social
application at the expense of systematic casuistry, and
remains "highest" only for the individual. But, as
soon as that individual tries to realise his nature in its
sole proper environment, society, the good is altered
according as utility or even circumstances may seem
to require.

Socrates was no more emancipated than any other Greek from the idea of the subordination of the individual to the state. He had not, because he could not have had, an adequate conception of the value of personality. No doubt he seems at the first to be approaching such an appreciation, but, whenever he begins to apply his principles, he feels the practical difficulty. When, for example, he insists upon freedom from the sensual passions, and upon independence of circumstances in which they might be excited,—and that with an earnestness to which his Cynic and Stoic disciples still bear witness in their historic doctrines,—he nowhere exactly determines what his temperance is to be, save by indicating generally the advantages of immunity from irresistible impulse. The good as it absolutely *is* cannot be abstractly fixed on account of practical difficulties. To accomplish this was not Socrates' mission. Just because he lived when he did, his aim was rather to impress man with a conviction of his own importance and permanence. The "good," whatever it was, came to be one among goods in practice. "The conception of 'the good' was a conception which had been largely insisted on in the philosophy of Socrates; but it was, at the same time, one which he had left indefinite and unexplained. Nowhere, and at no time, does he seem to have explained exactly what 'the good' was, or what he precisely and consistently meant by that term. That Socrates regarded happiness as the good is tolerably plain; but then it is equally plain that he regarded virtue as the good."[1] The resultant morality was not always moral, according to modern standards. Virtue as knowledge is the good;

[1] Greek Philosophy, Ferrier, p. 269.

therefore, for instance, fornication is better than adultery.[1] The reflective mind perceives that the dangers from social and legal penalties are not the same in both cases. But virtue is happiness; therefore gratification, in the more expedient yet still immoral fashion, is permissible to an extent which the individual's knowledge of his own requirements must determine.[2] There may be an absolute good, but circumstances alter cases, as the Cyrenaics and Cynics were afterwards to prove in their respective ways. While pursuing the good, the individual has a positive freedom, so far as he himself is concerned. But, when conditioned by social exigencies, this freedom becomes negative. And, this being admitted, all possibility of defining the good disappears. In respect of self-knowledge, and of the good which is its end, the individual may be an *imperium in imperio*. But the very fact that he is *in imperio* takes away practically, if not theoretically, the force of the Socratic maxim. The good of the family, to particularise, may conceivably be the highest good when the family is regarded as a unit. Still, in the state, custom and utility determine the kind of this highest good, and the family finds its final cause when it keeps the supply of sturdy citizens constant.[3] On the best ethical theory this is doubtless *a* good, but it is such only because it furnishes a means to *the* good. With Socrates, on the contrary, it is the highest good—the highest, that is, possible in the circumstances.

Thus, while Socrates knew whither to direct his search for a moral principle, and while he saw, though not so clearly, that ethical life is a continuous manifestation

---

[1] Cf. Memorabilia, ii. 1, 5. [2] Cf. ibid., i. 3, 14, 15.
[3] Cf. ibid., ii. 2, 4.

of one activity, the idea of the emancipation of the individual from external limitations had not occurred to him. The doctrine of personality had not yet reached the stage at which character could be viewed as a synthesis of individual effort realised in social antagonism no less than in co-operation. To have provided a better rule of conduct at a time of intellectual confusion and religious doubt was no small matter. To have insisted upon the obligation of the individual to self, in face of the objectivity of physical philosophy, and of the self-effacement demanded by the Greek state, was a still greater achievement. As yet a systematic theory of ethics, furnished with a definitely constituted *summum bonum*, was not only superfluous, but even impossible.

Genius must invariably stoop to conquer. Great men rise to eminence because they understand how to submit to limitation, and this is generally twofold. For, as Goethe said, only he who knows how to unite with the many at the right moment becomes great. The existence of the many, in the form of historical presuppositions and surroundings, limits greatness on the one side. On the other hand, discernment is creative, but it must be creative in a particular way; the conditions of activity have a determining power, and for that reason action is itself directed towards a particular end. Socrates was no exception to this general rule. Among the Sophists, he was yet not of them, although his permanent work derived alike its strength and its partial inefficacy from the relationship. Further, Greek civilisation as a whole, while it dated its distinctively ethical philosophy from him, confined his search for moral ideas to a limited and predetermined state of society. As great as he could be, Socrates was no greater. The limits from which he was unable to escape ought therefore to be clearly remembered, for, from their restraining influence he derived his force.

First, then, the intellectual cast of his ethical theory, which has already been partially noticed. Several serious objections may be raised against the maxim that virtue is knowledge. The plurality of virtues is denied by implication, and unconscious well-doing receives no recognition. In the former case, the absoluteness of the good is made subject of limitation. For knowledge may dictate that, on special occasions, a lie, or an unkindness, or a due gratification of passion at another's expense, is a "virtuous" act. In the latter case, an irrevocable difference is instituted between the good man and the bad. All that large class whose virtue is conventional, or at best regulated by haphazard, is ticketed as bad. No room is left for diversity of constitution. Struggle to obey a moral precept is precisely on the same footing as obedience easily rendered. One virtue is as good as another, because all *are* only on condition that they are known. In short, Logic is erected into a necessary presupposition of moral life. The immediate cramping of moral effort, to make no mention of the questionable elasticity of reason, is obvious. Calculation, or the knowledge of what is best for self in given circumstances, is not a sufficient principle for the regulation of the moral life, no matter how it may elevate the individual's estimate of his own worth, and may consequently affect his conduct. The Socratic morality fails here; nevertheless, Socrates himself died to vindicate something far higher. His theory of virtue was limited by unavoidable conditions, but the conviction which led him to propound it was better than its results. The value of the individual, which renders self-knowledge so necessary, is the great principle for which Socrates died. Only in man's nature as such could he perceive any necessity for the realisation of the systematic practice of good living. He discovered the whole source of ethical life, if he did not interpret all its implications aright. To this his life bears most conclusive testimony. "Every trait which Plato mentions adds to the clearness of that picture of moral greatness, so wonderful for its very originality, for the absence of all that is studied and artificial about it, for its exclusion of self-glorification and affectation."[1]

But, again, Socrates is in some respects even more Greek than in his intellectual theory of virtue. His whole career was of and for Athens. Wisdom cannot go beyond what the gods have given to men, but such as they have given, it must search out. The "good," therefore, is right conduct according to opportunity in the social life of Athens. Socrates was, in many ways, representative of all that to this day remains typically valuable in Greek civilisation. He did not know that the transformed character is at once the efficient and the final cause of moral being, but he was well aware that an essential part of ethical life consists in making the best of what one has. Not to get away from life after the manner of an ascetic, not to renew it like an apostle, but to use it in wisdom,—this is the specially Greek peculiarity of· the Socratic view. Moral responsibility is not an obligation to his god, under which the individual man somehow finds himself, but it is the duty of the Greek, seeing that he is a citizen, to live

[1] Zeller's Socrates, pp. 73, 74.

his best according as the laws,—that is, the wellbeing,
—of the community may determine.

If Socrates be thus limited by Greek thought in his
moral theory, he shares the permanent and practical
contribution of Greece to ethics. He knows what life
is, and accepts it as something out of which a good
result may be brought. Culture is possible for every
Greek,[1] and the materials are there, so be that the Athenians will only recognise and use them. Closely connected with this is the analogy from Greek art by which
Socrates was affected oftener than is always apparent.
"Socrate prêchait pour une élite qui aspirait à la perfection de l'esprit et à celle du corps; car les statues
parmi lesquelles ces Athéniens se promènent ne sont,
pour ainsi dire, que des échantillons choisis dans la
foule."[2] In art, which so dominated Greek life, the
tendency was to illustrate a principle of unity by sub-
ordinating details, so that they should form integral
elements in a perfect whole. Knowledge and skill
could accomplish this, and the Socratic theory was
but an art of life—a species of instruction, which
prevented men from ruining good material through
ignorance.

The moral courage, for which Socrates was so conspicuous, is of a piece with this. The individual is free
to mould the formless mass of his own being. Death
itself is preferable to a life which can only be disposed
under disadvantageous conditions. The moral artist
cannot change his ideal when his work is so far finished;
better to leave it fragmentary yet good, than to fore-
close the possibility of its final perfection. This was

[1] Cf. History of Greece, Curtins, vol. iv. p. 118.
[2] Origines, Havet, vol. i. p. 170.

the spirit of the Socratic argument before the Athenian court; it had also been the consistent practice of Socrates' life. When ordered by the Tyrants to form one of a party who were to fetch Leon from Salamis to Athens, where his judicial murder was deemed expedient, Socrates, at the risk of his life, refused to go. It were better to die than willingly to vitiate a character which ought to be flawless. "I then showed, not in word only but in deed, that, if I may be allowed to use such an expression, I cared not a straw for death, and that my only fear was the fear of doing an unrighteous or unholy thing."[1] The other side of this aim at statuesque completeness was illustrated in his action, after Amphipolis, when Epistates of the senate. The moral artist is under obligation to himself to use for the best that with which the gods have endowed him. Part of this divine gift consists in social life, with its accompanying state law. In disposing his life to the best advantage, the Athenian must do so within legal limits, and to this there is no exception. When, therefore, Socrates ruled the discussion of a collective sentence upon the accused commanders to be incompetent, because such sentence was not permissible by law, he but exemplified, on the negative side, the artistic consistency of his life. The most advantageous result must be obtained of which the artist's skill and the possibilities of his material are capable.

Nothing probably brings home to us with greater vividness Socrates' purely Greek character, than the relation in which he stands to the customary excesses of his day. Often, indeed, interested historians,—if such phrase be allowable,—have insisted too much on this

[1] Apology, 32.

point. The most that can fairly be affirmed is, that
Socrates treated publicly and without prudery matters
which sentiment, if not practice, now taboos. For him
asceticism had no merit in itself. As Emerson said, " He
can drink too ; has the strongest head in Athens ; and,
after leaving the whole party under the table, goes
away, as if nothing had happened, to begin new dialogues with somebody that is sober. In short, he was
what our country-people call *an old one.*"[1] But, at the
same time, does he not remember that virtue is knowledge ? He uses a wise moderation, which " appears
with him not to consist in total abstinence from pleasure, but in perfect mental freedom, neither requiring
pleasure, nor being ever overtaken by its seductive influence."[2] He quarrels with the body and its desires,
in fact, only when they impede right thinking. Once
more, in his conversation with the *heteira*, Theodota,[3]—
commonly instanced to his discredit,[4]—we have addi-
tional evidence that he was of, yet above, his age. Her
profession is evidently regarded as a matter of course.
But Socrates lets her know that even her calling may
be so far moralised. It is not to be a mere matter of
chance acquaintanceship, or of payment, but rather a
semi-friendship skilfully formed, and as skilfully maintained. Herself without virtue, she was not denied
the opportunity to gain it by knowledge. A living
illustration of the objective beauty in which the Greek
delighted, she received instruction from Socrates in the
proper method of rendering herself subjectively beautiful, by learning her own power, and so enabling herself

[1] Representative Men—Plato.   [2] Zeller's Socrates, p. 75.
[3] Cf. Memorabilia, iii. 11.
[4] Cf. The New Social Order, J. Fordyce, p. 69.

to put it to the most advantageous use. He only advised her according to his lights. Of Socrates' relation to the grosser vices of his time the same may be said.[1] Even Aristophanes, the severest and most unscrupulous of his critics, acquits him of "actual vice"[2]; and Döllinger, a censor of ancient morals so harsh as to be untrustworthy, bears strong testimony to his purity amid prevailing corruption.[3] Socrates was not Greek in personal indulgence, but in his attitude towards prevalent excesses. He did not hide them away, nor curse them, but tried to show how even they might be turned to means for the realisation of his conception of virtue. Yet, even at the best, we can only agree with Mr Burroughs, that "the Greek flexibility of intellect cannot be too much admired, but the Greek flexibility of character and conscience is quite another thing."[4]

Finally, Socrates was Greek in his attitude towards man the individual. He knew that every one possessed a mind, by which right conceptions regarding such things as the gods permitted could be formed, but he did not know that every one had a soul to save. Although he inaugurated the search for salvation, he was himself ignorant of its ultimate necessity, indeed that necessity did not then appear. In a manner he was emancipated from the rule of the Æschylean Zeus. That imperfect immortal was only able to act when aided by Might and Force, by Hephæstus, Hermes, and the other minions. Socrates saw, in his own way, that the rebel Prometheus could not be thus controlled. The indi-

---

[1] Cf. Plato's Charmides, 155.

[2] Cf. Zeller's Socrates, pp. 75, 76, note 5.

[3] Cf. The Gentile and the Jew, vol. ii. p. 240.

[4] Article on Matthew Arnold in 'The Nineteenth Century,' June 1888, p. 191.

vidual man is *in himself* what Zeus and his many
heralds are only in combination. He remains ever un-
changeable, save when he himself consents to be con-
quered. His life, in Socrates' view, provided he knew
how to act, was at his own disposal. Not external force
but internal consistency was the Socratic ideal.

Yet, although he went so far, Socrates failed to observe
the unavoidable implication—that every individual is
of absolute value. As his idea of the highest good was
limited, so too was his notion of individual worth.
Custom, advantage, utility, call it what you please,
deprives the one of its absoluteness, and by consequence
society denies the other the possibility of attaining such
an absolute end. Socrates' individual is a Greek citizen
first, and a man only secondarily. His ideal individual
is the wise man of the Stoics in embryo. But Socrates,
being still under the shadow of Pericles, was not country-
less like his successors, and therefore had no need to set
such store upon a self which, in more unhappy times,
appeared the sole inalienable possession. Even when
knowledge is conspicuous by its absence from the virtue
of the "ruling art," the consistent man, while remaining
obedient to the state, can retire into private life.[1] His
aim is to remain a submissive citizen, but never to
permit himself to become a slave. Socrates, although
conscious of his own inspiration, had no acquaintance
with the inspiration of humanity. His message was,
not "the *kingdom* of heaven is within you," but the
self to be known is within you. Just as he had but a
faint adumbration of the idea of immortality,[2] so he

---

[1] Cf. Zeller's Socrates, p. 169 *sq.*

[2] Cf. The Apology, 40-42. Whatever one may think of Mr Archer-
Hind's classification of the other dialogues, he is probably right in

had but a glimpse of the importance of man as man.
The individual is a part of the order of nature, and as
such he ought to put himself into the most favourable
position in that order. With the world beyond nature
Socrates does not concern himself, and so the individual
was worth knowing only as a citizen, never worth saving
for his own sake.

But, if limited by contemporary conditions, Socrates
also added something to them. The fruit of the past,
he was also the seed of the future. In this connection,
the difficult problem of his prosecution and death may
first be noticed. For Socrates was martyred on account
of what was distinctive in his doctrine.

"In the great work," said Goethe, "the great person
is ever present as the great factor." Socrates, as we
have seen, accomplished a great work; he was the
great factor in the turning-point of Greek life, and
because at that time he was a great person, he was condemned to die. The Greeks neither understood nor
desired great personalities. Any one who seemed to
rival the corporate state in power was liable to come
under suspicion. It is usual to trace the cause of
Socrates' prosecution and condemnation to several
sources, and in so doing Zeller, Church, and others
cannot be accused of error. Socrates was so far like the
Sophists that he adopted what seemed valuable to him
in their methods. His identification with the physical
philosophers, such as Anaxagoras, is less easily understood. But, doubtless, although he expressly denounced
their speculations, his attainments and the character of
his teaching led the public mind to accept in part the

placing the Phædo outside of the Socratic period. See his admirable
edition of the Phædo, p. 33 *sq.*

lampoons of Aristophanes and Eupolis. His accusers could not show that he corrupted the youth like the Sophists, nor could they substantiate the charge of heresy to which Socrates, as a presumed physicist, was liable.

Moreover, although "it told heavily against the philosopher that Alcibiades, the most mischievous of demagogues, and Critias, the most savage of aristocrats, passed for having been educated by him,"[1] the political charge was plainly manufactured for the occasion. However strong practically, its theoretical weakness must have been patent to all. It is perfectly reasonable to hold that the three main accusations which weighed against Socrates were all alike more or less far-fetched. They were perhaps the occasion of his condemnation, but they did not furnish the real reason for it. The Dicasts must have been perfectly well aware that Socrates was as different from the ordinary Sophist as from the representative natural philosopher, and that his connection with Alcibiades and Critias was in no sense productive of these statesmen's sins. It was for deeper reasons,—reasons not easy to be formulated in a court of law,—that Socrates suffered condemnation. He had sinned in being greater than his age—that is, in being dissatisfied with it. Thus some substance was given to the formal charges which in themselves had but a shadow of truth. No political crime could be recorded against him. But he was known to be thoroughly out of harmony with the political condition of Athens. Ever a good citizen, obedient to the laws, and without official influence whereby he might work harm, he had given offence by his references to demo-

[1] The Greek Philosophers, A. W. Benn, vol. i. pp. 163, 164.

crats and oligarchs as alike men who thought they had knowledge and had none. Neither popular election nor social position were considered by him capable of discovering, much less of producing statesmen. Only he who knows the art of ruling is fit to rule justly. Socrates was thus at variance with the democrats because he denied the capacity of all to rule, and he was out of sympathy with the oligarchy because he asserted that the same capacity did not necessarily accompany certain kinds of external advantage.

The other charges,—of corrupting the youth and of impiety, — are similarly explicable. They were the expression of a vague sense of the danger connected with Socrates' teaching, both in its social and religious tendencies. Socrates was himself without political influence, but his personal power in society must have been extraordinary. He did not specifically corrupt the youth, yet he taught men to seek guidance from their own independent judgment rather than from traditional rule. He did not insult the gods, but he felt that " the existing religion was not of a kind to be able to preserve a vigorous and sufficient life after the changes which had come over the general condition of the people's culture. The age, accordingly, needed another philosophy, a science which should be more practically useful for life, and enable every individual, since no general authority any longer existed, to take counsel with himself, and to acquire an independent judgment in all moral questions." [1] In other words, both in social and religious matters Socrates substituted the authority of the individual for that of the state—always premising that the former should not be brought into collision

---

[1] History of Greece, Curtius, vol. iv. p. 126.

with the laws of the latter. What else did he mean by self-knowledge and by the Dæmon ? He was condemned, as has been said, because he was a philosopher. And this implies that his presence gave rise to that undefined yet very real fear, which the mass of men always feel in presence of an individual whom they intuitively know to be great and good, whom they do not understand, yet who, as they secretly acknowledge with a grudge of self-reproach, " bears in himself the germ of a new life for thought." Never was more pregnant illustration that " God hath chosen the weak things of this world to confound the mighty." The Athenians, as we know, did not repent their decision, nor was there need for repentance. They had done Socrates the last service ; for, in spiritual life, a thing " cannot be quickened except it die." As for themselves, they were condemned already ; " Socrates was put to death, but the Socratic philosophy rose like the sun in heaven, and spread its illumination over the whole intellectual firmament." [1]

What, then, was Socrates' precise contribution to the course of psychological development ? Entirely unconscious of a division between spirit and matter, such as the middle ages exemplified, and largely without appreciation of the value of man as man, Socrates was the first to enunciate the principle that the moral universe is ruled by mind. Anaxagoras had discovered that the orderly arrangement of phenomena presupposed an agent like Reason. But this Reason of his was very analogous to what is now known as life ; it was physical rather than mental. Socrates' aversion to physical philosophy resulted in the perception that reason was

[1] On Liberty, J. S. Mill, pp. 18, 19 (people's edition).

essentially a spiritual force, and that its most characteristic qualities found scope in the control of human
conduct. He protested against a rule of life drawn at
haphazard from this or that set of opinions; he urged
the duty of learning one's own aptitudes; and he
claimed the right of the individual to develop these
powers, when ascertained, for his own benefit and for
that of the state. The old Greek idea of measure or
perfection, derived by artistic analogy, tended to con-
fine the citizen within certain predetermined limits.
The external expression of a living idea, such as is
furnished in art, is necessarily controlled by certain
principles which, in their general application, are identical for every instance. But in man's life it is otherwise.
No two individuals are exactly similar, and the results
to be obtained from the application of ascertained principles are thus of infinite variety. Every spiritual being
must fulfil some peculiar office. So far the analogy
from external art-work may be applied. But the office
is peculiar,—no man can achieve another's destiny.
Here the artistic analogy breaks down. Socrates'
creative act lay in the perception that each individual
soul in this world, or at least in the Greek world, must
be treated separately. Theoretically, indeed, he never
freed himself from the irresistible tendency to measure
all according to one standard. But in practice he himself was an exemplification of ideas which received
only implicit statement from him. The individual
is to know himself, and is to find out what his relations to others really are. As arbiter of his own fate,
and of the special manner in which he is, or rather
ought, to influence the lives of his fellow-citizens,
he *ipso facto* acquires a power wholly foreign to any

ever contemplated by conventional Hellenic moralists. Possessed of a right to speak authoritatively, he can discharge his duty, if disregarded himself, only by keeping silence. Socrates himself, in his everyday walk, was far from conforming to the ordinary customs of Athens. The luxury and refinement, incident to a life beautiful in its externals, were little affected by him, although he was well acquainted with their amenities. He was remarkable in his day no less for his manner of living than for his doctrines. Though retaining, in many essential points, Greek ideas and forms of expression, he was half conscious that his work tended in another direction. He knew that the end was not yet, for, like other wise men, he felt that he could not utter the whole burden of his message. He fully realised " the absolute necessity of a further illum-ination," and even ventured " in express words to pro-phesy the future advent of some heaven-sent Guide." [1] Socrates ever remained a searcher, and of this he was well aware. He understood the necessity for a principle regulative of moral life, and he knew when to look for that principle with greatest hope of success. Man must himself solve the enigma of his own existence. This was Socrates' contribution to the universal movement of thought. But although his method was on occasions more expository and less interrogative, he must ever be regarded as having given direction rather than form to ethical inquiry.[2]

In itself, therefore, the creativeness of Socrates, even setting aside considerations introduced by intervening development, was entirely different from that of Christ.

[1] Seekers after God, F. W. Farrar, pp. 318, 319.
[2] Cf. Zeller's Plato, p. 149 *sq.*

Socrates was the pioneer on a new way of ethical discovery, but he could not say, I am the way. He himself died, but others came who, if not greater, were wiser than he, and carried on his work as they had light. Philosophy, in short, did not come to life with Socrates, but a special department of it was instituted by him. Without Christ, on the other hand, there had been no Christianity. All Christians stand in a personal relation to Him, and the whole essence of their religion is concentrated in the possibility of this relationship. But neither philosophy nor philosophers stand in any such relation to Socrates. Plato and Xenophon alone, in their reverence for their murdered teacher, can be connected with him as every Christian must be with Christ. The Socratic schoolmen, the Stoics, and the Epicureans, who one and all owed their intellectual being to Socrates, are only his pupils, and even at this, owe him no personal allegiance. They depart from him, they reconstruct his work, and consequently but date their freedom from him. Christ is with His disciples always, and to His influence they trace their newness of life.

However, passing from this meantime, another aspect of the case now demands attention. Christ is different from Socrates not only in Himself, but also because He appeared several centuries later, and that in a vastly different environment. In the interval the world did not stand still, and the chief element in the contrast, which we desire to depict here, was contributed by the historical progress in question. Socrates was the precursor of Christianity as well as of ethical philosophy. Through the medium of the latter he paved a way for the former. Plato erected the general conceptions of

Socrates into a system of ideas,— ideas which are different from material things, and which pervade phenomena. Aristotle strove to correct the abstractness of the Platonic theory by showing that the division between ideas and things is not absolute. Matter is no longer μὴ ὄν, it is δυνάμαι ὀν. Man is no more regarded as striving after a far-off good, but it is enunciated that "soul is the primary reality of organism." Just as the world is progressing in an orderly sequence, so ought man's life to be growing. But all development tends to an end—towards that for the sake of which it takes place. This, according to Aristotle, is pure form. Form and end are identical ; therefore pure form is that which is an end in itself, which has an existence of its own, and that for itself. Thus, Aristotle's system, which was designed to overcome the Platonic separation between ideas and realities, itself ended in a far more deep-seated disruption. It culminated in a "dualistic theism."

All this, which cannot be discussed at length now, was a natural result of the Socratic teaching. For "Socrates was the first to impart the idea of teleology into the regions of speculative philosophy."[1] Moreover, he "taught in the most explicit way the doctrine of a divine purpose in creation."[2] Yet, with Aristotle the doctrine ends only in a theistic affirmation of the most abstract sort. God is required for the completion of a theory ; that He is near to every man is a very different and altogether unnecessary question. God's life is the life of pure thought, and deity is thus separated from the world. Men and things may be

[1] Philo-Judæus, James Drummond, vol. i. p. 51.
[2] Ibid., vol. i. p. 54.

progressing towards such a state, but the very fact
of its separation from them removes it to an infinite distance. The individual of Socrates, for example, may, out of his fuller Aristotelian knowledge,
desire to order his life towards the divine end. But
circumstances are against him. Evil is in the world
irrevocably, and nature leaves many designs unfulfilled
"because of the matter." The world, which we know,
may be a series of entelechies rising up gradually to
the highest in man, but he, despite his share in the
nature of deity, can only make the best of the incu-
rably bad. Circumstances contain a surd, as it were,
and the solution implied in a perfect life is thus put
beyond the region of realisation. Aristotle, in short,
raises Socrates' individual in that he makes him a
partaker of the divine nature, but at the same time
he removes all reason for the moral life by denying
man the ability to achieve what God essentially has.

On some such view as this, Socrates was the precursor not only of ethical philosophy, but of Christianity
itself. At the first man was forced to consider the
world ere he came to learn the power of his own mind,
and the perfectibility of his own nature. Socrates
revealed these in germ, and transmitted his discovery
to his successors. In the works of the later Greek
thinkers "wisdom dealt with mortal powers." Only
when the circle of knowledge, perfect in imperfection,
had come full, was the divinity of mind fully appreciated. What Socrates was to natural, Christ was to
moral philosophy. The Athenian saw that the true
end of life is the pursuit of the "good." But that
"good," half consciously sought and vaguely defined,
eluded the most searching and tenacious mental reason-

ing. There was need of a further revelation to free man from the dominion of sense, and to teach that he might not merely seek after a highest life, but that it could even be his to become a new creature.

Although doctrines such as those of the immortality of the soul and of a theistic God are attributable to Socrates, it is a mistake to suppose that in them specifically he did much to prepare the way for Christianity. Far rather he was the initiator of that movement towards the consideration of things spiritual which, in the end, produced thinkers who were conscious of a want that philosophy could not supply. The gradual development of this sense of helplessness, in its several phases, is the historical bridge between Greek philosophy and Christianity; it is also an essential cause of the difference between Socrates and Christ.

CHAPTER IV.

FROM SOCRATES TO ZENO.

ALTHOUGH few will agree with Mr Benn's statement, if supported only by the general considerations which he advances, yet there is a sense in which it is true that "the systems of Plato and Aristotle were splendid digressions from the main lines of ancient speculation rather than stages in its regular development."[1] The progress to Christianity by way of Greek philosophy is a record of man's growing consciousness of his own personality and its needs. This, emphasised with certain limitations by Socrates, loses itself for the moment in Plato and Aristotle. The Socratic self-knowledge, which culminates in virtue, is turned away from its subject, and is sent to explore every corner of thought and being. Plato institutes inquiry into the reality of knowledge and of its object; he seeks to discover the relation between knower and known, to show how mind and sense react upon one another, and to exhibit man's ethical character as it finds expression in a political organisation. Aristotle systematises these researches, divides philosophy into departments, origi-

[1] The Greek Philosophers, vol. ii. p. 1.

nates a scientific nomenclature, and applies principles of classification to concrete objects. With attention thus fully occupied there was then but little sense of the defect in life which impressed later schools so deeply. In Socrates the old unquestioning attitude of man towards himself had passed away; nevertheless, thought paused awhile in Plato and Aristotle, and, with a fuller knowledge, with a masterly application of the best methods afforded by past systems, these thinkers sought to theorise nature, or to state their own relations to the external worlds of the sensible and the supersensible. But the old unity could not be restored, for knowledge was unable to heal its self-inflicted wounds. "Plato opposes to the empirical world an ideal world, but is unable to find in this ideal world any explanation of the other; he can only explain matter as something non-existent, and can only subject human life to the idea by the arbitrary measures of his state. Even Aristotle keeps pure spirit entirely distinct from the world, and thinks that man's reason is infused into him from without."[1] Plato and Aristotle are thus "splendid digressions," not in the course of Greek philosophy, as Mr Benn would have it, but in their attitude towards the problem of *personal* life, which, beginning in Socrates, afterwards took such definite shape in the post-Aristotelian schools. Regarded even from this point of view, their digression is limited. They performed an indispensable service in rendering man aware of a contradiction in life, which, as his after-experience taught, he was unable to overcome of himself.

In looking, very briefly, at the work of Plato and

[1] Zeller's Pre-Socratic Philosophy, vol. i. p. 162.

Aristotle, it is important to notice how they prepared
the way for that new problem which was eventually to
be solved by the advent of Christ.   They go back again
to the inquiries of the early physicists, but they see
them deflected, as it were, through the Socratic medium.
Socrates was satisfied that in "general conceptions" he
had found the basis not only of true thinking, but also
of right action.   Yet he never proceeded very far towards clear determination of the office of these concepts
in the upbuilding of knowledge and character.   He did
not attempt any scientific metaphysic either for its own
sake or as a groundwork for morals.   It was enough
that he had the concepts: the metaphysical question of
their relation to the external world, in its several
aspects, did not trouble him.   Now Plato faced this
difficulty, and arrived at one answer.   Aristotle, who
had advantages over his master similar to those which
Plato had over Socrates, solved a cognate problem, but
in a different way.   Plato transfigures Socrates' conceptions into the permanent realities behind phenomena; Aristotle explains these realities as the permanent relations of things.   The passage is from the real
quâ thought, to the real as reflected into things, and
thence to the principle of reality in the system of the
universe.   To get behind phenomena to ideas, and if
possible to arrive at a highest idea, is Plato's aim ;
Aristotle's to see a rational principle working in things
and welding them into an organic whole.   In both
cases, then, there is a direct reference to external
phenomena which diverts research from the questions
incident to the life of man as an individual.   But
differences of temperament in the thinkers rendered
the relative value of their systems unequal.   Plato is

full of moral earnestness, Aristotle abounds in intellectual acuteness. They are thus inclined to busy themselves with widely divergent questions—at least so far as comparative importance is concerned; but they arrive at practically identical results—identical, that is, in their bearing upon the development of self-consciousness.

In modern times a tendency has sometimes been evinced to read too much into Plato. Hegel, for example, finds in him a specific confirmation of "absolute idealism." But this constructive exposition may be carried too far. In especial, it is often forgotten that Plato's ideas are not always "universals"; indeed, when the "universal" has been found, the older "particular" not unfrequently exerts a certain influence over it. For Plato never quite rids himself of hypostatised ideas, and precisely to this extent his philosophy comes short. In metaphysic, his separation between the ideas behind things, and the things themselves, largely determines any completed theory of the world. In the life of the individual there appears to be a parallel separation between thought and action. While, much more obviously, in the ethico-political theory of life, no adequate account of the connection between the individual and society is furnished. Plato, absorbed thus in the search for an all-pervading regulative power in the material order, and for a "supreme moral principle," had but little perception of the necessity for redemption either from the world or from self. In contradistinction to the Socratic "virtue is knowledge," Plato traces the cardinal virtues to a common source in wisdom. Wisdom partakes of the divine, and its proper exercise results in an assimilation to the nature of God. But how

the divine essence is to effect a transformation of life
we are never told.[1] The deception, which the lower
elements in man's psychological constitution are quick
to practise upon wisdom, must, no doubt, be carefully
guarded against. But what positively this solicitude is
to effect—beyond a knowledge of the "good"—is never
clearly defined. Ignorance of the right Plato ever
earnestly condemns, yet he nowhere adequately sets
forth the obligation under which one is to do the
right. To recognise fitness for certain work is one
thing; to feel constrained to perform that work is another. Moreover, who save the educated, that is the
few, can do the former, and where is the judge of fitness to be found? Virtue is not to be obtained by
wisdom, which, in its reaching forth towards the good
and towards likeness to God, attempts a *progressus ad
infinitum*. There will ever remain many baseless opinions and deceitful appearances from which deliverance
must be had. At the end the desired virtue is no
nearer than it was at the outset. Just as an innumerable number of ideas fall to be discussed, so an infinite
number of moral acts must be done. In both cases
equally, the ideal ever removes itself as it is approached.

The result is that, in Plato's philosophy, no unified
explanation either of metaphysical or of moral truth
is presented. Two gulfs, one in the spiritual, another
in the natural world, remain unbridged. The impossibility of attaining to the "good" appears to have
convinced Plato, if not of the absoluteness, at least of
the permanence of evil.[2] It is an accompanying condition of mortality. Plato was no advocate of suicide,

---

[1] Cf. Zeller's Plato, p. 454.
[2] Cf. Statesman, 273; Theætetus, 176; Laws, x. 896.

either implicitly like the modern pessimist, or explicitly like the ancient Cyrenaic; the world and the evil therein were to be used for the best. But through his moral earnestness he rose to a perception which was afterwards to be given to babes and sucklings in a fuller revelation. "Evils, Theodorus, can never perish; for there must always remain something which is antagonist to good. Of necessity, they hover around this mortal sphere and the earthly nature, having no place among the gods in heaven. Wherefore, also, we ought to fly away thither, and to fly thither is to become like God, as far as this is possible; and to become like him is to become holy and just and wise."[1] A more or less clear recognition of man's divinity is present here. The "well-considered practice of the good," however baffled by a contrary power in this world, still remains divine. It is not an appurtenance of the body, like the other virtues, but is of the soul which has its nativity in a pre-existent state. The result of this opposition between good and evil did not press upon Plato as it did upon later thinkers. He was too much engaged in the effort to formulate an explanation of things as they are here and now. At the same time it could be productive of only one conclusion. In this world there can be no redemption, for God alone has the perfect knowledge indispensable to the perfect life.[2] Man can so far eliminate evil, and train what is highest in his nature, but, strive as he may, he can never become a new creature.

This is further emphasised by the unmediated contradiction attendant on the theory of the universe. Just as, in the moral sphere, evil is finally opposed to

---

[1] Theætetus, 176.   [2] Cf. Zeller's Plato, p. 222.

good, so, in the material, phenomena—appearances—
stand over against ideas—realities. In both regions
an inexplicable residuum remains. The human spirit
goes out of itself to obtain satisfaction, and finds none.
Yet, in Plato, consciousness of this defect is not fully
developed. It is unfair to lay overmuch stress on his
latest work, because, however imperfect his final view,
he had had visions of better things.[1] He had grasped,
as in a picture, an ideal of the principle of the universe.
But he could not apply this ideal in all his measure-
ments of thoughts and deeds. He apparently grips
the essence of a thought, for example, and then admits
that after all his hold is uncertain. For he refers back
to a deity who has by nature the completeness which
thought, even with the utmost exertion, cannot now
comprehend. Consciously or unconsciously, an ac-
knowledgment of imperfection is present, confirming,
in relation to the material world, a hopelessness which
the inaccessibility of the "good," and the pattern of
the ideal state "laid up in the heavens," had already
established in other spheres. In the 'Timæus' particularly, the reality of things material is never
grounded on one homogeneous basis. The infinite is
rendered in a paralogism, like the ideal state in 'The
Republic.'

Plato's importance is that he consciously set forth
the highest thought of which his time was capable. He
travelled beyond the polytheistic gods, and had a vision
of the one true deity. Yet polytheism was not thus
deprived of vitality; Plato's god is little more than a sum
of attributes. Of personal immortality also Plato had
perception, yet he reserved it, in its fulness, for those

---

[1] Cf. Zeller's Plato, p. 544 *sq.*

who were enabled by superior knowledge to pursue the " good." There are different degrees of immortality, for moral life is a science, and according to scientific attainment will be the richness of a future state.

The Platonic community is a specially limited organism which subserves its own development by supplying the conditions best suited to the training of its individual members. Yet these members are so subordinated as to be practically deprived of self-determination. Plato's was the best state then possible; it is ideal because it was Greek. Plato's strength thus was that he represented the most mature speculation attainable under contemporary limitations; he was weak in that he could not escape those restrictions. To be more explicit, the conception of personality, out of which Christianity grew, and in which it largely consisted, was scarcely realised by him at all. His express purpose, as Hegel pointed out, was to construct a state in such a way that no room would be left for individual enterprise. This was the Greek ideal, and as such, in its perfect Platonic expression, it partook of all the excellences and defects inseparable from its very existence. Men had still to learn that no polity can be strong unless its institutions be nurtured on the consent of those for whom they are. The State, if there be such an entity, was made for man, not man for the State. By eliminating the analytic of personal interest apparent unity may be obtained, but the appearance can only result in a false sense of security. Because he thus disregarded the rights of the individual, there is as much irremediable opposition in Plato's political system as in his theory of man and the world. The oriental " right to be governed, and duty to be led " only issues in an antithesis between the unity of government and the plurality of governed. The link implied in free individual co-operation is entirely absent. Thus, so far as concerns the subject under consideration, Plato's work was the indication of inexplicables; their conflict and their clamour for solution belonged to later times. For this reason it is an absurdity to write about the Christian element in Plato.[1] His philosophy was but a stage in the preparation for Christianity. Certain formal likenesses may so far be found between the religion and the philosophy, but in essentials the comparison can be carried only a little way. Plato's righteous man is he who possesses certain powers, and by their aid alone lives as well as may be. The early Greek satisfaction with life, even if impaired, still exists. The recognised presence of evil was slow to abolish it. Christianity, on the contrary, appeared, and could appear only when that satisfaction had been swept away. Man had need to realise the limit of his own power ere he was able to contemplate the extent of his own imperfection, and consequent helplessness.

In the sense already admitted, Aristotle, even more than Plato, is a digression.[2] With him the Socratic concept is sent to explore every known region of the universe of thought. "He treated the Platonic dialogues as quarries out of which he got the materials wherewith to build up in consolidated form all the departments of thought and science so far as they could be conceived by an ancient Greek. He thus codified Plato, and translated him into the prose of dogmatic theory, at the same time that he carried further and

---

[1] Cf. Zeller's Plato, p. 505, note 47.

[2] Cf. The Secret of Hegel, J. Hutchison Stirling, vol. i., Preface, pp. 11 and 65 *sq.*

completed many of his results and suggestions."[1] Where Plato attempted to rise to a permanent ideal world, Aristotle sought to explain the presence and agency of the ideal in the real. Instead of trying to express matter in terms of something else, Aristotle put it to the question, and forced it to tell why it was there at all. Final cause, as seen operating in a definite object or group of objects, consequently comes to be the chief content of philosophy. And it is not difficult to see that the inevitable aim of such investigations must be to arrive at a final cause among final causes. Aristotle's conception of this highest entity, and his theory of its relation to the world, constitute his main importance for us in this discussion.

Aristotle had little of Plato's moral earnestness. This is partly traceable to his habit of mind, a habit which was doubtless confirmed, as in Darwin's parallel case,[2] by the character of his special inquiries. It was also due partly to the position which he assigned man in the economy of the universe. Not only does the Greek depreciation of personality cling to Aristotle, but, impressed by the might of things, he is inclined to regard man as a struggling pigmy. Freedom, which he frequently seems disposed to assume for man, is limited both from the side of the sensual and from that of the principle which orders phenomena. The aim of life is, therefore, to attain a certain attitude of contemplation. Reason, which is its own object, and which is an end to itself, must be of the nature of the highest possible being, and it alone can provide the best possible state of living. For the majority expectation is limited to membership of a community rationally ruled to the most

[1] The Ethics of Aristotle, Sir A. Grant, vol. i. p. 181.
[2] Life and Letters, vol. i. p. 101.

economical production of happiness; for some few, whose gifts are exceptional, the worth of moral life pales its ineffectualness before intellectual repose. In the one case personality is crushed, in the other it is developed only that it may negate itself into the nearest attainable likeness to the divine. Individuality, as now under- stood, is not merely undesirable, it is even positively bad.

God, who is the sole self-sufficient being, manifests himself, if at all, in no arbitrary acts. He simply *is*. Thus, according to the Aristotelian idea, God is εἶδος εἰδῶν—the form of forms. He is pure, free, and inde- pendent; as such he cannot be the subject of any deter- mination from without, nor can he enter into any express relationship with things material. God is, accordingly, *actus purus*, or, as Aristotle himself puts it, "the un- moved Mover."[1] This is the highest attainable concep- tion. What is to be said of its content? The great difficulty in Aristotelian speculation regarding things spiritual arises from an apparent recognition of man's divinity, which finds no adequate complement in a defi- nite account of the relationship between humanity and the distinctively divine—God. The conception of entel- echies in nature, gradually rising from lower to higher, would seem to warrant the most legitimate expectation of man's final connection with God. Sometimes, indeed, God takes his place as the immanent principle of the universe,[2] at others he dwells apart in a supramundane calm.[3] It is no injustice to Aristotle to take the latter as his prevailing view. The tendency of his system was towards a formal rather than a real deity. God is

---

[1] Cf. Meta., xi. 7 ; Zeller's Phil. der Griechen, ii. 2, pp. 280, 624.
[2] Cf. Meta., i. 2 ; Eth. Nic., x. 8, 206 ; De Anima, iii. 5, 430a.
[3] Cf. Meta., xi. 6 ; Eth. Nic., vii. 14, 146.

more above than in the world, for the opposition which Plato felt Aristotle explicitly stated. " He removes the divine spirit from all living contact with the world; but in his conception of nature as a uniform power working with full purpose and activity to an end, the poetic liveliness of the old Greek intuition of nature is apparent."[1] But the separation was emphasised even more. God is the final cause of things, the end " towards which the whole creation moves." Yet he is concerned only with himself. Plants, animals, men, all have their characteristic activity in which their peculiar nature is developed, so too has God. His activity is the life of self-contemplation. Thus, although he is the final cause of the world, his very existence shuts him off from it, and places him in a region of unattainable purity. In short, he is not a person but a state. As such he must ever remain beyond the reach of lower beings.

Man in his effort to explain himself is once more thrown back on self. A God who as " thinking activity relates eternally to himself" is a deity in name but not in reality. To nullify the moral government of the universe in this way is, at the same time, to deprive man not only of salvation, but also of any living connection with the power to do good. God is thus problematically blessed, but in order to his blessedness the whole creation must be cursed. It may be that the Aristotelian deity has developed an elementary self-consciousness.[2] Notwithstanding, he lacks that

---

[1] Zeller's Pre-Socratic Philosophy, vol. i. p. 156.

[2] Cf. Art. Aristotle's Conditions of Immortality, Thos. Davidson, in ' The Journal of Speculative Philosophy,' vol. viii., especially pp. 158-164.

consciousness of others,—in the case of deity, consciousness of the world as a whole,—without which
self-consciousness is only a name for an unrealised
possibility.   An active, self-contemplating being is
doubtless self-conscious by nature.   But, if he could
exist, he would not be the highest possible being.
Contemplation, however active, is the mark of an
unequally developed and one-sided life; contemplation
of self, no matter how perfect this object, attaches to
the hermit's living death, and can never have aught to
do with absolute reality.   Aristotle's conception of
deity may be nearer the Christian ideal than any other
attained by Greek thought.   But, granted this god, the
least in the kingdom of heaven is greater than he.

Like the Platonic, the Aristotelian philosophy resulted
in an opposition between God and the world, between
the real and the phenomenal, between the permanent
and the passing.   The problem of the individual life,
so near to every one, had been left unconsidered, and
the result of the omission was an unsatisfactory theory
of the universe—ethical, social, and material.   Just
as, after the death of Alexander, ambitious generals
quarrelled over the spoils of empire, so, after Aristotle, the complete kingdom of this world passed from
philosophy.   His *system* was forgotten with amazing
rapidity.   For, man having faced the question of material creation, had now to solve the problems of his own
being and destiny, on which little attention had been
bestowed since Socrates.   Philosophy, although ranging
over all regions of knowledge and discussing every im-
aginable subject, had failed to account satisfactorily for
individual personality.   The ultimate difficulties which
connected themselves with it were not yet realised.

CHAPTER V.

THE SEARCH FOR INDEPENDENCE AND WISDOM.

AFTER the death of Socrates philosophy was parcelled out, so to speak, and this with a certain relation to the martyr himself. He had not promulgated any complete system, and his immediate followers of the Megarian, Cynic, and Cyrenaic schools laid hold upon different doctrines which his conversation or life seemed to countenance. Thus, while they did homage to the greatness of Socrates by adopting his thought, they really misunderstood his individuality, and misread it by wresting it from its natural surroundings. The Socratic philosophy was full of suggestion, but the explanations thus put upon it served rather to show its limitations. Greek philosophy had yet much to attempt ere a richer theory of human life, as opposed to a mere account of the cosmical order, could emerge. After years of necessary but veritable wandering, in Plato and Aristotle, thought returned again to the Socratic " know thyself " in the decline of Hellenic civilisation. Philosophy was once more parcelled out, this time not with relation to Socrates as an individual, but in varied endeavour to comprehend human

personality as such.   The school of the Porch is largely
indebted to the Cynics, and in a much less degree to
the Megarians.   The Cyrenaics come to life again in
the Garden of Epicurus.   In Scepticism, with its universal doubt of the not-self and equally universal belief
in self, the dialectic of the Sophists reappears.   But, in
spite of the past, new aims are before philosophy.   The
secret of the world had not been found out in the days
of the Minor Socratics, and profiting by their experience, perhaps indeed dreading ills unknown, Stoics and
Epicureans alike sought to rescue man from difficulty
by teaching him to render all things subservient to his
own wellbeing.

In spirit, at least, the post-Aristotelian schools are
strictly constructive.   They strive to lay down a positive scheme of life for man, and, no matter how they
may have ultimately failed to find salvation for the
individual, the very idea that he had need to be saved
was the mark of a new attitude towards the problem of
existence.   External conditions formed a main influence
in effecting this change.   The exhaustion of Greece,
evident not only in material but also in mental pro-
ductiveness, and the descent from power to dependence,
doubtless reacted upon the spiritual life of the time.
But too much stress must not be laid upon these outer
causes.   There was a parallel movement in the mental
sphere which, although contemporary, was in large
measure self-originated.   Man was thrown back upon
himself no less by the final dualism of Aristotelian
philosophy than by the decadence of Greek political
life.   Discontent, if not despair, had origin in the state
of religion and in the results of speculation, quite as
much as in the disappearance of the once possible Greek

supremacy. And this is the more obvious when one remembers that the intellectual sceptre had not yet passed from Athens. Her scholars and teachers were still her glory, her learning still swayed the universe of thought. But the whole trend of speculation was altered; the object now was to furnish an ethical code, not to supply an explanation of external things. This, in turn, was suited to the requirements of the age. The Greek, not expatriated perhaps, but denationalised in a way, and tired of the philosophy which stood rooted in the past, was only too ready to lend an ear to any doctrine which might seem to bear promise of deliverance from the ills of life, both outer and inner. Thus the individual man is the problem of Stoicism and Epicureanism. The work of these later systems was to bring man to a consciousness of his own personal worth, and to set forth in part the conclusions to which the rise of this consciousness inevitably leads. How, then, was this accomplished, and in what way did it become an integral element in the preparation for Christianity?

The thought of rival schools, when sharply defined by several centuries of conflict, naturally presents many discrepancies in theory, which are often set forth with bitter tone. Yet nothing in the whole course of post-Aristotelian philosophy is more remarkable than the substantial substratum of agreement between thinkers of apparently the most diverse types. The common aim subserved by all the systems of this period asserted itself, whether the rival schools were aware of it or not. Indeed, the very agreement is the best proof that a certain need existed in spiritual life, which philosophy was striving to supply. Epicureans, Stoics, and the later Sceptics all desired to

frame a *schema* of life for the individual, such that the
largest possible amount of happiness might accrue to
him.   The individualism of the Minor Socratics, and
of Socrates himself, reappears, but with far more direct
reference to man as a person.   The highest life is now
put within reach of every one : according to all the
schools the end of life is the same ; the only differences
are with respect to the means whereby this end is to
be most easily and fully attained.   No doubt, as is
always the case, the opposition of means was at first
greatly emphasised ; but afterwards the likeness of aim
came to be observed.   For, Greek philosophy at Rome,
especially in the later years of the pre-Christian era,
became more homogeneous, and was made less an affair
of partisan rivalry than in the earlier post-Aristotelian
period.   The fact that man must inevitably free himself from the evils of this world, at last weighed far
more than the varied fictions concerning the proper
methods of obtaining freedom.[1]   Epicureanism and
Stoicism are important, in short, not so much because
they insist upon a certain manner of life, as because
they are agreed upon the value of the individual to
himself, and upon the final cause in relation to which
he must work out his own salvation.   " Individualism
in morals, subordination of all science to an ethical
end, and materialistic realism, are common to the two
schools." [2]   Scepticism also agrees with them on the first
point, which, take it at its worst, is always the remnant
of certainty that the most thorough-going doubter cannot

[1] Cf. The Moral Ideal, Julia Wedgwood, p. 88.   " When the Greek
spirit most approaches the contemplation of an Ahriman or a Satan,
there also it comes nearest to the sense of a Redeemer."
[2] Epicureanism, W. Wallace, p. 17.

doubt away. The serenity of the Epicureans is not different in kind from the passionlessness of the Stoics. If there be difference in degree it practically disappears through the mediating influence of the suspense of the Sceptics. All these states were valuable in their day rather on account of their immediate bearing upon common life, than for their place among the shibboleths of contending parties. It is of small moment that this later phase of speculation slowly broke away from Greek traditions. Its vitality was due to what preceded it, and its supreme moment lay in what it did to supplement older and less cosmopolitan thought. " The sublime intuitions of Plato had been found too vague and unsubstantial, and the subtle analyses of Aristotle too hard and cold, to satisfy the natural craving of man for some guidance which should teach him how to live and to die." [1]

The result of the Platonic and Aristotelian search for and application of concepts was in some respects well calculated to induce despair of philosophy. Plato's opposition of ideas and phenomena, Aristotle's antithesis between universal and particular, were as unsatisfactory in theory as the Macedonian domination was in practice. The god of the Aristotelian philosophy partook in truth of the nature of pure being, and was untouched by any defect incident to finitude. But, from his very "aloofness," he could neither sustain the world nor be worshipped by it. Man found no adequate explanation of the universe, no satisfaction for his spiritual needs in a deity whose godhead consisted solely in his difference and separation from things

[1] Epistle to the Philippians, J. B. Lightfoot, p. 270 (third edition).

temporal. As an immediate result the individual was cast back upon his own resources. Divided from God, and without knowledge of any possible mediator, the later Greek philosophers sought to make each man's life absolutely self-sufficient. Freedom from external restraint, with its suppositive attendant ability to dispose one's self as might seem best, became the ideal of existence. The three schools which flourished on the dualism of Aristotle, and made it their business to preach this new gospel, although contemporary, are of very different relative value to the present sketch. Stoicism, if for no other reason than its affinity for the Roman and the Jewish[1] character, is more important than either of its rivals. Epicureanism is notable, not so much for the widespread influence which it exercised, as for its absolute and unabashed individualism. It first pointed out the value of the individual, and then obtained a speedy recognition of its creed by systematic exaggeration. Scepticism, again, in so far as it can be treated by itself, is ultimately of small moment. It found its true mission in mediating between the other schools, and was thus resolved into a factor of later Eclecticism. The Epicurean solution of the problem of individual life may therefore be taken first. Its great significance lies in itself, and is not to be sought in the practical results—these were small—which it achieved through its exponents in after-years.

For whatever sins of commission the luxurious Roman may have found Epicureanism a convenient cloak, the "pleasure" which Epicurus himself contemplated had nothing in common with shameless gratification of the

---

[1] Cf. Art. Stoicism, E. D. Hicks, in 'Ency. Brit.,' vol. xxii. pp. 561, 562; Grant's Ethics of Aristotle, vol. i. pp. 206, 207.

senses.[1] Horace was no true disciple of his. Materialistic in its theory of things, Epicureanism was anything
but gross in its scheme of life. Indeed, the mechanical
view of nature is only the counterpart of the individualistic conception of man. The reaction from the wide-
visioned speculations of Plato and Aristotle is here
more marked than in Stoicism, even the sternest. Each
individual is set by himself, and his life is his to make
his own. The old problem of the universal is thus
narrowed into the question of finding the best practical
means for the ideal disposition of self. But the disposal
of self by self implies freedom from external conditions,
which only serve to stunt individuality and to disturb
self-culture. Hence both the absolute individualism
of the Epicureans, and the peculiar meaning which the
term "pleasure" bore for them. Pleasure, in the conventional sense, is an end, here it is only a means. It
has been placed in the hands of the individual as an
instrument for the perfecting of self. What, then, of
him who is thus to use it?

A century after his death the influence of Socrates
still remained strong. In him later disciples of philosophy saw a partial realisation of the ideal, which
increased knowledge, with its increased sorrow, was
now forcing upon them. In his person and conduct,
if not in his abstract thought, the post-Aristotelians
beheld an exemplification of the worth of individual
life. A particular interpretation of this life had been
emphasised by the Cyrenaics, and, following them, the
Epicureans attempted a more systematic account of
conduct on similar lines. The importance of self-
knowledge, as conceived by Socrates, and as partially

[1] Cf. Studies in Philosophy, W. L. Courtney, p. 31 *sq.*

applied by the Cyrenaics, in their revolt from existing conditions, became in Epicureanism a constructive theory of man, and of the world, directed towards individual self-determination. But, as ethical considerations predominated, the philosophy of nature was weak. Man, being concerned chiefly with his own happiness, had little need of any knowledge which did not appear directly to subserve this end. And the result is, that as a contribution to universal thought, and more particularly as an integral element in the development of religious consciousness, Epicureanism may be summed up in these phrases,—freedom, happiness, and the wise man. The first indicates the new problem before philosophy, the second implies its solution, while the third expresses the concrete result of this solution.

For the Greek, freedom had little of the connotation with which it is connected in modern thought. According to the interpretation now customary, freedom is almost invariably a name for certain relations, political or social, between men. The citizen is free if he be not conducted through life by a bureaucracy; the worker is free if he have the right of franchise; a country is free if it be governed by popular representatives duly elected. But in contrast to this, the freedom of Epicureanism is purely an affair of the individual. No doubt it touched contemporary philosophical theory in so far as it came to be a protest against the necessitarianism of the Stoics. Yet it protested only in defence of the individual. He must nerve himself to obtain freedom, because, lacking it, he is not in a position to take advantage of his single inalienable possession—his own life. On this showing each man is himself the subject of an entire ethical system. His nature is unique, his true life is to dispose it as best he may, and the one condition of proper disposal is individuality, which in turn implies freedom from the dynamic forces of society, and of the material world-order. Spontaneous activity of and for self must be gained at any price. For, the more the kingdom to be ruled is circumscribed, the more hopeful the task of governing. Escape from the world into self limits the dependence of self, and quietism of a kind is the indispensable prelude to realisation of the hedonistic ideal of self-development. "Not pleasure, but fulness, completeness of life generally, was the practical ideal to which this anti-metaphysical metaphysic really pointed. And towards such a full or complete life, a life of various yet select sensation, the most direct and effective auxiliary must be, in a word—Insight. . . . Not the conveyance of an abstract body of truths or principles, would be the right education of one's self or of another; but the conveyance of an art, an art in some degree peculiar and special to each individual; with the modifications, that is, due to his peculiar constitution, and the circumstances of his growth, inasmuch as no one of us is 'like another all in all.'"[1] When freedom has been attained, when self has actually laid hold on self, then the serious business of life may be said to begin—nay, this is the condition of its beginning at all. The problem must first be comprehended ere its solution can be attempted with prospect of success.

Now the aim of the individual is to obtain happiness or pleasure for self. The impossibility of "remembering to forget" had already been exemplified in the

[1] Marius the Epicurean, Walter Pater, vol. i. pp. 153, 154.

school of Cyrene, and, profiting by this experience, Epicurus was no advocate of momentary joys, but rather sketched a movement which was to culminate in a certain beatific state. Pleasure, with its accession of happiness, is not a kind of *noces de Gamache*, but a realisation — perfect after its species — of Aristotle's golden mean. It points more to an absence of pain than to a temporary fruition of pleasing luxuries, and curiously enough, it consists rather in the limitation of demands than in their satisfaction. "We want pleasure," says Diogenes Laertius, "when we feel pain at its absence; when we feel no pain, we want no pleasure."[1] The philosophy of Sybaris, despite superior practicableness, has no place here. To minister to the senses, as Epicurus saw, is the sure method by which to render serenity ultimately impossible. For the more the senses receive, the more they demand. Luxury is always a result of cultivation, just as unnatural vice is consequent upon indulgence in natural but vicious pleasures. To rid one's self of the occasion for gratification is, at the same time, to ensure permanent happiness. Freedom is the presupposition of the highest life possible for the individual, because only as a man can set bounds to himself—can dispense with external and then with internal necessities—is he able to enter upon the blessed state. His own nature, stripped of the fantastic accessories linked to it by culture and luxury, is the only power that can guarantee each one "a mind free from trouble, and a body free from pain."

He who lives with such aim and consciously subordinates his actions to the attaining of freedom, is the

[1] X.

wise man. He merits this title, not for his exemplification of the best life alone, but also for his knowledge
and observance of the conditions essential to that life.
He *knows* that pleasure is not a mere "Will-o'-the-wisp,"
and this because he is at home with self, — he *has*
satisfaction. Here remnants of Socrates' maxim come
to light once more. Virtue is still knowledge in a
manner. Man is wise for the simple reason that his
wisdom is now enabled to come to maturity. Lucretius,
in one of his most remarkable passages, really enunci-
ates the whole *raison d'être* of Epicureanism. "In our
flesh we are like children stranded in the darkness of
night, with no idea of our true position in the world,
and inclined to fancy terrors in the gloom which sur-
rounds us." Just because it is so, reason, and nothing
but reason, can be the means of our obtaining happiness. Wisdom is the one quality, by the very possession of which man becomes the architect of his own
life. To escape the terrors with which darkness seems
fraught, the child must comprehend it; so also man
must understand the world and his relation to it.
Then, when this has been accomplished, he may apply
his knowledge in the practical conduct of life. The
philosophy of nature is not absolutely desirable for
itself, it is of value only as a necessary prelude to
ethics. The complete man is thus "wise" because he
knows much, and has ability to make use of his knowledge. Undisturbed, no matter what may betide, he is
in harmony with self, and living in this peace he is
happy. For him pleasure is a continuous state, the
constitutive principle of which is so stable, that no evil
can enter in to disturb or cause pain. Life is now complete, not because it is virtuous, mark, but in that it

has or holds happiness. Yet, if it have the latter, it cannot but be virtuous, for virtue is one of the means to happiness. The unjust man is not miserable because he is unjust, but in his fear that one day his unjustice will find him out. His life is vicious in so far as it is subject to pain, or to possible invasion from without. Contentment, this time wanting godliness, is great gain.

Yet, after the ideal has been realised, is not the Epicurean wise man lacking in something? Does not his freedom recoil upon itself, as it were? It is easy, of course, to declare *post facto* that Epicureanism did not solve the problem of individual being in which it originated. But the failure was due more to the inherent nature of the system than to the difficulty of its task. External circumstances, such as the decadence of civic life in Greece, intensified the need for a new theory of life, which the Aristotelian separation of God and the world first occasioned. The aim of Epicureanism is so to endow the individual with an end and a means to it, that he may be practically independent of circumstances. But, in winning this independence, the ideally wise man sacrifices something of greater importance. Pleasure, or the state of being in which all things are indifferent, is hard to attain, for the very reason that pleasure exists. The main obstacle to the freedom of the individual lies in the very condition which is a *sine qua non* of that freedom. Man, to assuage the grief of living, must enjoy life, by ability to dispose it for the good of self. He must so conduct it that, to the greatest possible extent, pain may disappear as a *minus* quantity. But, by the very fact that conducting is necessary, pleasure can never be separate from pain.

Pleasure itself, if it is to be a continuous state, must stake its continuity upon the destruction of pleasure. The wise man is temperate because intemperance bears joyless results, and fosters painful cravings. Pleasure, in other words, is most likely to be attained when reduced to an infinitesimal point. The wise man realises his ideal, and finds his true freedom only when the ideal is a mere form, and the freedom a permission to do nothing. Epicureanism thus recoils upon itself. It attempts a theory of the pure individual, but, as the pure individual is nobody, the life which is suited to his nature comes to be a species of moral suicide. The individual cannot be a law or an end to himself; and Epicureanism represents but a particular case of this impossibility. Just as individualism finds its ideal man in the desert, and even then discovers nothing but a mirage, so Epicureanism only arrives at pleasure when pleasure, with its infinite series, has been ejected as a disturber of the peace. To liberate the individual by setting him in a vacuum, is to present him with a freedom which could exist only under the attribute of uselessness.

In spite of such disadvantages, however, Epicureanism was better suited to the wants of the average man than either of its contemporaries. Stoicism and Scepticism alike rested on a foundation of abstract reasoning. Epicureanism, on the contrary, although providing a theory of nature, did not so insist upon the application of logic to life. The pursuit of happiness was an aim comprehensible by the simplest. For some such reason, doubtless, the philosophy of the Garden long outlived its rivals. Nay, at a time when the panaceas of the schools were universally distrusted, it put forth fresh vigour.

The pagan reaction of the Augustan age, which reasserted the wish to believe, was contemporary with a remarkable growth of Epicureanism at Rome. The seemingly immediate practical value of the life-scheme which it gave was then, as always, the chief recommendation. For this reason also, four Christian centuries elapsed ere Epicureanism, in its old form, was finally laid to rest, and its periodical recurrence in various guises, ever since, may be traced to similar causes. It is not to be forgotten, on the other hand, that the Epicurean solution of the problem presented by individual life was, from its very readiness, wanting in scientific precision. For example, the meaning of the term pleasure, as used by Epicurus himself, is not always clear. Temperament might occasion various interpretations. It is certain that, while happiness partook of all the mildness incident to its Greek birth, in this form it had little kindred with Roman character. Mainly on this account, it is not always true to say that Epicureanism was changeless.[1] In its essential doctrine it remained almost without alteration, but the sense in which its chief tenet too often found acceptance, especially in Rome, was assuredly very far from that expounded by Epicurus at the first. To direct all action towards the elimination of fear and suffering is hardly a swinish doctrine. Yet, does not Cicero speak somewhere of the " swinish doctrines of the Epicureans " ? The connotation must indeed have changed since the days of the quiet Garden. Happiness, in short, is an aim easily understood by men, but it is capable of too many interpretations. The very ease with which it seems to solve life's difficulty is an earnest of inadequacy. The state of pleasure in which

[1] Cf. Hellenica, edited by E. A. Abbott, p. 247.

Epicurus sought to find deliverance from the ills of living is unattainable chiefly on account of the other meanings which can be put upon the term, and which appear to have been associated with it at Rome. Only in so far as Horatian morals are eschewed can the Epicurean reward be obtained.

The causes which favoured the growth of Epicureanism were also those that presaged its doom. The Aristotelian philosophy had cast the world off from God, and had driven man to seek the centre of the universe in himself. Epicurus met the consequent question— what am I ?—with an answer at once pleasing, according as each might interpret it, for himself, and, in its absence of theoretical difficulties, easily comprehensible by all. But this adaptability, grounded on indefiniteness, was the real weakness of the philosophy. " It tells the ignorant they need study no literature : it releases the niggardly from the duties of public beneficence : it forbids the lounger to serve the state, the sluggard to work, and the coward to fight. The godless are told that the gods are indifferent : the selfish and malevolent is ordered to give nothing to any one—because the wise man does everything for his own sake. The recluse hears the praises of solitude ; and the miser learns that life can be supported on water and polenta. The man who hates his wife is presented with a list of the blessings of celibacy : the parent of a worthless offspring hears how good a thing is childlessness : the children of impious parents are told that there is no natural obligation upon them. The weak and luxurious are reminded that pain is the worst of all evils ; and the brave man that the sage is happy even in tortures. Those who are ambitious are bidden to court the sover-

G

eign ; and those who shrink from usury are directed to avoid the place." [1] This, indeed, is no fair commentary, but it is important as being a very possible one. However suitable Epicureanism may have been to its early surroundings, it afforded no real solution of the pressing problem of individual life. *Λάθε βιώσας* is an excellent rule for one who seeks independence in self-limitation ; it affords no guidance to those who, like Epicurus himself, would secure for each individual life its own unique perfection.

Stoicism, though neither so persistent nor so changeless as Epicureanism, furnished a far more important reply to the problem then agitated. The influence of Zeno and his followers, especially in pre-Christian Rome, was immense. Their philosophy took the form of an articulated system, and it is a permanent link in that chain which unites Socrates with Christ, through Plato and Aristotle, Alexandrianism and the Jewish religion. How, then, did it meet the question presented by the individual's need for freedom ?

Face to face with the same special difficulties that exercised the Epicureans, Stoicism was naturally similar to the rival philosophy in many points. But, in an especial degree, its lineage may be directly traced to the personality of Socrates. As with Epicurus, the subjectivity of man's life forced itself upon Zeno, Aristo, and Chrysippus. For this reason, if for no other, Socrates was their great ensample. It is the more necessary to insist upon this, that Stoicism has often been regarded as a mere revival of Cynicism. One might indeed admit that, as Cynicism was foreign to

[1] Divin. Institut., iii. 17. Cf. Epicureanism, W. Wallace, pp. 259, 260.

Greek culture and love of the beautiful, so too was Stoicism. And in this sense it is certainly less Greek than Epicureanism. But such tendency is due as much to its Socratic as to its Cynic origin. Socrates was himself " in opposition" all his life. His thought was in many respects negative, and on its positive side it took the form of an earnest protest against current materialism and fraud. Stoicism is foreign to Greek civilisation in much the same way. It is prophetic of the passing of Hellenism to another and more practical people. The protestantism of the Cynics was the medium through which Socrates came to the Stoics,— Crates was Zeno's teacher. But doctrines of which Cynicism knew nothing rendered Stoicism incomparably more fertile than its alleged prototype. Take only one likeness to Socrates. With the Stoics, as with him, philosophy exists solely for the sake of its application in life. Even more than for Socrates, it was necessary for the Stoics to provide man with a sheet-anchor of the soul. In times of difficulty, theory is all very well,— it is invariably wise to explain the world, and prudent to possess a principle of reasoning. But this, and such as this, were worthless lumber, if not capable of application in common life, or if unable to teach man where to find his best nature. Moreover, the Stoic conception of the ethics which were to deliver Greece alike from the conclusions of Aristotle and from the sorrow of contemporary political decline, is strangely in accord with that favoured by Socrates. Virtue remains knowledge as before. The view that theory exists only for practice, has its complement in the idea that virtue must be based on abstract knowledge. Correct opinions concerning things are the exclusive means to right conduct

in life.   Aristo himself, though as inimical to theory as
the most orthodox Epicurean, saw in reason the sole
guarantee for goodness.   It may thus be legitimately
said, that Stoicism was a revival of the Socratic philosophy, tempered by the mature experience of Plato
and Aristotle, as well as by the fresh needs which
changed political surroundings were emphasising more
and more.

Stoicism, therefore, concerned itself entirely with
man the individual, and the conditions of his life.   Like
Epicureanism, its aim was to present each with his own
life—to give him freedom—and also to show how that
life might best be used when fully possessed.   And the
general tendency of historical events was to produce
a conviction of the necessity for deliverance from the
oppressive circumstances which had overtaken civic
life.   In particular, the Greek, ground under the heel
of Macedonia or Rome, had no refuge save in self.
Aristotle had not helped him to look for any salvation
from on high.   He was his own sole resource, and so
the philosophy which he favoured bore the gospel of
self-dependence with its implied self-possession.   " The
world and the thinker upon it, are consumed like a
flame," said Aurelius, " therefore let us turn away our
eyes from vanity ; and renounce ; and withdraw ourselves alike from all affections. . . . ' Folly ! to be lifted
up, or sorrowful, or anxious, by reason of things like
these !' "[1]   While the Epicureans had in effect assumed
that the individual can live for himself irrespective of
external things and persons, the Stoics desired to show
how it was possible to be a law to one's self, on the presupposition that the material universe and society are

[1] Marius the Epicurean, vol. i. pp. 215-217.

facts. As compared with the Cyrenaic school, Stoicism is a constructive individualism; as contrasted with Epicureanism, it is scientific. It is thus by far the most important of the post-Aristotelian sects. For although individualistic, it recognises the social environment incident to human life, and strives to make use of the world and of past accumulations of knowledge. A thoroughness, which none of its rivals possessed, consequently marks it.

Despite its practical character, Stoicism is among the most dogmatic of philosophies. Indeed its final decline was partly due to the impossibility of adapting hard-and-fast theories to the exigencies of everyday use. Hence we find that it starts from a first principle which is presumed to be applicable in all conceivable straits. As the aim of the system was to teach the individual how to live, it began with a definition suitable to every case. Ethical doctrine was the final cause of Stoicism, and as a result, the entire system was moulded by it. Accordingly, the one great maxim of existence, universal in application yet realised only by disconnected individuals, is "live according to nature." Given nature, Stoicism tries to sketch a career in which universal forces will fight for the particular end. To free the individual, not by taking him out of the world, but by teaching him both the good and the evil therein, this was the task. But to be susceptible of virtue, or to know nature in order to progress along with it, implies activity of reason. And if the Stoics be right, this rational activity transforms man's conception of the nature to which he ought to conform. Thus, life is not to be so much after nature, as after the interpretation of nature given by Stoic reason. Consequently, for the individual who finds himself in doubt or difficulty, the rule of reason is the only one possible. If he but exercise his intellectual faculties goodness will displace grief. To picture the state of being in which man is thus to find freedom and satisfaction is not an easy matter. Stoic inconsistencies, of which Cicero reminds us, are frequent. But, setting aside minor discrepancies meanwhile, a general conception of the ideal may be formed with tolerable definiteness.

The chief end of any organic being is the development of what is most characteristic in its nature. Stoicism here repeats in its own way Aristotle's distinction between the various kinds of soul.[1] In plants mere movement, in animals activity under pressure of irrational feeling, in man reason subduing feeling, are severally the *propria* of life.[2] Man's chief end is therefore the development of reason. But at the same time, he has to consider his surroundings as well as himself. He is what he is in virtue of an all-pervading reason which distributes itself over the universe. Yet reason alone enables him to apprehend this principle. So, in the end, the Stoic ideal is not the culture of individual reason solely, but also the harmonising of it with another and greater power, whose nature it seems to share. Freedom is attained *in* the world; *out* of the world there is no sphere in which a rational being can act. Man stoops to conquer in that he only appreciates his own value when he understands the meaning of the universal order in which he is a part. With the Stoics, then, as with Socrates, ignorance would appear to be the arch-enemy of moral attainment. Clean-

---

[1] Cf. De Anima, book ii., 2 foll.
[2] Cf. Zeller's Stoics, Epicureans, &c., p. 227, note 4.

thes' famous hymn contains a prayer for deliverance from this very ignorance, to the end that the universal order may be eulogised :—

> " But Zeus, all-bounteous, wrapt in sable cloud,
> Thou ruler of the thunder ; oh, redeem
> Mankind from mournful ignorance ! Do thou
> Dispel, O Father, from our souls this fault,
> And grant that we attain that wisdom high
> On which relying thou dost rule the world
> With justice ; so that honoured thus by thee,
> Thee we in turn may honour, and may hymn
> Unceasingly thy works, as doth beseem
> A mortal, since nor men nor gods can know
> A grander honour than to justly hymn
> The universal and eternal law." [1]

It therefore follows, that only in so far as the individual understands and is able to fit himself to the universal order, has he realised the conditions inseparable from the ideal life. When his knowledge is perfect, then his conduct cannot fail of sinlessness. Now, in spite of its admittedly prominent application to individual lives, this scheme is as abstract as may be. The initial dogma, of a universal changeless order of reason, is perhaps satisfactory enough after its kind. But when the maxim associated with it comes to be applied to the endless variety presented in life, the want of that elasticity which alone could bring it serviceably near, is very obvious. It is little suited to regulate special needs. And after all, the aim of a philosophy such as Stoicism, more especially in view of problems which then pressed for solution, must be to convince each separate individual that such and such a line of conduct is for him and for none other.

[1] Cf. Philo-Judæus, James Drummond, vol. i. pp. 88, 89.

The very universality of the rational world-principle, however it may manifest itself by successive reproductions in human reason, cannot but cause the frequent failure of this intense personal application. As often as not, the Stoic ideal is condemned to remain an ideal—for it is too ideal at the first. Stoicism, like Epicureanism, derived its strength and its weakness from the same source. While it gifted the individual man with a conception of his own value, it surrounded his actual possession of his personality with difficulties too great to be overcome. "While the main object of the Stoics was to popularise philosophy, the high standard of self-control they exacted rendered their system exceedingly unfit for the great majority of mankind, and for the ordinary condition of affairs. Life is history, not poetry. It consists mainly of little things, rarely illumined by flashes of great heroism, rarely broken by great dangers, or demanding great exertion. A moral system, to govern society, must accommodate itself to common characters and mingled motives. It must be capable of influencing natures that can never rise to an heroic level. It must tincture, modify, and mitigate where it cannot eradicate or transform."[1]

Yet, as a concrete doctrine, Stoicism had the highest value. Man finds himself in this world, and is there exposed to certain unavoidable vicissitudes. From such fortuitous, but inevitable circumstances he seeks some measure of relief, and is taught to find his true rest neither in himself nor in momentary externals, but in the permanent order to which both his nature and his surroundings may be referred. Nor is the implied concrete or practical rule of life confined to

[1] History of European Morals, W. E. H. Lecky, vol. i. p. 204.

an individualistic application. The existence of the universal reason, on the recognition of which morality rests, is a direct negative to the abstract reason of Aristotle. God is once more brought back to the world. The instinct of the Stoics, whatever the defects in its formal expression, was a true one, and the truth which it involved was the cause of the very appreciable influence exercised by its originators. What, then, was this influence, and towards what did it tend?

The Stoic conception of virtue is an important link in the development of the ethico-religious consciousness mainly for two reasons. As regards its origin it is neither an idea of pure individual wellbeing nor of universal law. As regards its results, it gave rise to certain ethical doctrines which in later history proved to be of the deepest importance. First, then, in respect of its origin. Virtue faces two ways. It consists in conformity to nature, but conformity is explained as an activity of the individual. Thus Stoicism, while regarding man as a part of one great whole, lays upon him the responsibility of fulfilling his own special duty. It might reasonably be supposed that the universal element in this virtue would bring about its approximation to Christian ethics. But it was not so. And herein lies the peculiarity of the universal contemplated by the Stoics. Man is a part, not so much of human society, as of the natural order of the world. Hence he is indebted more to the controlling law in things than to the limiting yet fostering relations of the social organism. Conditioned more by the abstract infinity of Aristotle's god, than by any conception of man's dependence upon man, the universal element in Stoic ethics only became more intensely individualistic in application. He who recognises the universal reason, and conforms to its commands, has everything sufficient for happiness. He is therefore able to despise his less-informed fellows, and from the height of his own goodness to look down upon them as fools, if not sinners. By assuming that there was a reason in things, and that man, were he but to recognise it and subject himself to it, would thereby attain absolute goodness, the Stoics implied that the individual was capable of perfectibility. And the universal element in their ethics proved to be the condition of this perfection. The natural completeness of the world-order passed over into the individual whenever virtue was attained. Nature, as it were, is specially created to conduce to man's perfectibility—nay, the rationality of the universe is only perceived when some men have linked themselves with it by an effort of their—and its—common reason.

The implicit tendency of a theory such as this, is gradually to lose hold upon the universal, and to substitute an exaggerated estimate of the individual. Stoicism, in its intuition of an all-present reason, was legitimately protesting against Aristotle's separation between God and the world. But the time to bring deity back to earth had not yet arrived. The cry of the age was not for a theory of universal being, but for a practical aim which individual men might follow. Here, as with Aristotle, reason comes to be nothing more than an abstraction, which, however, exerts influence fragmentarily in this or that man. Now the innate logic of this theory had three very important results. It ended by universalising the individual. It set up an ideal man who, by the very fact of his own self-contained perfection, was absolutely valuable. And it developed, if it did not originate, the conception of virtue for virtue's sake—that is, of duty. In all three alike, the presence of the universal is traceable in the individual. The Stoic is a citizen of the world, for the universal order in which he partakes is not confined to this or that portion of the earth or of mankind. He is completely independent of his fellows, for in the possession of virtue he has all possible good. Is not happiness itself but the *umbra* of virtue ? Moreover, is not virtue its own reward ? Man cannot reach it if he seek it for the sake of happiness, but only if he practise it for the mere love of so doing. The first of these Stoic characteristics fitted the philosophy for its reception into the world-empire of Rome, and also familiarised finer spirits with the Christian conception of a human brotherhood. The second formed the first stage in the evolution of the idea of personality, which has had such enormous influence on the progress of civilisation. While the last laid deep foundations for the doctrine of self-sacrifice, by which Stoicism itself was to be afterwards superseded.

Thus, by a different and far more thorough-going method, Stoicism at length reached the same conclusion as Epicureanism. Freedom for the individual is the end—the use of his own life for his own highest good is man's sole worthy aim. But the likeness did not stop here. The Stoics also present us with an individual whose salvation in self, simply on account of its kind, is illusory. The wise man is all-perfect in his complete conformity to nature. Paradox though it may seem, he is happy in that he needs no happiness ; his struggle with the passions, curiously enough, enables him to declare that "never to have been miserable is

to be miserable;" his imperturbability is the quality
which causes him to regard "the ills of life as no
ills except to those who bear them ill." But when the
perfection of this ideal being—the Stoics admitted that
their wise man never was—is subjected to scrutiny,
wherein does it chiefly consist? The constant reply is,
that it consists in the supremacy of reason; and this, as
every one will admit, is good. But regard must also be
had to the reverse side; this supremacy must needs be
purchased at a price. The rule of reason is subject to
danger from one quarter—from the passions, namely.
Thus the ideal life is not, as with Aristotle, that of the
man who has his lower nature well in hand. It depends rather upon the total extirpation of impulse.
But it is to be remembered that Aristotle was not
very far from the truth when he grouped his virtues
into classes. Virtues are not products of indifference
to vicious desires. True virtue is rather the transformation of tendencies which, with less conscientiousness,
would only be causes of vice. To ensure family life,
with its thousand unrecorded acts of goodness, it is not
necessary at the same time to make certain that the
race shall die out. Virtue comes from passion changed,
not from passion destroyed. The morality of the
Stoic sage has all the appearance but none of the
reality of living virtue. It is the life of indifference,
the attitude of the agnostic towards the Church, of the
blind towards painting, of the *dilettante* towards philosophy—this, and such as this, is the position of the wise
man towards evil. And its result is proof of its character—realised in characterlessness.

Here, just as true good is found only in absence of
what might produce evil, so true freedom only accom-

panies absence of want. The individual, as with the Epicureans, attains his apotheosis at the moment when no appreciable remnant of him is left to be deified. *In se revocandum, est ; in se recedendum, est.* True. But if the *se* be passionless, into what is the withdrawal? And if a withdrawal be the end-all of life, to what purpose is living? Isolation, the freedom of self only in relation to self, is a doctrine that cannot preserve its balance. Even could it maintain its equilibrium, no credit would accrue; it is equally easy and difficult to adjust nothing. From setting man in a universe to which he must be subordinate, the Stoics retrograde to taking him out of society—that is, to making him independent of everything which might furnish him with material for the construction of an ideal life. They set him the task, godlike but impossible, of creating something out of nothing. From extreme optimism in theory they finally arrive at extreme pessimism in practice. For, to the wise man his fellows are fools or madmen, nay, worse, they are "mostly fools." "In the belief of the Stoics, all men, with few exceptions, and those rapidly disappearing, are fools. Even to the most celebrated statesmen and heroes at most the inconsistent concession is made that they are afflicted with the common vices of mankind to a less degree than other people."[1] Under such conditions again, little wonder that to the possible wise man himself his perfectibility seemed further and further from realisation. Life itself, for the sake of which these excessive sacrifices to duty must be made, may conceivably become indifferent. Circumstances detrimental to utter apathy may force themselves upon the wise man to the exclusion of his ideal imperturba-

[1] Zeller's Outlines of Greek Philosophy, p. 248.

bility. Then it is meet to seek release, and "the door is ever open." Rare as are the cases in which this extremest extirpation is unavoidable, the very fact of their possibility shows that the freedom contemplated can never be won by man. Reason is not greater than brute force if it be shut out from contact with the material world. In a complete universe it is the mightiest of known powers. Of this the Stoics were well aware, but they mistook the shadow for the substance. To free man they sought to find for him in some far-off clime that life which he can only possess here and now. The problem of human nature was to be solved by a negation of its existence, or by a laboured process of rendering it indifferent to humanity.

The defects of Stoicism, which had influence on its own later development as well as on the progress of philosophy in general, relate, as is natural, to its main component elements. They are connected either with the theory of individual life or with the conception of a universal reason controlling the world. To the former, sufficient attention has perhaps been given already. So far as their theory of individual life is concerned, the Stoics must be numbered among the many good men whose doctrines contain an evil taint. Apathy, taken even at its best, is a purely negative state. The knowledge on which Stoic virtue was based might fairly be called positive. But no such plea can be advanced on behalf of virtue itself. It is ever entirely negative, and necessarily so. What the wise man is not, we are constantly informed; what he is, we learn only in a formula. Reason is so abstract that, even in action, it sinks back into simple identity with self. Development of self may indeed be the ideal, but even thus life is reduced to a shade. The pure self, like pure being, may possibly form a peg on which to hang the attributes of definiteness; yet as such it has no qualities. At the same time, it is but just to add that the criticism of Stoic morality, which assumes that a rule of external law is intended, goes beyond the facts. The morality of law makes mere performance of pre-scribed acts good, altogether without reference to the spirit of the actor. Stoicism did not contemplate any-thing of this sort. It actually delivered man from such an external yoke. It sought to reveal to him a manner of life in which practice should indeed be an expression of inner principle. But in its conception of the nature of this life it was at fault. In so far as its aim was to deliver men from evil it was good. But the condition of being in which, according to the theory, such deliver-ance could be accomplished was not attainable; and even could it have been realised, it would not have been de-sirable. The ideal set up as good was essentially not good. The eradication of the passions has, as such, no final moral significance. To erect it into an end much to be desired is the result only of a confusion of thought. Man finds himself in a world of conflict, and he wishes to lay hold on his own life so as to dispose it to the best moral advantage. But conflict is in itself no final account of human nature. It, in turn, is traceable to imperfection. So, true freedom for the individual is not to be found in the destruction of one part of his being, but in training it all round, to the end that continuous growth may at last obliterate original imperfection. A formal obedience of the passions to rational will, nay, more, their absolute disappearance, serves but to im-poverish the individual. He may progress towards the

Stoic ideal, but, as in all progress by negation, the imperfection becomes more and more, the individual less and less. The wise man never existed, for the excellent reason that a ghost cannot be clothed in flesh and blood. The Stoic attempt to gain freedom for the individual was in its way crowned with failure as complete as the Epicurean.

Further, Stoicism was defective on its universal side. The world, if governed by a permeating reason, cannot fail to be the best of all possible worlds. Yet the stern logic of facts seems to be entirely against this inference. So far from being the best of all possible worlds, this earth is evil to such an extent that even the wise man himself is sometimes forced to succumb. The Stoic explanation, or rather explanations, are various. They are, however, germane to our present inquiry only as they throw light upon the obliviousness of sin, which still characterised the ethico-religious consciousness. The most common and obvious account of moral evil is that offered by Chrysippus. He apparently assumes that good exists only as the contrary of evil.[1] "Bugs do us good service by preventing us from sleeping too long, and mice warn us not to leave things about."[2] Like many analogies, this one is misleading. We may be unable to *think* good except as the other of evil: it by no means follows that good *exists* only as a contrary. In any case, a thoroughgoing explanation of evil is here implicitly postponed as concerns this world. Some day evil may be turned into good; now it *is*, and the fact cannot be denied. This view is partly responsible for the common Stoic doctrine—a doctrine which did noth-

---

[1] Cf. Plutarch, De Repug. Sto., 35, 36.
[2] Zeller's Stoics, &c., p. 189, note 2.

ing to assuage the despair of dying Paganism—that sin is a defect rather than an offence. The other main accounts of evil point in the same direction. If "sin" be due to the imperfection of the parts when isolated from a great whole, then defect is still the tenor of the solution. And the same may be said of the explanation which makes evil but an incident in some mighty evolution of good. Stoicism, in short, had not been able to rid itself of the Platonic dualism which always connects evil with the very existence of matter. " In the economy of the great world evil is like chaff falling —as unavoidable and worthless." [1] Except as a foil to good, its existence is without aim. Yet the end of man's life is to eliminate all tendencies on which evil might flourish.

Parallel with this negative account of evil runs the Stoic conception of deity. Although it will be necessary to return to this later, in connection with the discussion of the Logos, it is important to note its relations to preceding doctrines now. The course of religious evolution shows that it is possible to view God under three different aspects. Of these, two are distinctively monotheistic, while the third is pantheistic. In the Jewish theocracy God is represented as a being of infinite power, who has an indisputable right to dispose of his creatures according to his own good pleasure. Here the idea of a royal prerogative dominates, if it does not quite efface, all other attributes by means of which the conception of deity might be extended. The unavoidable consequence is, that God is set over against man and the world, in the form of an external law which demands and enforces unconditional

---

[1] The Gentile and the Jew, Döllinger, vol. i. p. 351.

obedience. Needless to say that this conception of deity
was entirely alien to Greek genius.[1] Had any such
notion been integral to the religious consciousness of
the Hellenic peoples, their supreme joy in the world
would have been blighted, and the whole course of
their civilisation would have been different. Yet, the
second monotheistic view of deity, — less markedly
monotheistic than the first, no doubt,—is to be found
in the later period of Greek reflection. Aristotle's
purely intellectual god is not so far removed from the
deistic deity of last century as the lapse of time might
lead one to suppose. This self-contemplating being is
out of relation to the world, and unaffected by it. His
nature is divine only because he is exalted above matter
and its imperfections. God is god, not so much in that
he is a being of infinite power and majesty and love, as
in that he has a self-sustained existence, which is perfect for the very reason that it is abstract. In extreme
antagonism to this view stands the pantheistic explanation of deity, according to which God is a part of the
world, and diffuses himself throughout its visible frame-
work. This was the Stoic theory.

"The inconsistencies of a great philosophical system
are best explained by examining its historical antecedents."[2] In its conception of God, Stoicism is a
reaction from Aristotelian dualism. It sought not only
to free the individual from control of external forces,
but also to bring him, and the world which he in-

---

[1] By this I mean Greek genius as a factor in universal civilisation.
The instructive parallel which Quinet draws, between Jehovah and the
Dorian Hercules, does not affect the truth of the statement. Cf. Génie
des Religions, Part I. sec. 5, "The Migrations of the Human Race."

[2] The Greek Philosophers, A. W. Benn, vol. ii. p. 25.

habited, into connection with the universal power which was believed to order everything. Whatever may have been the defects of the resultant theology, the Stoics are not to be blamed overmuch. The inevitable course of Greek speculation, no less than the events of contemporary history, led them to protest against Aristotle's barren doctrine. Their encyclopædic knowledge, covering the whole field of previous philosophy, could not fail to find, in at least one former system, just the suggestion which was then needed. Nor is this wonderful. The Stoic elevation of knowledge very naturally took the direction which past research had prepared for it. Physical speculation had no small part in Zeno's teaching, and it occupied a prominent place in Chrysippus' voluminous writings. The form of their system forced the Stoics to formulate a theory of the univèrse, and this caused them to redirect attention towards the pre-Socratic philosophy of nature. Here they discovered, at all events in outline, the anti-Aristotelian theology which they required.

The physicism of Heracleitus, with its god who " is day and night, summer and winter, war and peace, satiety and hunger,"[1] and with its substratum of universal law which is the one changeless fact amid unending flux, furnished the Stoics at once with a god who is in the world, and with a world which is determined by the nature of that god. This conception, as developed by them, was often self-contradictory. The failure to procure freedom for the individual, and to sublate moral evil in a growth towards perfection, has

[1] Frag., 36 (Bywater). Cf. Art. A further Study of Heraclitus, by G. T. W. Patrick, in 'The American Journal of Psychology,' August 1888, p. 587 *sq.*, and throughout.

its parallel in a wavering account of deity. God is at one time personal, at another impersonal. Stoic sentiment tended towards an individualised providence, but the facts of nature seemed to imply a general principle, revealed with no definiteness save in the orderliness of things. The Stoic god, then, is *in* matter—that is, he is united to the material world. Not indeed that they are always inseparable. God, in one point of view, is more than the world. He has a homogeneity with self which the world, as an order in time, would appear to lack. But, as Zeller has shown, this admitted distinction is not essential. " The world is the sum of all real existence, and all real existence is originally contained in deity, which is at once the matter of everything, and the creative force which moulds this matter into particular individual substances." [1]   It is important for the present purpose to note, that whatever expressions to the contrary [2] are to be found in Stoic writers, the tendency of the theory is to regard deity as impersonal. God is not the "absolute subject," as Hegel thought, nor yet "absolute substance," as Spinoza contended. He consists rather in a diffused force, unlike the Hegelian "Subject" by absence of individuality, unlike the Spinozistic "Substance" by presence of activity. He is the soul of the world—that is, a determining principle, which, however, can be known as it manifests itself in the systematising of things material. Providence, in the shape of certain irresistible laws of matter, is god. A double movement of thought is here traceable. According as one side of the conception predominates, god appears in the idealistic guise of the

---

[1] Stoics, &c., pp. 156, 157.

[2] Cf. The Greek Philosophers, Benn, vol. ii. p. 11.

rational part of the world; according as the other is pressed, the original material mass, in relation to which his power is displayed, keeps deity down. God, in short, is an efficient cause, and as such is abstract and ideal. But a cause of this kind is efficient in a certain sphere alone. Therefore, god is concrete and material, and is only able to *be* provided that he put on the world for a body. This conception of deity is not unlike the freedom with which Stoicism gifts the individual. In opposition to Aristotle, god is brought back to the world; but in the process of reconveyance his *divine* nature disappears. The difficulty which beset the Stoics in formulating positive virtue for the moral life, repeats itself in inability to explain the relation between humanity and god.

Seeing that reason controls the world, the course of things takes place inevitably. The universe was, is, and will be an order in time for the plain cause that what has been, is, and will be, must come to pass. "Nothing *happens*, but it *comes*." [1] Thus, the restoration of god to the world results in fatalism. There is one cause of the universal order, and as it is necessary, so too must its effects be. Just as freedom was obtained by emptying life of content, so god's presence seems to imply the total disappearance of the self-determining individuality, which with the Stoics was the sole instrument of morality. Thus the problem came to be, how can this predestined order of the universe be reconciled with the moral responsibility of man? In attempting its solution the Stoics were forced to limit both man and god. Man is saddled with responsibility for his own acts, because they are pro-

[1] Seneca, De Prov., v.

ducts of his will. It does not lighten the burden one whit that, given the foreordained order of events, the deed could not have been other than it was. So, freedom of the will is limited to mere activity within a pre-ordered set of conditions. But responsibility remains the same as if those limitations were non-existent. God, too, must needs be limited. As he pervades all, he pervades man. The good man differs from god in his mortality alone.[1] No doubt he is enjoined to imitate god. But, being under the law, how can he? God, it would therefore seem, is himself necessitated, for he is but a less imperfect edition of man. He too must develop himself within the limits of the universal law. Just as the Stoic depicts the perfect life devoid of passion, so he represents god devoid of imperfection. In both cases alike reality is conspicuous by its absence. God is interpreted in terms of his own cosmical order; whereas, if deity be worth the name—if he can stand in any real relation to sinners—the cosmical order must be interpreted in terms of him. Truth to tell, the Stoics had not yet grasped the idea of personality, which was afterwards to transform the religious consciousness in humanity.

But Stoicism, as a theoretical system called forth by contemporary needs, did not end with Greek civilisation. It passed over into Rome, and there assumed a practical importance—in Roman law—which remained without parallel till the present century, when English Utilitarianism so deeply influenced politics. But what now interests us in this migration is rather the change which overtook the philosophy when it came into contact with a character so alien to the Greek as the Roman was.

[1] Cf. Cicero, De Nat. Deor., ii. 154.

Mommsen, whose account of Greek philosophy is, one would hope, the least meritorious portion of his great work, declares that "the Romans became in philosophy simply inferior scholars of bad teachers."[1] Yet, he seems to contradict himself shortly afterwards. The influence of Greek philosophy and culture did originate something new. "As the aggregate result of this modern Roman education, there sprung up the *new idea* of 'humanity,' as it was called, which consisted partly of a more or less superficial appropriation of the æsthetic culture of the Hellenes, partly of a *privileged Latin culture* as an imitation or mutilated copy of the Greek. This *new humanity,* as the very name indicates, *renounced the specific peculiarities of Roman life*—nay, even came forward in opposition to them, and combined in itself, just like our closely kindred 'general culture,' a nationally cosmopolitan and socially exclusive character. Here, too, we trace *the revolution* which separated classes and levelled nations."[2] When Greek culture penetrated to Rome, the result was precisely that which invariably follows in similar circumstances. The product was neither a mere debased reproduction of Greek genius, nor a cleverly veneered example of Roman character, but an entirely new compound. Cato was perfectly right when, with instinctive conservatism, he opposed the inroads of Hellenic learning. He was more or less clearly conscious that the foreign influence would appreciably affect the old Roman character, which, perhaps by its very defects, had won so many triumphs. In all likelihood he was unaware that the strange doctrines would themselves undergo transforma-

[1] History of Rome, vol. iii. p. 427 (pop. ed.)
[2] History of Rome, vol. iii. p. 444. (The italics are mine.)

tion. Yet, this was but the other aspect of the fears which inspired him. To what, then, did this contact amount, and in what direction did it tend? Speaking generally, it may be said that, under the influence of Roman character, Stoicism departed from its quest for individual freedom, and concerned itself more with practical virtue—that is, in the statement of a rule of life, by reference to which man might obtain guidance how to act in given circumstances.

The type of Rome was narrow and intense, rather than flexible and amiable. Duty, as represented by some particular thing to be done at a specified moment, was the prevailing conception, and that to the exclusion of beauty, or the harmonious realisation throughout a lengthened period of a plastic ideal. Brutus and Cato may have been extreme, but the *severitas,* which was the peculiar characteristic of their countrymen, rendered them possible. The tendency to satire in poetry, the absence of dramatic freedom, the historical bias of literature in general, as well as the confusion of styles so apparent in art,[1] and especially in architecture, are traceable one and all to the decisive bent of Roman genius. Eminently strong in body, these rulers of the ancient world were withal weak in faith. They could destroy kingdoms as could none others, they could construct roads and waterways which bade defiance to decay. But for all this, they could not crush invisible forces, nor had they sufficient spiritual originality to transform alien religions, as they incorporated foreign principalities. I think it was Quinet who remarked, that though they swallowed whole empires, the inner

---

[1] This point has been fully worked out by Dr Burn in his recent book, Roman Literature in relation to Roman Art.

emptiness of their own city remained to them. Their attitude towards everything that did not bear on its face the mark of practical service remained unsoftened even long after Greek thought had held sway.

> "Dixeris hæc inter varicosos centuriones ;
> Continuo crassum ridet Pulfennius ingens,
> Et centum Græcos curto centusse licetur." [1]

In the same spirit is Cicero's story of Gellius the pro consul.[2] "On his arrival in Athens he called together the philosophers and urged them at last to put an end to their disputes, offering his assistance as umpire if they were unable to settle matters peaceably without him."[3] The very coinage still remains bearing witness to this determined process of magnifying externals. "J'insiste sur cette grande qualité de la numismatique de Rome. Peu d'imagination, beaucoup d'énergie, et un sentiment profond de la vérité historique. Là est sa force et son intérêt."[4] All this testifies conclusively to the existence of a Roman temperament entirely different from that which characterised the Greeks and other contemporary peoples. And the question which naturally occurs is, had this national bias any special affinity for Stoicism ? To this hour, even the physical eye of the restless tourist can see that it had. Ruins, extraordinary in destruction, such as the Thermæ of Caracalla, and the Basilica of Constantine, are but evidence of the application of the distinctive Roman genius to that form of architecture from which Stoicism

---

[1] Persius, Sat., v. 189.   [2] Cf. Leg., i. 53.
[3] Ancient Philosophy, J. B. Mayor, p. 217, note 2.
[4] W. Frœhner, quoted by Dr Burn in Roman Literature in relation to Roman Art, p. 101.

derived its name. The porch of the Greeks—another
proof that theory and practice are but the reverse sides
of the same shield—is the basilica of the Romans.
Zeno's doctrines took powerful hold at Rome on account
of their very hardness. "Roman virtue found its
highest expression in Stoicism. Roman vice sheltered
itself under the name of Epicurus."[1] Mutual inflexi-
bility, strange as it may seem, was the cause of the
ready reception with which Stoicism met at Rome. At
the same time, Stoicism had a "transcendental" element,
if such phrase be permissible, which could not fail to
affect and to be affected by Roman prosaicness. The
philosophy itself both gained and lost by the change of
environment, but, partly owing to circumstances altogether different from the influence of Roman character,
the gain was more than counterbalanced by the loss.

From 150 B.C. Greek culture exercised much influence
at Rome. In particular, the sons of rich or noble fami-
lies were considered uneducated had they not sat at the
feet of Hellenic teachers. In this way Stoicism, as well
as the other Greek philosophies, became naturalised.
The process of assimilation, however, did not leave
the materials on which it wrought altogether unchanged.
Something new was superadded. Stoicism acquired influence, but it departed somewhat from its classical
traditions. The teaching of Panætius, as Aulus Gellius
avers,[2] had less abstract harshness, less dialectical difficulty, than that of Zeno or Chrysippus. In brief, it was
better adapted to the wants of everyday life. The
theory of the individual's relation to the universe—that
is, the search for freedom—lost importance, which was
now transferred to the furnishing of practical aid in the

---

[1] Hist. of European Morals, Lecky, vol. i. p. 243.
[2] Cf. Ferrier's Greek Philosophy, p. 458 ; Cicero, De Fin., iv. 28, 79.

moral difficulties incident to private life. Teachers of "wisdom" contrived to give lessons in rhetoric because pupils required some really "useful" return for fees paid. Stoicism thus became influential in proportion as, like the Romans themselves, it ceased to trouble itself about the origin of the world, or the destiny of man, and devoted attention to the discussion of the immediate needs inseparable from ordinary life. By adapting itself in this way to surrounding requirements, it formed another among the many evidences that Roman civilisation developed new affinities the more it came into contact with Greek thought and culture.

At this stage, then, Stoicism found its individual man ready to hand. Freedom was no longer the problem, but rather the more casuistical one of drawing a dividing line between specifically right and specifically wrong deeds. The old theory embodied in the maxim "live according to nature," which was supposed to be a guide sufficient for eternity, found itself jostled in the streets of Rome by a questioning mob, all of whom spoke at once, asking each a different question. A philosophy put to such test could not but exercise a very definite sway. It practically stood in place of religion,[1] and like religion, it tended to treat all men as equals.[2] Stoicism thus became more cosmopolitan during its sojourn at Rome. Humanitarianism, if implicit from the first, was its latest doctrine. In this shape it entered Roman law, moulding man's conceptions of his natural relations to his fellow-man for centuries after the Roman system had been dead or crystallised. Ceasing somewhat to

---

[1] Cf. Roman Stoicism as a Religion, in Essays and Addresses, Rev. J. M. Wilson.

[2] This point is brought out by Mr Lecky in European Morals, vol. i. p. 252 *sq.*

minister to an ideal, it grasped real life, and breathing into the narrowness of local or national institutions a larger spirit, it evolved a positive code of duties, which the individual ought to fulfil in social life.   And so it achieved its own immortality.   For a principle was thus formulated which Christianity afterwards adopted and spread over the whole civilised world.

While, then, Stoicism gained in one respect by its contact with Roman civilisation, it lost in another.   And, so far as the development of the religious consciousness in humanity is concerned, the loss, even if necessary to progress, was, relatively speaking, greater than the gain.   As a theory of the universal, Stoicism waned more and more.   The constant demands of the individual that *his* particular difficulties should be met, while they pointed to an increase of respect for man as such, kept limiting the philosophic outlook.   The relation between the universal and the individual no longer absorbed thinkers.   The isolated individual himself, nay, even his momentary mood, had become the important object of inquiry.   Self-examination, directed no doubt to the disclosure of imperfection, took a leading place among Stoic doctrines. This apparently unavoidable tendency to attach undue consideration to the man of the moment, was fatal in its effects upon Stoicism regarded as a witness for highest truth.   Assuredly there were some few brilliant exceptions.   But, as a general rule, the philosophy was reduced to the level of an officially authorised cult. Grounded now on the exaltation of man as an individual, it readily lent itself to the degrading deification of the Emperor.   In the absence of any other effective *universal* faith, and amid the conflict of individuals, all equally valuable in the eyes of the cosmopolitan philosopher, Cæsar, who *ex officio* had many advantages, became *the* individual,—the only god possible for the Roman world as a whole. With Nero for "their Lord and their God," the later Stoics might well question the efficacy of the salvation which their wise man could achieve for himself. Of old it had been the strength of their system to perceive one ever-present power reproducing itself in the endless variations of the pagan pantheon. Now, this very god was found shut up in human form. Theoretically he might be in every man, practically he reserved his self-revelation for the person of the Cæsar. The contradiction was unavoidable. Reason—the deity—is everywhere, but he is limited by the circumstances now and here operative. The friction of the world, as it were, is too strong for the moulding force even of divinity. And if God be thus constrained, what must be said of the individual man in whom he is alleged to find habitation?

In Rome, the philosophy of Zeno and Chrysippus chanced upon elements which were essentially incompatible with its continued existence as an explanation of man and the world. At the last, indeed, it proves itself "the most incongruous, the most self-contradictory, of all philosophical systems. With a gross and material pantheism it unites the most vivid expressions of the fatherly love and providence of God: with the sheerest fatalism it combines the most exaggerated statements of the independence and self-sufficiency of the human soul: with the hardest and most uncompromising isolation of the individual, it proclaims the most expansive view of his relations to all around."[1]

[1] St. Paul's Epistle to the Philippians, Lightfoot, p. 296.

CHAPTER VI.

SCEPTICISM, COMPLACENCY, AND SUPERSTITION.

IN addition to Epicureanism and Stoicism, a third post-Aristotelian school appeared in Greece, bent on similar aims, but prepared to solve difficulties by another method. Pyrrho and the Sceptics, like their contemporaries, desired that the individual should be enabled to make the most of his own life. But they promised subjective freedom only on condition that the problems presented by the phenomenal world, and by the strange contradictions incident to human life, should be severely left unheeded. The harmony with self of Epicurus and Zeno was obtained by Pyrrho in a veritable suspense of judgment with regard to everything except self. Here too, as with the other schools, individual salvation was only achieved by a *tour de force*. If the Epicureans had sought pleasure principally by avoiding pleasures, if the Stoics had tried to bring about the fuller development of life chiefly by destroying its only possible content, the Sceptics arrived at self-possession by narrowing the bounds of certainty down to self. They did not observe that, if self be certain, the harmony is no longer with self, but with all that makes self in any respect real.

At first, under Pyrrho and his immediate followers, Scepticism was the creed of a comparatively feeble folk.[1] But afterwards, in contact with the other individualistic schools, and more especially at Rome, it gained many adherents. Carneades is its chief historical representative. The disturbing force, which his negative criticism brought to bear upon the progress of thought at Rome, was much more important in its results than is sometimes supposed.

Dogmatic theories, such as Epicureanism, and more conspicuously Stoicism, are always open to easy attack. Whenever dogmatists begin to formulate positive doctrines, they are liable to criticism on the part of those who are not burdened with any inflexible conscientiousness. And Stoicism, being the more constructive of contemporary systems, attracted the larger share of hostile comment. At Rome, despite an ingrained horror of irresponsibility in matters of conduct, there was a special reason for the widespread scepticism of the Academy. Scepticism, as a suspense of judgment, did not bind men down to any "cut and dried" abstract creed. As a theory of such suspense, it left the individual to himself, and so was well able to accommodate adherents whose ethical practice was of the most varied description. At the same time, as an integral portion of the philosophical organism, its importance was relative rather than absolute. Carneades and his friends kept up a constant irritation by criticising the other competing systems. When Stoicism first began to gain ground at Rome, nothing hindered its growth more than the continuous, and, it may be added, well-founded and well-informed opposition of the Academicians. This

[1] Cf. Zeller's Stoics, &c., p. 517.

served to propagate distrust, and to rally the remnants of that antipathy with which Greek philosophy was at first regarded. Moreover, its influence was increased by the fact that it was not wholly negative, as indeed its authors claimed.[1] The theory of probabilities, with its sufficiently elastic application to the unforeseen necessities of practical life, recommended Scepticism to a people who, though devoid of taste for abstract speculation, always desired to adjust to a theoretical standard actions which seemed the unavoidable results of utilitarian demands made by the work-a-day world. In itself a theory of this sort has no "grit." It only exists in relation to something else, and it enters into that relation for a specific purpose alone. No better example of this general truth can be found than the career of the New Academy. It fulfilled its destiny as the parasite of Stoicism, and this, its allotted task, being done, it disappeared. From the widest diffusion under Carneades, about 150 B.C., it had scarce a representative at the close of the century.

In relation to the other schools, then, what office did Scepticism perform? Reference has already been made to the likeness between Epicureanism and Stoicism.[2] In certain aims and tendencies these systems, however divergent in details, were practically agreed. Yet this agreement was obscured by the seeming antagonism of their several distinctive tenets. In Rome this difference became more and more obvious. Epicureanism was congenial to the sybarite, whilst Stoicism attracted men of purer mind and more earnest spirit. Carneades devoted himself to exposing the errors of both schools, though the Stoic theology and naturalistic

---

[1] Cf. Sextus, Pyrr. Hyp., i. 226.   [2] See above, p. 85 *sq.*

ethics were the favourite objects of his criticism. "To the appeal to the universality of belief in gods he opposed, in part, the denial of such universality; in other part, the little value to be set upon what the ignorant multitude believe. He contested the assumption of a divine order in the world, and a providence, by pointing to the general misery of man, the bad use the great proportion made of the pretended gift of reason, and the abundant happiness and prosperity of the evil: there was nowhere any indication to be discovered of a world-soul or a government by a deity. The idea that God was an infinite being, and at the same time a personality existing and living for himself, involved a contradiction. Were God a living being, he must be also capable of suffering, and therefore exposed to death; while, as a corporeal being, he must besides consist of parts, and therefore be divisible and destructible."[1] Argument such as this could not produce any positive results. But it caused both Stoics and Epicureans to reconsider their dogmas, and to bethink them of the insufficiency of their creeds. It also occasioned a distrust of the rival sects, and led to their partial rejection by all. In short, Scepticism did not destroy Epicureanism, much less Stoicism, but its very negativity did originate an entirely new movement in the sphere of philosophy. A narrowed Stoicism and an adulterated Epicureanism were brought together by its destructive action, and at length partially sublated in a fresh philosophical form. Thus the importance of the New Academy lies, not in its solution of the problem of individual life, but in the relation in which that solution stood to the other explanations of the

[1] The Gentile and the Jew, Döllinger, vol. i. pp. 367, 368.

same difficulty.   Carneades is remembered because his
negative criticism presaged that despair of philosophy
which, but a century afterwards, was to work such
momentous results in the preparation for Christianity.
Strange to tell, however, the immediate influence of
Scepticism went to aid construction.   Philosophy did
not despair ere it had rallied all its forces for a final
desperate attempt.   Reason had first to make an in-
ventory of its own most useful goods : only thereafter
was faith called in to supply an irremediable want.
Scepticism, acting upon Stoicism and Epicureanism,
was therefore the principal cause of Eclecticism.   And
Eclecticism implies that the systems from which its
formative elements are chosen have lost their original
vitality.   To Cicero and to Varro the problem of philosophy was not the serious affair of human wellbeing
which it had been to the early successors of Aristotle.
The sudden efflorescence of Roman genius in the Ciceronian and Augustan ages obscured for the moment the
eternal necessity of Fate, which, in its conflict with
Freedom, as Schelling says,[1] rendered the close of
Paganism so tragic.

Scepticism usually causes positive thinkers of various
opinions to unite for the preservation of thought.   So
it was at Rome, where the leading schools had certain
elements in common.   On the basis of the post-Aristotelian philosophy and of the classical Greek systems,
a new school arose to combat the unbelief of Carneades.
Several causes, which have been partially indicated
already, co-operated to bring about this result.   In the
first place, Epicureanism and Stoicism were not the
mutual contradictories which Hegelian theory would

[1] Cf. Journal of Speculative Philosophy, vol. xii. p. 209.

have them labelled. On many points they were in substantial agreement. The ethical aim of philosophy; the subservience of physical science to the scheme of moral life; appeal to the evidence of the senses; the proof of the substantiality of knowledge by the fact of action,—all these were subjects about which the two schools had no quarrel. The ideal of life too, presented as individual independence of the world, was alike for both. Again, the destructive criticism of Carneades left a certain constructive residuum.[1] The theory of probability hinted at—if no more—a standard of truth in individual consciousness. Philosophy had been brought down from the high moral sphere of Stoicism to the facts of man's life. It thus became valuable in proportion as it could provide *criteria* for common use. The larger problems of speculation, such as the origin of the universe, and man's relation to the cosmical order, had to give place to smaller but more clamant questions. Positive theory was discredited by Scepticism, with the result that practical ethics, about which the philosophical sects were in general accord, came to have a vastly increased value. This result was also accelerated by the reaction of Roman character upon Greek culture, which has been already noted[2] in the discussion of Stoicism. Indeed, it was mainly in connection with that school, owing doubtless to natural affinities, that the influence of Rome on Greek philosophy found example. Hence, as Zeller points out, "this eclecticism first appeared in the Stoic school."[3] The Stoics became conscious of their defects.

---

[1] Hume's "memory reviews experience by the aid of association" presents a striking parallel to this.
[2] See above, p. 119 *sq.*   [3] Outline of Greek Philosophy, p. 276.

So, too, did the Epicureans. Mr Pater's remarkable chapter entitled "Second Thoughts,"[1] is full of constructive significance. "Cyrenaicism, then, old or new, may be noticed, just in proportion to the completeness of its development, to approach, as to the nobler form of Cynicism, so also to the more nobly developed phases of the old, or traditional ethics. . . . It was some such cramping, narrowing, costly preference of one part of his own nature, and of the nature of things, to another, that Marius seemed to have detected in himself, as also in his old masters in the Cyrenaic philosophy. If they did realise the $\mu o\nu\acute{o}\chi\rho o\nu o\varsigma$ $\acute{\eta}\delta o\nu\acute{\eta}$, . . . if, now and then, they apprehended the world in its fulness, and had a vision, almost 'beatific,' of ideal personalities in life and art; yet these moments were a very costly matter: they paid a great price for them, if we duly consider it, in a thousand possible sympathies, and things only to be enjoyed through sympathy, from which they detached themselves, in the mere intellectual pride of loyalty to a theory which could take nothing for granted, and assent to no hypothetical or approximate truths."[2]

The new Eclecticism, then, was constructed from the more commonly accepted elements of the preceding systems. Stoicism took on a certain amount of tenderness from Epicureanism; Epicureanism was so far braced by Stoicism.[3] Yet, despite advantages of this kind, Roman Eclecticism, like all its kind, was mainly a stop-gap theory. With it philosophy ceased to strive after man's eternal welfare. The problem of life as a whole received but scant attention at a time when the

---

[1] Marius the Epicurean, vol. ii. ch. ii.   [2] Ibid., pp. 23-25.
[3] Cf. Mr Lecky, following Plutarch, History of European Morals, vol. i. pp. 263 *sq.*

all-absorbing pursuits of the present limited the intellectual outlook. It is to be remembered that, taken even at its best, all Eclecticism must in a manner be a confession of failure. Systems set about to solve the riddles of knowing and being, and so long as they are vigorous, they turn neither to the right nor to the left from their search after truth. But when a moment comes, as come it often does, in which the deep plummet seems but to tell of a bottomless abyss, then there is faltering. A philosophy seeks aid from without only when it begins to be doubtful of itself. And when such doubt is abroad, the earnest single-mindedness necessary for grappling with higher problems cannot but be wanting. Stoicism, ere it arrived at Rome, was filled with strength for the resolution of Aristotelian dualism. But changed circumstances rendered the worse Stoicism the more successful philosophy at the great city.

Hence the Eclecticism which grew out of it no longer pursued the essential search of speculation, but paused in order the better to adapt itself to numerous momentary demands. Adaptation was the new but barren principle which it thrust upon philosophy. Amid the busy practical life of a ruling people, the desire to escape from the world's limitations vanished awhile. Scepticism occasioned a sense of need for some sort of certainty in things spiritual. Eclecticism, quarrying in previous systems, heaped up a miscellaneous pile of doctrines applicable to life, and, as an addition of its own, proceeded to impress the individual with an idea of his resultant ability. The business of the philosopher is, therefore, to justify each man's particular acts to himself, and that in accordance with a standard of truth or right which recommends itself to the person whose knowledge or morality happens to be under judgment. The "probability" of Carneades naturally becomes respectable when invested with the cloak of Stoic virtue, and in displaying the adaptability of Epicurean happiness inevitably makes itself useful. Theory is now degraded to the menial task of discovering for citizen or slave what he had best do in a minor difficulty, or of justifying, *post facto*, such actions as a little forethought might have prevented. Not what is eternally true and right, but what is expedient and justifiable for this man here and now—that is the question. And as "one man's meat is another man's poison," the ethical value of this philosophy may easily be gauged. Eclecticism, in fact, is not only no effectual answer to Scepticism, but is itself the cause of further doubt. To find and describe "the immediately certain" is unquestionably a laudable object. Yet the search must be initiated with the question, what is "the immediately certain"? Each individual must be left to judge for himself, or, to every man a specially measured and clipped system must be supplied. Knowledge, as it really is, becomes one thing for the judge, another for the criminal. Doubt concerning punishment is the unavoidable result. Knowledge is known to exist, yet, somehow, man is apparently unable to arrive at it. In some such way Eclecticism reproduces the very doubt against which it arose to protest. It applies itself to the endless task of adjudicating on each individual's every act, and that with a special standard for each. "*Non numero hæc judicantur sed pondere.*" Assuredly. But who is to be the judge? Here, as ever, the casuistry which begins by regarding all doubts as duties, ends by reducing all duties to doubts.

Philo of Larissa and Antiochus of Ascalon were the chief founders and teachers of Eclecticism as a formal system. The influence of the new tendency on the life of the day, however, was represented not by the professional thinkers, but by a pupil of Antiochus, who was only an " amateur in philosophy." Marcus Tullius Cicero, to whom one would willingly devote much more consideration than is here possible, was the microcosm of the thought of his age. In him the decline of Stoicism into a system of mere utility, and the subordination of ethical research to casuistical argument, found full exemplification. It has long been the custom to disparage his power as a thinker; probably it were fairer to blame the period than the man. To tell the honest truth, Cicero was no original thinker. The conflict of contending opinions effectively prevented the tranquillity essential to achievement in abstract thought. At the same time, he was a diligent student who possessed unusual faculty of selection and restatement. Without the learning of Varro, he had the more effective gift of lucid exposition. Neither an Academician, an Epicurean, nor a Stoic, his varied practical experience fitted him to cull from all these schools such sentiments as were best suited to contemporary requirements. If he doubts, it is more because he despairs of theory than of thought. Firm footing is to be found in none of the competing philosophies; therefore, as a last resort, the would-be thinker must look to himself for the criterion of truth. On this account Ciceronianism has been stigmatised as time-serving. In one sense it was. Cicero never saw that the ideal of Stoicism, and of his own revered Plato, had nothing in common with the variegated individual utilities which, with him, went

to make up "the good."   But, on the other hand,
everything that has any meaning must be time-serving.
And this blindness was the distinguishing characteristic
of the Eclecticism of the day. Philosophy was philosophy then only so be that it transformed itself into
obiter dicta as quickly as possible.[1] The Ciceronian
ethical code advises a well-considered compliance with
use and wont. The 'De Officiis,' with its careful anat-
omy of moral probabilities, is a fitting introduction to
the 'Tusculanæ Disputationes' and the doctrine of individual complacency. This pliability in action was
the immediate result of a train of thought which made
provision for guidance on particular occasions only. To
" know nothing with absolute certainty," even if we do
" know that which is most important with as much
certainty as we require to know it,"[2] is a species of
assurance that may do well at rare intervals, but
which, as a universal principle, is certain to break
down at all other times. Macaulay's characterisation[3]
—sweeping, *suo more*—overshoots the mark; but Plato's
gentler phrase prophetically sums up Cicero's case—
" the last garment which the pure man doffs is the
love of fame."[4]

From a rounded theory of man and the world,
philosophy had now sunk to the level of a machine
for the production of virtue as required. The heart's
desire of the old Stoics,—to bring God back to earth,
and to raise man to a divine state,—ended here in an

[1] Compare the interesting parallel drawn between Cicero and Socrates in Mr Benn's The Greek Philosophers, vol. ii. p. 170 *sq.*
[2] Zeller's Eclectics, p. 157.   [3] Cf. Essay on Bacon.
[4] Quoted by Niebuhr in his Lectures on Roman History, vol. iii.
p. 24.

amazing inability to make any ethical use of the idea of deity, and in an equally curious attempt to square moral precept with customary practice. For Cicero's reputation, the incidence of "the power of the man and the power of the moment" was unfortunate. Yet he was great for the very reason that he represented his age so completely. Constant dissipation of energy in other directions left neither time nor inclination to the Romans for the pondering of problems which did not directly affect the pursuits of the hour.

With Marcus Terentius Varro—*Doctissimus Romanorum*—the Ciceronian epoch gave place to the Augustan. And, indeed, time was ripe for the transition. For, Varro's Eclecticism bore no such recommendations as that of Cicero. This "able man was unfortunately too much a scholar to confess that he neither could nor would be a philosopher, and accordingly as such throughout life he performed a blind dance — not altogether becoming—between the Stoa, Pythagoreanism, and Diogenism." [1]

As contrasted with a busy age, represented by a busy man, the Augustan era was a time rather of rest and literary reflectiveness. Save for the interesting school of the Sextii, to which we owe Seneca, philosophy remained very much as it had been. The disquietude of republican political life was succeeded by the comparative calm of imperial rule, and mere appropriation of Greek culture, at high pressure as it were, gave place to its more unobtrusive appreciation by the finished scholar.[2] The empire at last contained but one people,

---

[1] History of Rome, Mommsen, vol. iv. p. 593, note.

[2] The change in the influence of Greek culture is well depicted by Jahn in his Populäre Aufsätze,—Höfische Kunst und Poesie unter

and the Romans paused a while to enjoy their con-
quests, material and spiritual. At such a time a distinctive development of Roman genius was only natural,
and the remarkable efflorescence of literature formed the
memorable feature of this revival. But another tendency
also made its appearance—a leaning towards the old
religion—which was later to work momentous results.
At first this rehabilitation of the ancient Roman gods,
and of the characteristic national *pietas*, had a somewhat close connection with philosophy. The old deities
were so many "familiars" or reproductions of their
worshippers, just as ethical philosophy consisted in a
series of concessions to popular use and wont. But
this likeness, even founded as it was on the genius
of a people, could not withstand the progress of universal religious consciousness. The pagan reaction,
which soon followed, involved issues immeasurably
more important than any incident to a simple re-
adoption of a former faith.

Meanwhile, although changed much by the course of
thought, Stoicism had not been destroyed. And the
school of the Sextii, as represented by Sotion, had the
honour of training a man who, while clinging to the
older philosophy of Zeno, was also heir to "the fulness
of the time." Seneca might indeed be of the Stoa, but
Christian Fathers claimed him after as almost their
own. Nor was their contention without justification,
unconscious of it though they were. For Seneca was
not only a Stoic of the later eclectic kind, he was also
a man of the world, and open to influences as powerful
as any exercised by abstract theory. As a consequence,

Augustus. See also Professor Sellar's Roman Poets of the Augustan
Age, ch. i.

like Cicero, he has been variously denounced without measure, or indiscriminately lauded by modern
writers. Gibbeted by Macaulay,[1] partly, one fancies, for
the mere words' sake ; damned with faint praise by Niebuhr ;[2] dubbed "rhetorician" by Döllinger ;[3] he has also
been considered capable of regenerating "an age desper-
ately overrun with drolls and sceptics"[4] by Sir Roger
L'Estrange. Thoroughly representative of his age,
Seneca has either been made its scapegoat unfairly, or,
to his equal misfortune, he has been judged by reference
to one portion of his work alone. A less partial view
might result were he to be regarded in three different
aspects. He is typical, first, of the reaction to Stoicism,
which, in the early empire, was the only creed with
sufficient affinity for the old Roman character that the
cultured sought to revive. Again, and operating in
another direction, the eclectic tendency of philosophy,
particularly as it attempted to adapt itself to the common difficulties of ordinary people, affected him strongly.
Moreover, his own private circumstances favoured this
influence. A theory that inculcated poverty lost a
portion of its power when practised by a rich man, and
the independence of the ideal Stoic suffered certain
rude shocks in the person of an emperor's adviser.
Thirdly, Seneca, no matter how he might flout the
popular religion, was himself swayed, far more than
he knew, by that deep-seated "wish to believe" which,

---

[1] See Essay on Bacon towards the close—just before the characteristically valuable "smut and stubble" estimate of Greek philosophy.

[2] Cf. Lectures on Roman History, vol. iii. p. 185 *sq.*

[3] Cf. The Gentile and the Jew, vol. ii. p. 125.

[4] Cf. Seneca's Morals by way of Abstract, edited by W. Clode,
Introd., p. xiv.

originating in the Augustan era, continued for long years to increase in fervour.

When one remembers that Seneca was not a professional thinker, but rather a reflective man whose position entailed much practical work, his contribution to philosophy at once appears less inconsiderable. His office was in no sense that of a schoolman or of a system-maker. Brought into constant contact with common life, his reflections were primarily directed towards the amelioration of society by a comparison between what it was and what it conceivably might be. His meditations, as has been well said, "took the place of religious principles among the educated circles of the Roman empire; were a protest of real value against the coarse materialism of the old heathen world; taught the choicer spirits how to live with dignity and die with honour."[1]　To such protest Stoic doctrine was, of all others, best suited. Accordingly, Seneca reproduces many of the ideas usually associated with the teaching of Zeno and Chrysippus. In particular, the ideal of the wise man, with its accompaniment of freedom from aught but self, figures prominently; physical speculations also receive some attention. But, for all this, Seneca could not escape the "down grade" of philosophy. For him, as perhaps for no other Stoic, the wise man remained a mere ideal. Eclecticism, having accommodated itself to the wants of the time,[2] was not to be easily displaced by the reintroduction of any former theory, however desirable. The monism of

---

[1] Stoicism, W. W. Capes, p. 161.

[2] Seneca's respect for Epicurus—whose philosophy was most adaptable—and his frequent quotations from him, are important in this connection.

the Stoics might indeed be the mainspring of Seneca's
physics, but the logic of accomplished changes forced
him to a dualism. The wise man of Zeno might be his
pattern, but rude use defaced it, if not beyond recognition, at least beyond reproduction. Seneca sometimes
takes good heart enough to give a species of theoretical
reality to man's self-appreciation—to the complacency
which, under the name of *honestum*, played a prominent
part in Ciceronian ethics. But, alas! experience is
against even such justifiable pride. " Conceive in this
vast city, where without cease a crowd pours through
the broadest streets, and like a river dashes against
anything that impedes its rapid course—this city, that
consumes the grain of all lands—what a solitude and
desolation there would be if nothing were left save
what a severe judge could absolve of fault! We have
all sinned (*peccavimus omnes*), some more gravely,
others more lightly—some from purpose, others by
chance impulse, or else carried away by wickedness
external to them; others of us have wanted fortitude
to stand by our resolutions, and have lost our innocence
unwillingly and not without a struggle. Not only *have*
we erred, but to the end of time we shall continue to
err. Even if any one has already so well purified his
mind that nothing can shake or decoy him any more, it
is through sinning that he has arrived at this state of
innocence."[1] So far as he was able to overcome this
deep sense of defect, Seneca still clung to the abstract
freedom of the Stoics. The ideal man is he who
attains liberty in loneliness. Longing for retirement
from the world—the consequence, no doubt, of inability

---

[1] De Clementia, i. 6. Cf. Grant's Ethics of Aristotle, vol. i. p.
356 *sq.*

to accommodate his ideal to circumstances, and yet to keep it—gradually grew upon Seneca. Anxiety to show a balance to the right side in a life which ended here, naturally filled him with a desire to isolate himself from the contaminating influences of ordinary society.

Here Seneca's essential affinity for the religious reaction of his time appears. Truth to tell, it is not so much freedom that is now the ideal, as salvation from a self which finds its only life amid circumstances entirely unsuited to the evolution of goodness. The old Platonic conception, that body is somehow indissolubly associated with evil, affected Seneca's final account of man not a little. The problem of existence, as it presents itself to the sage, has almost passed from the search after freedom here, to the vague groping for individual perfection to be realised in another state, where earthly hindrances do not obtain. The deep religious tone displayed by Seneca is only a result of this, the altered mood of self-examination. He was not acquainted with Paul,[1] neither did he adopt phrases from Christian sources. But he felt the need of which Paul had conviction; he saw, if only "through a glass darkly," that man in his common state is unable to rebuild life to his own soul — his materials are far too scant. Seneca's supreme contempt for the popular religion was not unlike Voltaire's hatred of theological dogma. After his own manner, he illustrated the attitude of mind expressed in the "si Dieu n'existait pas, il faudrait l'inventer." The official resuscitation of religion

---

[1] Compare Aubertin's Rapports supposées entre Sénèque et St Paul; Lightfoot's Epistle to the Philippians, p. 268 *sq.*, especially p. 276, note 1; Farrar's Seekers after God, chaps. xiv. and xv.

by Augustus was but the prelude to a spontaneous popular movement towards a faith of some kind. The struggle against evil, the depreciation of man as he is, in short, the perception that this life was not what it ought to be, proved that, despite the circlet of philosophical culture, Seneca was himself in no wise exempt from the needs which originated the popular religious revival. Superstition he hated, but he did not perceive that such *bizarre* beliefs as then prevailed were, to the uninstructed, what the conviction of the good man's divinity was to himself. Seneca was a " Platonising Stoic," just in proportion as he felt the inadequacy of the old Stoic freedom. Neither longing for the possession of self, nor necessity for expulsion of the passions, was the conclusion which persistence of evil forced upon him, but the half-consciously apprehended search after a new life, or after a positive end to which the passions might be subordinated. In another sphere and in a different fashion, the same alteration of man's attitude towards the present life was expressing itself in a quickened sense of an indefinable spiritual need, and in a remarkable up-growth of superstition. An hungered and without proper sustenance, man " would fain have filled his belly with the husks that the swine did eat."

Stoicism failed to satisfy the spiritual necessities of the ancient world. Even when tempered by the adaptations of Eclecticism, it was unable to remove man beyond the reach of evil, either by raising him above it, or by teaching him how to control it. After all its theorising, the explanation of things appeared as ineffective as before. The demand for a cause sufficient to account for the universe, which is the invariable accompaniment of self-consciousness,[1] finds satisfaction, of a rough and ready sort perhaps, in religious doctrine. "The first function of religion is to furnish an answer to the question of the origin of the world and the phenomena of human life."[2] And, at Rome, the movement towards Eclecticism which, among the educated classes, indicated a sense of Stoic failure, found parallel, among the people, in an eclectic religious revival.

The steady effort of Augustus to rehabilitate the ancient Roman worship was prompted not only by reasons of statecraft, but also by a desire to divert support from foreign deities, some of whom had numerous devotees. But paganism was not simplified in this way. The idea of an imperial religion, of one faith for the whole empire, was doubtless thus originated. But the form which it ultimately took was more that of a wise toleration, permissive of all gods, *plus* the deified emperor, than of a state religion, selected from the rest, and enforced by government authority. For long years scepticism had been undermining the sanctions of religion, and, when the natural reaction came, credulity of the most abject kind abounded everywhere.[3] Superstitions, as endless in their variety as the people of the great metropolis, were rampant. The worship of Isis, of Serapis, of Mithras, and of the Idean Mother, belief in omens and miracles, flourished with oriental luxuriance, beside the cult of Jove and the other old

[1] Compare the suggestive discussion in Mr Crozier's Civilisation and Progress, p. 263 *sq.* (new ed.)

[2] Ibid., p. 264.

[3] Cf. Friedländer's Darstellung aus der Sitten Geschichte Roms, Part iii., chaps. iv. and vi. Cf. also The Greek Philosophers, A. W. Benn, vol. ii., chap. iv., especially p. 224 *sq.*

Roman deities. While, more remarkable than any, the religion of Judea, despite its despised votaries, began to attract many adherents. Paganism, in short, took a new lease of life in the absence of any authoritative source of spiritual comfort.

The tendency of the time, towards living for the moment, had philosophical effects which have already been noted.[1] Here it was exemplified in the multiplication of rite and ceremony. Outward observance seemed to do duty for depth of inner feeling or conviction. In this connection Mr Benn's remark,[2] that the Jewish proselytes were attracted more by Sabbath observance than by theological doctrine, is full of meaning. The existence of this craving for something concrete receives further proof from the spontaneity with which the worship of the emperor was often carried out. It was not a mere fashionable foible. For, when the Cæsar had bestowed real benefits upon his people—as in the case of Augustus,—or was himself a saintly man—as in the case of Marcus Aurelius,—the veneration of his person became the more sincere and permanent. As regards "the philosopher ruler," this is specially remarkable. Without entering into further details, it may be said that the pagan reaction during the Empire marked the transition from the abstract problem of man's individual freedom to that of concrete individual salvation.

A widespread sense of failure and defect existed. Paganism received an unexpected respite in that it so far ministered to this need. It was not so utterly dead as the philosophers had thought, otherwise it had fallen before Christianity far more unresistingly than proved

---

[1] See above, p. 136.
[2] The Greek Philosophers, vol. ii. p. 218.

K

to be the case. But the very necessities which cradled the new religion of the Cross also revived beliefs which, in speculative theory at least, had long been set aside. Greek influence had softened Roman hardness; and Stoicism, taking on in its eclectic form unwonted tenderness and adaptability, had lent itself to its own destruction by cultivating "passions" which only tangible realities could satisfy. Not an abstract rule of life, but a plain statement of duty, no matter how absurd, was acceptable to a people whose corruption naturally followed from a sufficiency of things for this world, and whose spiritual emptiness found no satisfaction in State grants of grain, or in luxuries fetched from the ends of the earth. Paganism flourished as it provided, in positive ritual, a seeming performance of virtuous acts. But it furnished no lasting salvation from self and the evil that is in self, because it could not set a pattern of manhood in the midst of sinners who longed for such exemplar.[1] "We too desire, not a fair one, but the fairest of all. Unless we find him, we shall think we have failed."[2]

The causes of the pagan reaction lay deep down in the civilisation of the Roman world. Then, as at no other time, sin and suffering triumphed over holiness. Philosophy, reasoning to an impersonal God, could not satisfy the head, nor was the old religion, with its array of pretty tales, sufficient to stay the cravings of the heart. Stoicism, in its search for a first principle, only arrived at self-contradiction. To live in conformity with Nature the best must needs be made of irresistible natural law. Yet the wise man is, or ought to be, free; for he is wise because he deliberately chooses the good.

[1] Cf. Virgil, Eclog. iv.   [2] Marius the Epicurean, vol. ii. p. 191.

God is far from man, and even the theism of Cicero fails to connect morality with religion. The Stoic theory of self-dependence arrives at a consciousness of its own inefficacy in Seneca.[1] A readiness is evinced to link man with God, and to emphasise the necessity for redemption from self. Asceticism, while driving away the grosser passions, at the same time occasioned the loss of many opportunities for developing the more pleasing graces. Remnants of faith, and even of hope, remained, but no charity could abide with cynicism. Indifference took the place of pity for suffering, for sin scorn served instead of shame.

Nor did the outburst of superstition promise any more permanent satisfaction. It bore witness to a diffused need for a revelation of truth. But the whereabouts of the desired light was unknown, and worse, was acknowledged to be unknowable. Yet such were the necessities, that multitudes deceived themselves into thinking that time was when the gods dwelt upon earth. With many mysterious rites and significant ceremonies, they sought to propitiate the departed deities, so as to win their presence here below once again. Behind all these undoubtedly lay the deep thoughts concerning things unseen accumulated by the ancient world. The harmony with self of the philosopher had relation to a harmony with a material or spiritual not-self, as the case might be. Duty, conceived as obedience to a law,[2] could not be explained unless the double application of law itself were regarded. A command is from the outside inwards, and to obey it is virtuous only when the act implies a transformation possible alone in a movement

---

[1] Cf. Baur's Church History, vol. i. p. 16, note 1.
[2] Cf. Plutarch, Sto. Rep., ii. 1.

from the inside outwards. Philosophy failed to set forth
the true freedom of virtue, just as religion could not
reveal the one source of moral obligation. Yet the Roman citizen yearned for knowledge and for faith alike.
What other interpretation can be put upon the fourth
Eclogue ?[1] A conviction of defect was abroad, like-
wise an ardent longing for better things, if only for the
return of some mythical golden age. Nor, in succeeding
years, did the dire social fortunes of the dominant people fail to quicken their recognition of present imperfection. "Long before death ended the astute comedy
in which Augustus had so gravely borne his part, he had
experienced the Nemesis of Absolutism, and foreseen
the awful possibilities which it involved. But neither
he, nor any one else, could have divined that four such
rulers as Tiberius, Gaius, Claudius, and Nero—the first a
sanguinary tyrant, the second a furious madman, the
third an uxorious imbecile, the fourth a heartless
buffoon—would in succession afflict and horrify the
world. Yet these rulers sat upon the breast of Rome
with the paralysing spell of a nightmare."[2] With such
divinities a large class might well rise who regarded all
conviction as fanatical and all enthusiasm as ill-man-
nered. Yet Pilate's question only represents the post-
ponement of man's inevitable reckoning with his own
nature. To pass "the impracticable hours" is a way of
living; it is not a way of life. And, as if in answer to
this deeper need, a new philosophy, with a message
akin in some sort to the "good news," arose to mark
the "fulness of the time."

[1] Cf. Roman Poets of the Augustan Age, W. Y. Sellar, p. 144 *sq.*
[2] The Early Years of Christianity, F. W. Farrar, pp. 10, 11 (pop.
edition).

CHAPTER VII.

THE IMPORTANCE OF THE CONTACT BETWEEN JEW AND GREEK.

THE world peace forced upon the nations by Roman supremacy had, as its counterpart, a certain feeling of general unrest. Just as the social bonds so congenial to Plato and Aristotle proved obstacles to the individual freedom of the Stoics, so this very freedom, guaranteed now by Roman citizenship, issued in a desire to escape from self altogether. When self-sufficiency and self-indulgence fail to fill life—when human nature, weary both of the world and of its own disquiet, begins to take thought concerning itself—then the too obvious method of suicide is supplemented by some more efficient, if less speedy plan of salvation. The anxiety to escape from self engenders the belief that there is some beatific state, or some divine person in whom exist none of the defects so bitterly experienced by man. Set over against the world, pure in contrast to its impurity, is a higher individual, communion with whom may mean deliverance. The great problems for the sin-oppressed thus come to be, what is the nature of such a being? and how is he related to this world? The latter is plainly the more important question; for, the connecting link between God and the world is also the bridge across which the sinner must escape to rest. A mediating essence of this sort, a power lying behind things and revealed in them, was not unknown to the Greeks. "To the most cultivated, it was awe and acceptance of the fact of mystery, and not the thrilling at the consciousness of realised beauty in stone or otherwise, that ruled their souls. The same thing is patent in our own popular holy feasts of Baptism and the Supper. Beauty is there as the attendant to solemnity, the awfulness of life and death."[1] This is the key to the view of deity taken by Plato. There is here a great mystery; and because that mystery was acknowledged, the Platonic philosophy recommended itself, towards the close of ancient order, to all who were searching vaguely for some transcendent being or state. To this correlation of supply with demand must be traced the wonderful renaissance of Platonic influence in the Græco-Jewish school of Alexandria.

Mysticism, particularly when it takes the form of religious philosophy, commonly concerns itself with soteriology. Salvation from self, by means of union with God, is the end, and abstraction from the things of sense is the method. Mysticism of this kind presupposes a deity separated from and superior to the world. Now the rehabilitation of Platonism, in certain of its aspects, was caused by its obvious ability to supply such a deity. In 'The Republic' or 'Parmenides' God is a transcendent being, who not only possesses freedom by his very nature, but is also untouched by mundane imperfections. In short, he *is*

[1] Quest, T. Sinclair, p. 101.

what the mystic desires to *become*. Nor is this all. According to the Platonic metaphor, God, *quâ* "Idea of the Good," stands definitely related to man. Persistent evils notwithstanding, man knows "the good" in part, just as he sees the light in part, and he can trace it back to its source. Should he desire to rise to a higher state, he already has a certain conception of the one being whose life is a realisation of that state, nay more, he feels, indefinably perhaps, that he bears kinship to this being. In such a case, consciousness of the imperfection, if not of the unreality of life, is, as it was to Plato, the earnest that a perfect being, and a state to which perfection is organic, exist. Personal salvation does not depend, therefore, on conformity to a law of nature, but rather on such wise direction of life that, in a moment of supreme exaltation, a vision of deity may be obtained. The Jewish-Alexandrians were not influenced so much by Plato's later idea of love to a Divine Person. They were attracted more by his enunciation of the *fact* that such a Being existed, and of the necessity that man should assimilate himself to this deity. The idea involved was thus religious rather than moral. Not purity, but individual perfection— especially in the shape of freedom from temptation—was desired. And the element of extreme mysticism in this conception sprang from the belief that likeness to God, with its attendant disappearance of evil propensities, could be attained only in proportion to the severity of self-negation. Accordingly, the first factor in the new philosophy was the transcendent God of Plato—the simple unity removed beyond all possible differences, at once perfect and without attributes. Man's sole way of salvation lies in striving to liken himself to

this abstract entity.   The dualism between God and
the world, between the divine and the human, will
disappear when the latter have been absorbed in the
former, but not till then.   God is ; *what* he is can be
revealed only in a state of union with him.

Platonism alone, however, did not supply all the
elements formative of this new school.   Nay, its more
characteristic doctrines were originally derived from
the Stoics.   God may transcend the world, yet if he
is to be a real deity, he must relate himself to creation.
The Platonic conception of the Divine Being, as set forth
in the ' Timæus,' doubtless formulates such a relationship.   But the world-process of Chrysippus illustrates
it in a far more developed form.   While, therefore, the
origin of the Alexandrian Logos may be credited to
Plato, it is referable more properly to Stoicism.[1]   The
transcendent view of deity, as taken partly by Plato
and completely by Aristotle, was here exchanged for
a doctrine of immanency, in which both the world and
man were included.   The universe is ruled by an all-
present wisdom which, even if impersonal, constitutes
the sole *simulacrum* of deity.   God is no longer set over
against the world, but becomes practically identical
with it.   Mediation between God and creation is not
necessary, because the deity only exists in so far as he
is seen causing all things to work together.   Now the
advance towards a solution of the constant question respecting the relationship between man and God, which
was signalised in the Jewish-Alexandrians, was largely
due to their adoption not only of the Platonic, but
also of the Stoic theory.   They accepted the Platonic

---

[1] Cf. Philo-Judæus, R. B. Drummond, vol. i. p. 75 *sq.*   Heinze in
Theol. Litztg. (1877), 112; and in Die Lehre vom Logos, p. 140 *sq.*

conception of an absolute and abstract entity which is above all imperfection. But they provided themselves with a way of escape from the conclusion of God's aloofness. The Stoic pantheism taught them the proper direction in which to look for a link of connection with the hitherto transcendent deity. But their materials did not end here. Yet another, and that the most important influence, affected them.[1]

As its name purports, the Græco-Jewish school of Alexandria was the first in which Greek philosophy experienced the action of Jewish religion. Reason, which had thus far gone about to provide man with freedom, god, and salvation, was now to be impinged upon by a faith that had postulated a certain view of deity as its starting-point. The result, thanks to favouring cosmopolitanism, was highly instructive. Greek philosophy received what it had so long sought in vain ; Jewish religion lost much that had hitherto cramped its inner development. An excellent indication of the character of the new factor, with which Judaism was able to furnish Hellenism, is supplied by the causes of the successful Jewish proselytism at Rome during the pagan reaction. Broken as a compact nation by the Captivity, and only retaining place as a state by in-

---

[1] It seemed unnecessary, for the present purpose, to enter upon a consideration of possible Neo-Pythagorean influences, more particularly as this question has been connected with theological controversies which it was desirable to avoid. Compare Zeller's Phil. der Griechen, iii., Abth. 2, p. 281 *sq.* ; Lightfoot's Epistle to the Colossians, p. 394 *sq.*, especially pp. 382-386. The statement on p. 383—that the Pythagorean school *entirely* disappears before the middle of the fourth century B.C.—appears a little too strong in view of Nicomachus of Gerasa, P. Nigidius Figulus, and of the Augustan works purporting to be of ancient Pythagorean origin. Probably Keim's view is truer. See Jesus of Nazara, vol. i. p. 365 *sq.*

trigue with successive heathen rulers, the Jews were
scattered abroad among all the kingdoms which rose on
the ruins of Alexander's empire. Yet, wherever they
happened to be, in Athens, or Rome, or Alexandria,
they preserved their peculiar religion intact. The *punc-
tum stans* of Judaism was the revelation of himself
vouchsafed by a monotheistic God; and the resultant
conviction — of almost fanatical intensity — regarding
the divine nature and presence, could not be exchanged for the flexible doctrine of any less spiritually
grounded creed. The force of this belief, and the clear
views of deity which it embodied, were the qualities that
attracted men towards the religion of a despised people,
at a time when scepticism and superstition flourished
remarkably. In the same way, the Græco-Jewish philosophy of Alexandria added the monotheistic conception of deity to the many elements furnished by Greek
reason. Men might now "know him that is."[1] And, indeed, this addition was inevitable. For, "the one God
of heathenism was another than that of Israel; he was
not like the latter—if I may so express myself—ethical
to the very core. Certainly he had moral attributes
also; in the system of some philosophers—in that of
Plato, for instance—they came even prominently into
the foreground. But it is very doubtful whether this
would have been the case also in the popular belief,
even though it were granted that it could have been
developed on the ground of philosophical reflection.
But, on the other hand, holiness, righteousness, mercy,
formed the very nature of the God of the prophets.
And—a thing which above all we must never lose
sight of—that which they themselves possessed, and

[1] Wisdom of Solomon, chap. xiii. 1.

therefore could awaken in others also, was *religion*, no speculation, but a reality of life. The influence of philosophy would have always been more negative; it undermined polytheism, but it did not show at least that it could build anything better on its ruins."[1] An ethical conception of God—of a deity who is the postulate, and not the mere goal, of thought—was the Judaic contribution to the new philosophy. Moreover, this was the most important, because the distinctive, element that it contained. For the school remained Hebraic rather than Hellenic in nature. The old Palestinian exclusiveness was never entirely broken down, nor was its resultant bias corrected. Gibbon gauged the case rightly, when he said of the Jews, that "a larger acquaintance with mankind extended their knowledge without correcting their prejudices." Well for the world that it was so. The distinctive Jewish ideal reached Greek philosophy intact, with the result that a flood of fresh light was thrown upon the dark problem of God's relation to mankind. In Franz Baader's phrase, "Not only salvation but also wisdom comes from the Jews." Possessed of God, Judaism could offer conditional salvation, and recognising the transcendence yet essential moralising power of the divine nature, it knew where to seek for hidden wisdom.

Like every movement of thought, the Græco-Jewish philosophy had a history. It did not spring up and grow to maturity in a night. The Jewish *diaspora* not only rendered its existence possible, by bringing East into contact with West, but the condition of *Judenheit*, particularly as regarded its literature, also indi-

[1] The Prophets and Prophecy in Israel, A. Kuenen, pp. 590, 591.

cated mental peculiarities which very largely determined the character of the early Alexandrian school.
In a word, the literature, of which the Book of Daniel
is the prototype, was the outgrowth of a longing for
better things, of a desire for salvation from present
evils—evils which, in their kind, the Jews shared with
the Romans. "The majority of those writings were
occasioned by times of trouble and distress, or by the
depressed circumstances of the people generally."[1]
And the literature "shows with what indefatigable
energy the depressed spirit of Israel still strove, amid
all the vicissitudes of the age, to hold fast its eternal
hope, and, at least, to avoid again losing the blessings
of its earlier days."[2] With Jewish Hellenism and its
varying fortunes, from the time of Alexander's entry
into Jerusalem in 332 B.C., till the defilement of the
temple by Antiochus Epiphanes in 167 B.C., and the
consequent foundation of the Asmonæan dynasty of
Judas Maccabæus (164 B.C.), we are not now concerned.
But it may be inferred that, if Israel were subject to
Greek influence at home, the Jews of the Dispersion
would be far more deeply affected by "heathen" philosophy. And, with curious propriety, the memorial
city of the great conqueror who played so important
a part in the diffusion of Hellenism, was the scene of
the contact between Eastern faith and Western reason.
The translation of the Hebrew Scriptures into Greek[3]

[1] The Jewish People in the Time of Jesus Christ, E. Schürer, vol.
iii. p. 47.

[2] History of Israel, Ewald, vol. v. p. 462.

[3] B.C. 221-150. Cf. Schürer, ibid., p. 159 *sq.* ; Philo von Alexandria,
Siegfried, p. 6 *sq.* ; Life and Times of Jesus the Messiah, Edersheim,
vol. i. p. 26 *sq.*

set free influences, the importance of which it is difficult to overestimate. The new language introduced
the Jews to vistas of thought hitherto unsuspected by
them. While the sacred record, now rendered accessible
to the Greek, revealed a God and a rule of life, sought
in vain by him after the wisdom of this world. Of
necessity, the mutual interaction that ensued was at
first less intense than it afterwards became. Accordingly, we find that the earlier products of Jewish Hellenism at Alexandria are coloured not only in matter
but also in form by Judaism. In short, the religious
element predominates completely over the philosophical
or scientific. System-making is discounted in favour
of a rationalising of history as read by the Jews.
Greek ideas are here rendered subservient to Jewish
propaganda, just as, in the time of Antiochus, exhortations against the heathen are put into the mouth of
Daniel. In the various spheres, of history, of osten-
sible revision of the Hebrew Scriptures, of poetry, and
of pseudo-prophecy, such as the Sibylline, this movement took form. Nor was philosophy any exception
to the general rule. The elaborate 'system' of Philo
was foreshadowed in the 'Wisdom of Solomon,' and in
the 'Explanation of the Mosaic Laws,' attributed to
Aristobulus. These works show how the peculiar results of the contact between Judaism and Greek philosophy began to take definite shape. Just as, in the
Platonic and Stoic systems, and in the pure Jewish
conception of deity, specific elements formative of
Philo's philosophy are to be found, so here other factors,
compounded of Greek and Jewish ideas, came to light.
Difficulties regarding God's relation to the world, and
conscientious scruples about the attitude towards sci-

ence to be adopted by the " peculiar people " present themselves, and receive a partial solution.

The author of the Book of Wisdom,[1] while convinced of the natural superiority of the Jews, departs from the distinctive doctrines of Hebraism, or rather supplements them by the addition of Greek elements. He appears to have come under obligation to the Stoics more particularly. At the same time, traces of other Hellenic influences are not wanting, even in the form of the work.[2] The Platonic conception of the soul's pre-existence,[3] with its complementary view of the body as a prison,[4] and the Platonico-Stoic enumeration of the virtues,[5] are all clearly of Greek origin. These, however, are of minor importance, as contrasted with the conceptions of God and of Wisdom presented in the book. As in untainted Judaism, the deity stands over against the world. " For the whole world before thee is as a little grain of the balance, yea, as a drop of the morning dew that falleth down upon the earth." [6] The Almighty transcends all that he controls. But the writer does not stop here. From the Stoic philosophy

---

[1] Cf. Schürer, ibid., p. 230 *sq.*; Heinze, Die Lehre vom Logos, p. 192 *sq.*; The Book of Wisdom, W. J. Deane ; and especially Principal Drummond's Philo-Judæus, vol. i. chap. v.—one of the most excellent parts of a work which has removed a long-standing reproach from English scholarship.

[2] Cf. Deane, p. 29, on the remarkable sorites in chap. vi., vv. 17-21—

> " The desire of Wisdom is the beginning of Wisdom,
> And the truest beginning of Wisdom is the desire for instruction,
> And the care for instruction is love,
> And love is the keeping of her laws,
> And attention to her laws is the assurance of immortality,
> And immortality maketh us to be near unto God ;
> Therefore, the desire of Wisdom leadeth unto a kingdom."

[3] viii. 20.   [4] ix. 15.   [5] viii. 7.   [6] xi. 22.

he obtained, and used to great purpose, the idea of the immanence of deity.[1] God's wisdom pervades the world. Acting through it, the deity is omniscient and omnipresent. What was a mere poetic conception with the authors of ' Proverbs ' and ' Jesus Sirach,' as Schürer points out,[2] here emerges as a philosophical theory. God may, indeed, transcend the world, but in virtue of Wisdom—an intrinsic part of his nature—he became one with that world, and, as a result, directly controls the universal order. Wisdom, in fact, *mediates* between God and the world. Further, with our author Wisdom does not remain the same vague impersonal principle as the Stoic world-spirit. It is endowed with specific attributes,[3] and in the very possession of these qualities it appears to attain a being of its own. If it be the "only-begotten," surely it must be distinct from if not independent of its begetter. Here, then, in addition to the ordinary Jewish conception of God, is the idea of a power that connects deity with the world; it is *of* the one, and *in* the other.

The precise value to be put upon the writer's conscious personification of Wisdom very naturally remains a disputed matter. But there can be no doubt that he sometimes regarded the divine quality as endowed with a real being of its own.[4] It is something which stands, as it were, outside of God, and is yet inseparable from his nature,—a hypostatic attribute. This doctrine, in the form of the pre-existence of Wisdom, is evidently present in Proverbs,[5] and the theory that God created Wisdom is also foreshadowed, without much distinctness how-

---

[1] vii. 22 *sq.*   [2] Ibid., p. 232.
[3] Cf. Drummond, ibid., vol. i. p. 219 *sq.*
[4] ix. 4.   [5] Chap. viii.

ever. The author of the Book of Wisdom, then, is the precursor of Philo, in that he formulated, in germ if not finally, the doctrine of a mediating quality, which certainly *quâ* knowledge, perhaps *quâ* being, connects the transcendent God with the world.[1] The probability is that the personality of this mediator was only adumbrated at so early a stage. Wisdom was an attribute, —a *genus* of other attributes, but still an attribute,— rather than a person. But, by the fact that other attributes were often attached to it, it naturally tended to become an individualised subject. In either case it was an abstraction, and perhaps the remarkable facility with which Philo afterwards transformed abstractions into persons was not altogether denied to our author. At all events, in this its first philosophical product, the Græco-Jewish school has already laid hold on the element essential to any scheme of salvation. A method has been indicated of uniting the absolutely perfect and good being to the imperfect and evil universe, without in any respect impairing his transcendence or holiness.

The little that we know of Aristobulus[2] goes to prove that, whether he lived after the date of the Book of Wisdom or not, he represents a later stage in the development of Græco-Jewish philosophy. So far as form is concerned, Judaism has disappeared. Aristobulus, under Greek influence, had moved so far beyond the orthodox Jewish stand-point, that he found it necessary to pause in order to discover how the new

---

[1] Cf. Article " Philo " in Dictionary of Christian Biography, vol. iv. p. 362.

[2] Cf. Clemens Alex., Strom., i., vi. ; Eusebius, Præp. Evang., vii.- ix., xiii.

might be made to tally with the old. His solution of this problem constitutes his importance; for by its means he contributed a permanent element to the philosophy of Philo. His 'Explanation of the Sacred Laws'—that is, of the 'Pentateuch'—was composed in order to show that Greek philosophy must have derived all its most valuable doctrines from Moses. "It is evident that Plato has imitated our legislation, and made himself thoroughly acquainted with all that it contains. Before the conquest of Alexander and the Persians, parts of the law had already been translated, so that it is obvious that the said philosopher borrowed a great deal from it. He was indeed a very learned man, just as Pythagoras has included in his own system much that is ours."[1] In the same place, Socrates also is subjected to similar Judaising; so too are Homer and Hesiod.[2] From this the complementary proposition follows as matter of course. If the Greeks took their highest ideas from Moses, then the Mosaic writings already contained all that was most valuable in Greek philosophy, *if one only knew how to disentangle it.* Thus, Aristobulus supplied the Græco-Jewish thinkers with a ready answer to those Jews who disliked Hellenic influences, and also indicated, if he did not fully formulate, Philo's famous allegorical method. In such of his philosophical views as have come down to us, traces of his wide acquaintance with Greek philosophy are to be found. Plato and Pythagoras, and more than either, the Peripatetics, influenced him.[3] From the last he derived his doctrine of deity. According to Aristobulus, God is invisible, and entirely separated from the

---

[1] Eusebius, Præp. Evang., xiii. 12.　　　[2] Ibid., 12, 13.
[3] Cf. Schürer, ibid., p. 241; Zeller's Outlines of Greek Phil., p. 319.

world. Like the Aristotelian *actus purus*, He affects the world solely as δύναμις. This doctrine is important only as illustrating the manner in which Aristobulus endeavoured to fuse all kinds of philosophical dogmas with the Jewish traditional faith. His ingenious defence of this position, though in one sense predetermined, marked a distinct advance in the development towards Philo.

Thus, at the time when the ancient world was sick of life, and longing for deliverance, and when Stoicism, in the person of Seneca, was realising what it had long furtively suspected—the impracticableness of its stern creed—the Græco-Jewish school, as represented by Philo, once more attacked the great mystery of man's being. This, the last attempt to know God by the intellect, and to gain atonement by the exercise of reason, is notable because it gathered to its aid all the best that ancient civilisation had to bestow. Philo came very near a solution of the dark problem concerning God's relation to the world and man. He had inherited the doctrinal elements necessary to a theoretical or abstract removal of hitherto impassable difficulties. From Plato he had the conception of God's transcendent nature; the Stoic doctrine of God's immanence in the world descended to him; and as a Jew, he could grasp the idea of a moral deity who, by His ethical nature, stood in a personal relation to each individual man. Further, the Græco-Jewish school, as it developed, had furnished him with the means of mediating between the transcendent God and the world from which it was of His very divinity to remain aloof. It had also put into his hands a method of reconciling extremest Hellenism with the revelation once delivered to Moses.[1] To what uses, then, did he put this unique wealth of wisdom?

[1] Cf. Siegfried, Philo, p. 160 *sq.*; Zeller, Phil. der Gr., iii. 2, p. 265 *sq.*

CHAPTER VIII.

PHILO-JUDÆUS AND HIS SIGNIFICANCE.

NOT a few critics of the Jewish-Alexandrians have
made it their habit to decry Philo.[1] He has been
condemned as a mere commentator, or characterised
as an artificer who, though commanding many materials, failed to infuse any synthetic power into his
work. His attempt to combine faith and reason has
been stigmatised a failure. "Philosophy gained little
by it; faith suffered great loss."[2] Such criticism is
usually founded on the supposition that Philo's philosophy was necessarily artificial, because it tried to
unite doctrines which were not of its own invention,
but which were derived from many external sources.
Now, while it is true that Philonism inherited nearly
all its integral elements, it is also true that certain
contemporary conditions combined to effect their
fusion. The system, it may be fairly claimed, is not

---

[1] Cf. Histoire Critique de l'École d'Alexandrie, E. Vacherot, vol. i.
pp. 161-163; St Paul's Epistles, Jowett, vol. i. pp. 369-371; Herzog's
Encyclopædia of Theology, vol. iii. pp. 1832, 1833; History of Philosophy, Stöckl, Part i. p. 170; Church History, Neander, vol. i. p. 89;
Early Years of Christianity, Farrar, pp. 146, 153, 154.

[2] Book of Wisdom, Deane, Introduction, p. 14.

artificial, in so far as it unites and reproduces in a new form theories of the connection between God and the world, which had previously been isolated from one another. For example, Philo renders Platonism, Stoicism, and Judaism to a large extent complementary, and so tries to eliminate the imperfections of each. His plan of salvation is better than that of his predecessors just on this account. Moreover, he represents a most important, and in later times a most influential, phase in the evolution of religious thought.[1] His philosophy is not artificial, again, because it ministered to certain needs, and because, more than any other, it indicated the high-water mark of pre-Christian thought concerning the graver questions of religion.[2] No doubt there is a sense in which Philo's want of system may be most reasonably urged.[3] He does not work out any architectonic of salvation,—the very fervour of his idealism prevented this. Yet, using the resources of Greek philosophy with rare skill and amazing range of knowledge,[4] he defends the Mosaic revelation, now in this, now in that aspect. His importance in the history of thought, which has so often been too little appreciated, is mainly due to his clear consciousness of the ultimate value of the Jewish religion, and to his unremitting efforts to show that, in some way or another, man's highest conceptions must be interpreted in the light of an intelligible revelation of God. He may have universalised

[1] Cf. Philon d'Alexandrie, F. Delaunay, and C. G. Prowett on Philo in Fraser's Magazine, August 1874.

[2] Cf. Ewald, History of Israel, vol. vii. pp. 199, 200 ; Dr Jowett, notwithstanding his immediately following judgment, appears to allow this—St Paul's Epistles, vol. i. p. 368.

[3] Cf. Schürer, Jewish People, vol. iii. pp. 366-368.

[4] Cf. Siegfried, Philo, pp. 32 *sq.*

Judaism, as the Tübingen school contended, or he may not. It is certain that he was the first to counteract the one-sidedness of Jewish theism by the introduction of a Greek pantheistic element, and thereby to lay the foundation for a characteristically complete—that is, a Christian—theology. He felt, if he did not fully comprehend, the insufficiency not only of abstract monotheism, but also of ubiquitous polytheism. Particularism played little part either in his religious doctrines or in his learning. Appearing when he did, he was destined to formulate, with such materials as he had, an explanation of God's relation to the world and to man in many ways meet for the " fulness of the time."

For the purposes of the present brief survey Philo's philosophy may be conveniently divided as follows. First, the existence and nature of God; second, God's relation to the world; third, man's nature; and lastly, man's life in the light of his own and of God's nature.

Philo makes no attempt to prove, in the strict sense, God's existence. His arguments,[1] such as they are, appear rather as poetical ideas than as philosophical principles. Reasoning from analogy, he contends that God must exist to control the material universe, just as man's mind must furnish the central cause of all his bodily actions. Further, he holds that matter has no causal power in itself. It is not self-determined. Hence, arguing once more from analogy, man intuitively relegates the origin and ordering of the world to a being who, though infinite, is like, though by no means identical with, the self-determining element in human nature. Mind is the only principle of this kind,

[1] Cf. Drummond, Philo-Judæus, vol. ii. p. 3 *sq.*

therefore a supreme mind must exist which is the first
cause of the world.   Philo's most interesting " proof,"
however, is that in which he proposes to utilise the
Socratic knowledge of self [1] as an introduction to the
knowledge of God.   The individual as such is possessed
of a certain personal identity, which remains unchanged
throughout the varied occurrences of life.   A proper
appreciation of the inner nature of this permanent soul
is but a beginning in the perception that, behind the
constant flux of phenomena, resides One Self-existent
Being, unseen yet most real.   He it is who " compre-
hends all things, but is not comprehended." [2]   Philo's
attitude towards the nature of God is largely determined by those so-called proofs.   *That* God is, he is
fully persuaded; *what* God is, he can never exactly
tell.   Indeed, the doctrine of the transcendence of
deity forms an essential portion of Philo's metaphysic.
Like Jehovah, Philo's God is separated from the world,
but this separation is itself of the last importance.   For,
seeing that he is unaffected by the imperfections of the
world, God represents precisely that state of being for
which the entire civilised world was then longing.
Here dualism is not an obstacle to salvation, as some
would always have us believe; it is rather a condition
without which the problem of salvation would be rendered insoluble.   Only as he is removed from this
sphere of sin and suffering can God be the possessor
of such desirable qualities as infinity, unchangeableness,
simplicity, freedom, and self-sufficiency. [3]   Because he

[1] An interesting reference—all too brief—to Socratic principle in
Alexandrian philosophy occurs in E. B. Bax's History of Philosophy,
pp. 91, 92.

[2] De Mig. Abra., i. 464 (Mangey).

[3] Cf. De Mundi Opifico, i. 3.

is thus elevated, he transcends in his ordinary nature the very highest that man can ever hope to attain. He is of perfection all compact.[1] Yet his being is of the most mystical kind. For, such is its transcendence, that it cannot be conveyed in any attribute or series of attributes. This conception of deity, which was doubtless coloured by Jewish views of the exaltation of Jehovah—" I am that I am "—is in the main philosophical rather than religious. Obtained by analogy from the human mind, it naturally has reference more to a self-sufficient principle than to a self-sacrificing person. On the religious side it represents a desirable state, but affords little comfort as to the possibility of attaining it hereafter, much less of realising it here. God, in short, is pure being. " Ce n'est plus," as Havet pointedly says, " qu'une idée d'idée; on est monté à un sommet bien nu et bien dépouillé. C'est l'*Un* du *Parménide;* mais, dans le Parménide, il n'est pas question de religion." [2]

Seeing then that God remains a great mystery, Philo finds himself forced, while preserving the transcendent nature of the deity, to mediate between him and the universe. The peculiarity of the dilemma, and the means by which extrication was sought, form one of the most important features of Philonism. In previous times the mysteriousness of God had impressed itself upon man's mind with at least as much force as it did now. But, hitherto, one of two consequences had invariably followed. Either the material particulars and God were mixed together in inextricable confusion, as by oriental pantheism, or God was banished from the world, as by Aristotelian metaphysic. But Philo was

---

[1] Cf. Legum Alleg., i. 52.   [2] Origines, vol. iii. p. 391.

privileged to stand upon the shoulders of such explanations, as it were, and was thus able to face fairly the
obvious contradiction between the idea of an absolute
person and the clouded conception of a multiplicity of
phenomena in which this deity *ought* somehow to be
present, transcendence notwithstanding. His it was to
provide in vague outline, if nothing more, an answer to
the inevitable demand of the religious consciousness.
For religion, when stripped of all fortuitous accretions,
imperatively insists upon two things. It asks for a God
who, in his purity and exaltation, shall be a worthy
deity. But it also demands that a definite relationship
should subsist between this God and his worshipper.
No thinker ever urged the former with more eloquence
and persistency than Philo. And he accounted for the
latter—at least so far as thought concerning God, apart
from life after God's model, could enable him to surmount a theoretical difficulty. Philo, like Socrates,
saw God through self; but he did not stop there. He
attempted to render the spiritual unity adequate to a
full explanation of the natural universe. Now the
character of this mediation was determined for Philo by
existing philosophy. Stoicism had rendered the personification of the universe, and its consequent elevation to
divine honour, out of the question. The time for mythology was past, and the endless inventions of polytheism were consequently useless. The mediatorial power
desiderated must not be presented in any fantastic naturalism, nor in a mere fable, however pleasing. A real
mediator was required who should form a tangible link
between the world and its heart's desire—the transcendent God, through relationship to both. Here a difficulty immediately emerges, which, as one must admit,

Philo could not effectively meet. How is it possible to endow God with attributes which essentially connect Him with the world, and yet to preserve His purity by the mediating presence of the same attributes? As has been pointed out,[1] Philo never reconciled the conception of these divine powers as, on the one hand, independent of God, and on the other, as determinations immanent in deity. Yet he so far succeeded that he was often able to relegate the duty of mediation in general, and of the unification of God's special powers in particular, to one divine activity.[2] Of the divine powers "the oldest and best, acting as the metropolis, is the divine Logos."[3]

The doctrine of the Logos is at once the most obscure and the most distinctive portion of Philo's system. Influenced in practical application, as it is, by conceptions drawn indifferently from Platonism, Stoicism, Jewish and rabbinical learning,[4] any accurate reproduction of it, in tolerable unity of form, is almost impossible. At one time the idealism of Plato determines it; at another, Stoic pantheism, with its immanent world-reason, causes Philo to foreshadow here the Christian doctrine of the Trinity; once more, the endless ramifications of rabbinical lore lead the Logos now to a priestly office, again to an atoning function. But, apart altogether from these considerations, of which mention only can be made, Philo's doctrine is ambiguous in itself. The Logos is not presented under any one well-defined aspect. Philo identifies intelligence and soul, idea and

[1] Cf. Schürer, Jewish People, iii. p. 373.

[2] Cf. Drummond, Philo-Judæus, ii. p. 161; Heinze, Lehre vom Logos, p. 248 *sq.*, especially p. 253. F. C. Baur and Zeller hold a contrary view.

[3] Cf. De Prof., i. 560; given at length by Drummond, vol. ii. pp. 83, 84.

[4] Cf. Siegfried, Philo, pp. 142 *sq.*, 219 *sq.*

power, in the nature of the Word.[1]　Or, to put it otherwise, that which is seen and external proceeds from an
unseen and internal principle.　The Logos is not only
the word, it is also the thought by which that word
is formed and put forth.　That is, it has equal reference
to reason, and to specific effects of rational activity.
It may therefore be defined, with Zeller,[2] as the *power*
of God, or the *active* Divine intelligence in general.
But, although it is thus possible to evade the difficulty
of confusion between capacity and activity, the am-
biguities of the doctrine are by no means at an end.
The Logos may be the practical exercise of the potentiality of divine intelligence, yet what do we know of
its relation either to God or to the world?　Has it any
being of its own apart from God, or does it possess any
actuality out of relation to matter?　Philo's dualism
would seem to preclude a negative reply, and at the
same time to render it the only possible one.　If God
be the transcendent being, and if matter pre-exist in
chaos, then the Logos must be different from both, in
order to mediate between them.　But, on the other
hand, it must partake of the nature of both, if its
mediation is to bring them into any vital connection.[3]
This apparent contradiction constitutes the irremediable
difficulty of apprehending the significance of the Logos,
and it is further aggravated by Philo's intensely rhetorical style.　Indeed an exact statement of his doctrine on this point cannot be given—at least according
to modern standards of accuracy.　A clue may possibly be found in the sphere of Platonic idealism, rather
than in that of Stoic pantheism.

[1] Cf. Vacherot, L'École d'Alexandrie, vol. i. p. 150,
[2] Cf. iii. 2, 371.　　　　　[3] Cf. Schürer, Jewish People, iii. 375.

In its relation to the world the Logos appears to be a generic name for what is permanent and efficient in material phenomena; it is also the only sphere in which divine activity can be conceived as existent. "The world of ideas has its place in the divine Logos, just as the plan of a city is in the soul of the master-builder."[1] God's thought may become objective in the universe by being impressed upon things, but on account of its subjective nature, it can only be apprehended in a subjective sphere—that is, by one who is capable of entering that sphere. The Logos exists solely in the same realm as deity, and it can mediate between the transcendent and the mundane only if an element proper to the former be discernible in the latter.[2] The Logos, in other words, is a mediator between God and the universe, but it partakes of the divine nature only. So its mediatorial office is limited by the fact, that neither in itself, nor in the lower objects which it connects with deity, does any change of character take place. We have, in short, a piece of machinery, a useful, and indeed a superior, kind of *deus ex machina*, but not a living principle in any sense capable of transforming evil into good. It may account for creation, after a manner, but it cannot induce man to become better than the presumed limitations of his spirit permit. Salvation, if it be, can only last one moment; and even that, at what expense! Man and the world may be fashioned in the image of God, through the instrumentality of the Logos; but they are so surrounded by the barriers of sense, that elevation to the transcendent sphere is impossible.

[1] De Mundi Opif., i. 4.
[2] Cf. Drummond, Philo, vol. ii. pp. 222, 223, note ††.

This, then, raises the whole question of the personality of the Logos, particularly as it is affected by the idea of mediation between God and the world. On this subject much diversity of opinion exists, and that with good reason. For, " in his utterances respecting the Logos, Philo wavers between the attributive and substantive conception of it; the latter, according to which the Logos is hypostatised to a person, is already developed in his doctrine to too firm a consistency for us to suppose the personification was for Philo's own consciousness a mere poetic fiction (all the more, since in Plato the ideas are not mere attributes, but possess an independent and almost a personal existence), and yet not to a consistency of so absolute a character that Philo could be interpreted as teaching, as a positive doctrine, the existence beside God of a second person, in no way reducible to a mere attribute or function of the first person."[1] While it is thus hard to arrive at a precise estimate of Philo's doctrine on this all-important point, it is not absolutely impossible to draw certain definite conclusions.

The Logos as such is dependent upon God for its being. It stands in the same relation to the deity as human thought, particularly in the form of " genius," bears to the mind from which it proceeds. We say, for example, that Homer, Dante, and Byron created certain ideas which remain permanent possessions. So, it would appear, Philo's God created the Logos. From him it proceeded, and any independence which it has consists not so much in its hypostatised personality, as in the fact that it does not return again to God. It abides as his revelation of himself. In the same

---

[1] History of Philosophy, Ueberweg, vol. i. p. 231.

manner, for instance, the so-called "suppliant" Logos,[1] which has so often occasioned misunderstanding, is a manifestation of the peculiar nature of the Israelites. They possess the Logos of God in part, and thus have a special means of communicating with deity. Certainly this conveys the conception of a mediator, but the reference is more to a medium — which represents mainly an identity of attribute in the two beings whom it connects—than to an individualised person. And not only this. It is also a medium which, apart from its divine source, remains a mere potentiality. The Logos must therefore be viewed as entirely dependent on the transcendent God. In this sense it is subjective, nor does it ever become truly objective. When it appears in the universe, it does not assume any specific material form. The subjectivity remains in the notion that the Logos is the diffused power behind things, and not a quality resident in this or that object. Indeed the Logos may be fairly characterised as a generalised repetition of Plato's earlier doctrine of ideas.[2] Ideas are the realities behind phenomena, and in the same way, the Logos is the diffused reality which, though immaterial in itself, holds the cosmos together. It passes from God's transcendent state into its own proper immanency, but it never becomes materially objective. It represents a middle kingdom which can be inherited only by those who are able to abstract from objective conditions. It thus mediates between God and the world, not in the sense that it raises the lower to the higher, but in that it

[1] Cf. Drummond, Philo, vol. ii. p. 235 *sq.*

[2] It is a reply in some sort to Aristotle's question,—which of the Platonic ideas could connect the other ideas with sensible things?

accounts for the reasonableness of the lower by reference to a specific attribute of the higher. This attribute it itself is.

When discussing the mediatorial work of the Logos,
with regard more to its activity than to its origin,
Philo not unfrequently personifies it.[1] Here Philonism achieves its distinctive characteristic as the nearest
pre-Christian solution of the difficulties presented by
the relationship between God and man. Philo's work
in this direction was always retarded by his original
doctrine of the entire transcendence of deity, and the
consequent impossibility of connecting the divine with
the human, even through the Logos. Hypostatise it
as he might, the Logos ever remained a principle
rather than a person. An abstraction at the first, it
lost little of its abstractness by the gift of personality.
The movement in this direction represents rather a
true instinct on Philo's part, than any particular realisation of the intuition to which that instinct testified.
His comparatively slight appreciation of the messianic
hope bears abundant testimony to this. He conceived
a salvation wrought out, not by a personal mediator
who should himself be God, but by an abstract essence
flowing from deity, an essence which found full expression in the entire cosmic order, rather than in a
member of the human family. His God is of Jewish
origin; but, personify as he may, he is unable to
deliver himself from the Greek or impersonal presentation of the mediator. He proclaims such salvation
as the Logos can effect, but the "other worldliness"

---

[1] Cf. Dr Drummond's very cautious treatment, Philo, vol. ii. p.
222 *sq.*; a list of personifications of the Logos is given in St Paul's
Epistles, Jowett, vol. ii. pp. 397, 398.

of the immanent saviour necessarily postpones redemption for an indefinite period.[1] The scheme is
theoretical, and no amount of lavish rhetoric can
render it practical. Philo indeed realised man's necessity, but his conception of God's nature precluded
a fruitful perception of divine opportunity. All the
elements of Christianity were present in his philosophy,
but the living force requisite to weld them into organic
unity was as yet absent. His Logos orders the universe, and so reveals the divine presence in things and
in man. But whether called the " Second God," the
" First-born of God," the " Messiah," the " High Priest,"
or the " Mediator," it remains in essence a principle of
unity amid plurality, of permanence in change, or of conscious thought swaying chaotic matter. It can never
become a being who is " touched with the feeling of our
infirmities, and in all points tempted like as we are."

Philo's view of man's nature and duty is a natural
consequence of his metaphysico-religious theory of the
universe.[2] Spiritually, man is made in the image of
God ; reason, which he possesses in common with deity,
is a divine gift. But Philo's knowledge of Platonic
doctrines modified his anthropology. Man, though he
partake of God's rational nature, does not represent the
highest type of reason. This " pattern is laid up in the
heavens," and the actual man is but a baser reproduction. The bodily frame, in which human reason must
needs take up its abode, vitiates original purity, and, in
its contact with this lower form of being, reason ceases
to be of the same quality as it was in its pre-existent

[1] Cf. History of Israel, Ewald, vol. vii. p. 231 *sq.*
[2] Cf. Drummond, Philo, vol. ii. p. 274 *sq.*; Zeller, iii. 2, pp. 389-
416 ; Siegfried, Philo, p. 249 *sq.*

and divine state. And, in the lapse of ages, the remnant of the highest nature has become more and more debased.[1] Yet, sense and its obscuring pleasures notwithstanding, a seed of divinity remains, ready to spring forth with purifying growth in the life of him who nurtures it. Man's salvation, therefore, consists neither in transformation, for which there is no need, nor in becoming as God, of which there is no hope, but in crushing bodily desires and their attendant evils as far as may be. The aim of existence must be to substitute the higher for the lower nature, as completely as conditions permit, even although the mere presence of the body implies an influence for evil which cannot be removed. "It is this possession of a higher and a lower nature that makes man a moral agent. Beings above man and beings below him are . . . alike exempt from sin; but with the possibility of following a better or a worse course of life the whole problem of ethics arises."[2]

The more man appreciates his own nature,[3] the more distinctly do questions of duty formulate themselves. Self-knowledge is the presupposition of self-judgment. The aim of life must be in the mortification of the corrupt members. For, only by their subjugation can man imitate the deity.[4] He who disregards this duty, like Ishmael, or Cain, or Joseph, extinguishes the spark of divine reason, and is shut out from the number of those who have the privilege of practising the higher life.[5] But he who follows moral-

---

[1] Cf. Mundi Op., i. 33 *sq.*   [2] Drummond, Philo, vol. ii. p. 283.
[3] Cf. Vacherot, L'École d'Alexandrie, vol. i. pp. 157, 163.
[4] Cf. De Mundi Op., i. 35.
[5] For Philo's distinction of lower and higher in life, see Siegfried, Philo, p. 249 *sq.*

ity will, in the end, attain true wisdom. Philo's ethics are in many ways kindred to those of the Stoics. They inculcate a vigorous asceticism, which has as reward a certain ecstatic state of being. In a moment of exaltation, attainable by long quietism, the saint may perchance obtain a vision of deity. More than anything else, this conception of practical life proves that Philo, although conscious of the need for a saviour, did not fully understand in what form salvation must present itself. Virtue, which in one aspect of it is the proper end of life, becomes so far self-contradictory, that its realisation implies the destruction of certain natural faculties. It is abstract in character, and therefore represents an ideal of being which requires the elimination of the sole opportunities whereby this very ideal might be achieved. Purity, based on a knowledge of the evil that is in the world, is not less desirable than withdrawal from all society because some men are bad. Yet Philo would have it that the active life is pardonable only as it gives occasion for battling with evil. In fact, man is to save himself by approximating, as far as possible, to the mystic transcendence of God. Salvation is not elevation in the world, rewarded by a power to draw all men to it; it consists rather in retiral into self, so that a portion of the natural man may, in some ecstatic mood, be able to bring itself face to face with a perfection which it can never hope to enjoy.

Admirable in its insistence upon purity and sincerity, no less than in its anti-pharisaic pursuit of virtue for its own sake, this moral philosophy fell short of the teaching of true holiness. Its gospel was for the children of culture, and, even to them, its message was but the preaching of a half-truth. Philo saw the eternal in

the temporal, and hoped that good was present in evil.
But he did not understand that "love for a divine person" might be so diffused throughout a human life as
to render evil and unreality means to the attainment of
good and to the revelation of truth. He did not grasp
the fact that salvation is desired not *from* but *in* self.
Opportunity to flee from self is presented to a few only,
for it implies much tuning ere the strings of human
nature can be harmonised to divine music. Nay, does
not Philo himself tell us, that this harmony with God
"is an incomprehensible mystery to the multitude, and
is to be imparted to the instructed only"?[1] Deliverance
from sin on this wise must ever remain a mere idea.
The personal example, in which an actual demonstra-
tion of the transformation of an entire human life to
divine ends is given, fails us. But moral principles
operate upon men only through individuals who have
lived according to them. Consequently, the ideal of
withdrawal into self, of an absorbing pursuit after that
Will-o'-the-wisp—an ecstatic vision, is of no practical
value save for one individual, and even for him it may
never leave the range of enigma. Of "the ethereal
flight beyond" none can tell. So salvation is bereft of
power to touch all men. Philo was indeed of them
that also serve who only stand and wait. It was reserved for another to show by his life that renunciation is not desirable of itself, but is good only in so far
as the effort which it presupposes has part in the production of a richer personality.

The significance of Philo in the development of religious thought consists chiefly in what he attempted.
It is neither fair nor wise to judge him according to the

[1] Gentile and Jew, Döllinger, vol. ii. p. 408.

rigorous standards of modern systematic criticism. He was the first who tried to construct a philosophy in which all the elements supplied by ancient religion and speculation should have a place. If he did not universalise Judaism, he at least broke down barriers between Jew and Greek, and between Greek and Barbarian. So mighty was his intellectual inheritance that he seemed to stagger beneath its weight or to lose himself in its maze of doctrines. God remains inaccessible to man, in Jewish-Alexandrian theory, not because the elements of divine revelation and human unrighteousness are lacking, but rather because accepted Jewish tradition had separated the Deity from creation, and accepted Greek philosophy had brought Him back to earth only as an ineffectual mode, all-present yet of no reality. Judaism and Hellenism had been slowly preparing for Christianity, and all the dry bones into which the breath of life was to be breathed by the prophet of Galilee had been collected, skeleton-like, by the great Alexandrian.

It is easy to discount Philo's importance by reference to his comparative want of influence. The truth rather is, that this very lack of "roots in actual life"[1] forms the main testimony to the indispensableness of his philosophy. Contemporaneous with the events from which we date our era, Philonism, the idea, immediately passed over into Christianity, the fact. The philosophy was taken up and transformed by the religion. It disappeared before the face of Christianity, not from any inherent weakness, but as the star becomes invisible at sunrise. Both were akin in nature, and both arose under similar historical conditions. They came to

[1] History of Israel, Kuenen, vol. iii. p. 206.

solve a clamant problem, and the "ought to be" of the solution was naturally absorbed in the solution itself. Philo recognised God's infinite purity, and man's imperfection by reason of sin. He was clearly conscious of the need for a mediator. The thought of mediation, and its mystical explanation, are the main subjects of his philosophy. But there was no call for further allegorical formulæ when a personal mediator appeared among men, realising in his own life the long-sought unity with God. The partial, its work well done, gave place to the perfect. Philo imagined himself a devout Jew, but, as the mouthpiece of an epoch, he was not entirely his own. His age forced him, all-unconscious, to quit the old religion once and for ever. To this his want of immediate influence on life, and his immense after-influence on dogma,[1] were both due. Had he not adumbrated Christianity, Philo might have been the greatest of the Neo-Platonists; he would never have spoken to the Christian world to-day through the Gospel of John and the Epistle to the Hebrews.[2]

Christianity is, in the strictest sense, a historical religion. And even in these times of destructive criticism, nothing testifies more to its supernatural or spiritual character than its natural origin. Neither a higher Judaism, nor a transfigured Greek Philosophy, it united, in an entirely new form, ideas drawn from both these sources. As the Roman Empire was the practical preparation[3] for its reception, so the course of

---

[1] Cf. Siegfried, Philo, p. 273 *sq.*

[2] Cf. Church History, F. C. Baur, vol. i. pp. 18-20.

[3] Cf. Neander, Church History, vol. i. p. 6 *sq.*; Baur, Church History, vol. i. p. 2 *sq.*; Hausrath, New Testament Times, vol. ii. p. 3 *sq.*; G. P. Fisher, The Beginnings of Christianity, chap. ii.; History of Israel, Ewald, vol. vi. p. 1 *sq.*

Hellenic thought and the development of Jewish faith were its speculative and religious presuppositions. Amid the degeneracy of the antique world, when the awe-inspiring[1] mystery of the sculptured Zeus had been replaced by the reckless fatuity of the Roman Emperor, Philosophy found itself helpless. In this the hour of direst need, man could minister no soothing comfort to man's necessity. The humane spirit of Hellenism fathomed the depths of human weakness, which, as if in mockery of material power, was displayed with accompaniments of unparalleled horror in the empire that " devoured the whole earth, and trod it down, and broke it in pieces." And, as if to teach that " things which are despised hath God chosen to bring to nought things that are," the religion of a small Roman province, born of a people weak in war but mighty in prayer, was to reveal the righteous deity whom by searching man could not find out. Greek philosophy taught that the human spirit was worthy of salvation; Jewish faith pointed to the one God in whom and through whom alone deliverance from sin was possible. Each supplied an element which the other lacked. Hellenism, with its joy in man and all his works, softened the harshness of the exclusive Jewish religion, and claimed the blessings of providential care for the whole human race. Judaism, with its overmastering intuition of deity, set holiness before the Greek in place of happiness, and spiritualised practical as well as speculative life. A Jew by birth and a Greek by education, Philo was in possession of all the elements requisite to the new revelation. But no metaphysical alchemy could amalgamate them. The power which

[1] See above, p. 150.

could create and diffuse higher spiritual force must needs spring from the midst of religious influences, and not from logical abstractions. That the travail of the ages might bring forth a lasting blessing, one was required who should do more than take thought concerning God and His relation to man,—who should Himself be man, yet live the divine life.

The Greeks, thanks to Socrates, were able to appreciate in some sense the absolute value of a human soul, but they could not understand how that value might be vindicated. Jesus, who in the course of historical development became the Christ—the type of salvation —is different from Socrates because he came out from religion and lived for it. Socrates died to teach Greek thought that man is his own noblest study. Jesus appeared to lead man, however full of self-knowledge, up to that higher, and then unrevealed, state where thought takes its proper place as one element in a perfect life. He was moulded primarily by religious influences, as all who reveal God to humanity ever have been. His revelation was the end of Judaism and of Greek philosophy alike; it was also the beginning of a religion grounded more deeply in human·nature. As a religious teacher he found his only possible place among the one religious people of antiquity. And, in superseding their faith, by setting the heavenly seal on all work well done, he at the same time transcended an ethical theory which sought to command salvation by surrendering the nearest duties of daily life.

CHAPTER IX.

THE JEWISH IDEAL OF GOD.[1]

THE long development of thought, some features of which have now been reviewed, goes to prove that Christ was absolutely different from and greater than Socrates. But this is not the whole truth. He was also differentiated from the Greek proto-martyr by the totally diverse set of influences under which his life was spent. Not in their own estimation only were the Jews a peculiar people. Like the Greeks, they performed a unique office in the progress of civilisation. Theirs was the charge of moralised religion. The consequent characteristic qualities which marked them off so completely from the other nations, were in large part formative of Christ's intense spiritual consciousness and moral exaltation. Some account of these qualities must therefore be taken.

Like every other phenomenon of history, Jewish religion was the subject of change. Moses and the Prophets

[1] I am here indebted specially to the following works—viz., Kuenen's Prophets and Prophecy in Israel, History of the Religion of Israel, Hibbert Lectures, The Hexateuch, and Histoire Critique des Livres de l'Ancient Testament; to Wellhausen's Prolegomena to the History of Israel, and article on Israel in the Encyclopædia Brit.; and to Dr Robertson Smith's The Old Testament in the Jewish Church and The Prophets of Israel.

on the one hand, and the later Priests and Talmudists
on the other, represent phases of this alteration. These,
and the many intricate questions which they involve, are
not so much connected with our present study as the
general character of the inner faith of whose original
nature and gradual growth in depth they were the visible manifestations. In the history of Israel religion
underwent many vicissitudes, but its great central idea
remained ever the same. When the Jews had emancipated themselves from the bonds of a crude polytheism,
Moses formulated their nascent religion on what was
to him, and is to every theist, the *fact* of revelation.
Jehovah[1] was at once the origin and the object of his
faith. Jewish knowledge of Jehovah increased from
this time forward, and at length culminated in the
appearance of a deliverer, not from principalities and
powers, but from that sin which prevented the realisation of Jehovah's holiness. Yet, despite this progressive
revelation, the divine source of it never became other
than the " I am that I am." The ideal of the Godhead
gained in sublimity under the prophets, but it was
brought to birth in the wilderness.[2] The conception of
God by the proclamation of which Moses supplied the
motive force for the complete deliverance from Egypt,
may not then have had any definite connotation.[3] But
at Sinai it assumed specific form which no after-growth
could hide or supersede. " In the world are two visible

---

[1] Written thus for the same reason for which Mr Arnold would write
The Lord or The Eternal. Cf. Isaiah of Jerusalem, p. 7.

[2] Cf. The Philosophy of Religion, Pfleiderer, vol. iii. p. 122 *sq.*

[3] Cf. Wellhausen, p. 453 ; The Idea of God, J. Fiske, p. 74 *sq.*   In
the Theologische Tijdschrift, Sept. 1888, Kuenen shows, as against
Renan, that the religion of the wilderness was not a pure monotheism,
—Article, ''Three Ways; One End.''

figures of Eternity, the Ocean and the Desert. Each
has left its imprint on the genius of the religions.
The changing gods of India have arisen from the capri-
cious and tumultuous Ocean; the Desert, without voice,
without succession, without apparent form, can never
reveal any other than the God-Spirit, immutable, inexorable, incorruptible as itself." [1] The Jew was thus
early intrusted with the keeping of a germinating
monotheism which ultimately attained the most pure
and exalted ideal of God—an ideal which, at the right
moment, became the nucleus of a new universal religion. Accordingly, the entire career of the people thus
chosen—historically chosen—is dominated by the exigencies of their unique mission. The Old Testament
literature, criticise it, alter its chronology, and rearrange
the internal relationship of its parts as you please, is a
veritable record of intercommunion between the divine
and the human. Man here relates himself to a perfect
being, the fact of whose existence is the one pervading
principle of life. Israel's faith differs from all other
pre-Christian religions in this, that for it man is made
in God's image,—the conception of deity is no human
imagination. By a true instinct the Jews perceived
that God alone is adequate to the proof of His own
existence. Accordingly, as Greek philosophy tended
towards monotheism with more or less uncertainty, [2]
Jewish religion, even at the time of the exodus, was
implicitly monotheistic, and in its later developments
the ideal of deity became richer in all the attributes of
true divinity.

[1] Edgar Quinet, R. Heath, p. 321.
[2] Havet insists upon this point with much skill, Origines, vol. ii.
p. 319 *sq.*, vol. iii. p. 485 *sq.* Cf. Kuenen, Hibbert Lectures, p. 321 *sq.*

So long as the cult of Jehovah found no serious
competitor in the worship of another deity, the nation
which had adopted it went forth conquering and to
conquer. Strengthened by the remembrance of what
the Eternal had done for them in the great deliverance, they subdued hostile clans and tribes by the
indwelling power of something very like fanaticism.
In other words, the practical effect of the religion for
the moment displaced theoretical development. But
when contact with the strange peoples, and with
other gods—whose existence was as yet admitted—
threatened to bring about apostasy from Jehovah,
then the spiritual fervour of true monotheistic conviction began to be asserted with ever-increasing force.
The sublimest thoughts of the ancient world concerning things spiritual were uttered by the Hebrew
prophets. Theirs it was to insist upon the grand
central idea of deity, altogether irrespective of the
various doctrines and ceremonies which might have
attached themselves to it. What, then, was the idea?

The national unity of Israel was dependent upon
the belief in a tutelary deity—in Jehovah. When
the circumstances which served to stimulate national
sentiment were wanting, the correlative religion, especially in the presence of alien worships, was apt to
waver. It then found enlivening warmth in the fer-
vent poetic utterances of the prophets, who, with
deepened religious insight, called the people back to
the God who had revealed himself to Moses on Mount
Sinai.[1] But their mission was itself progressive. The
earlier prophets performed in the main a practical,
the later a theoretical, service to Jehovah. Samuel

[1] Cf. Wellhausen, p. 399.

turned the people from Caananite apostasy, Elijah [1] and Elisha stemmed the tide of Baal-worship. But their successors, of whom Isaiah is the great type, revealed God in a new character, and demanded that service should be rendered him in more spiritual fashion. The earlier conception of the Lord had always been abstract, and time had only tended to intensify this characteristic. [2] To maintain his exaltation Jehovah remained far from earth. His supremacy might be freely acknowledged, and yet no perceptible effect might ensue in the life of his professing servant. It was in this crisis that the insufficiency of prevalent Jewish religion first dawned upon the more spiritually minded among the chosen people. A God who lived apart from the world, and who revealed himself only in the disastrous defeats which he enabled his elect to inflict upon common foes, was a Being of power but not of holiness. The assumption of God's existence, on the basis of his self-manifestation in might, was the initiatory stage in the religion of Israel. The germinating idea of a pure godhead was then impressed upon the Jews. But they had failed in their office as the guardians of this conception, had not the "canonical prophets" insisted that Jewish predilections were not Jehovah's chief characteristic, but rather his holiness. "They laid the chief emphasis on the *Holy* One of Israel, and understood by this designation Jahveh's exaltation not only above the physical but above the moral imperfection of earthly life, that moral elevation and unconquerable energy which manifests itself in judg-

---

[1] Cf. Prof. Cheyne's Hallowing of Criticism.
[2] Cf. The Prophets of Israel, Robertson Smith, p. 224 *sq.*

ment and justice upon all evil, whether outside Israel
or within: they knew in fact that the Holy One of
Israel, since he was a just judge, must set to work
first on Israel, that judgment must begin at the house
of God, and therefore that his 'day'[1] would be darkness and not light to the sinful people."[2]

But, in a sense, the tendency of the new ethical
conception of God was to render Jewish monotheism
too monotheistic. During the wresting of the Promised
Land from its aboriginal possessors, God in a manner
came down from the high heaven to help his people.
He was so far prejudiced in their favour, that he might
even bring himself to disregard their lesser backslid-
ings in order to vindicate himself against alien deities
through them. But with the enunciation of Jehovah's
holiness all hope of his revealing himself on such wise
vanished. He became not only infinitely exalted above
sin, but also absolutely inexorable towards the sinner.
Inhabiting a sphere of his own, he was a law to himself, and ethical changelessness formed the prominent
feature in his new character. By the very dynamic
force of his holiness he is separated more and more
from an unholy world. But although monotheism
may thus have been limited by over-abstractness, it
gained both in distinctness and in superiority. The
God whom the Jewish people were now preserving
for humanity was no longer a mighty adjunct of the
Hebrew fighting force. He had become *the* Holy
One—that is, no other deity was possible beside him.
This, at last, was the supreme Jewish contribution
to religious development. Set apart from the world

---

[1] Amos v. 18 *sq.* ; Isaiah v. 16 ; Jeremiah xxv. 29.
[2] Philosophy of Religion, Pfleiderer, vol. iii. pp. 130, 131.

maybe, but existing nevertheless, is One God, absolute in holiness, without susceptibility to sin, and of infinite power. This is the true Eternal who was afterwards to be the desire of all nations. The peculiarity of Jewish religion, then, no matter at what point in history it finally emphasised itself, was the conception of God as a transcendent *person*. Deistic in tendency though it was, and continued to be, the prophetic addition of the attributes requisite to holiness raised it to a unique place. Greek philosophical monotheism could enunciate the transcendence of intelligence *quâ* deity, but not of a holy One.

> "Thou, in the daily building of thy tower,—
>
> . . . . . .
>
> Hadst ever in thy heart the luring hope
> Of some eventual rest a-top of it,
> Whence, all the tumult of the building hushed,
> Thou first of men mightst look out to the East :
>
> . . . . . .
>
> And get no answer, and agree in sum,
> O King, with thy profound discouragement,
> Who seest the wider but to sigh the more."[1]

But the prophets, filled with religious fervour, saw in their nation's deity the One God who, by his very holiness, was the sole possible pattern for sinful man. They knew where to look for the answer that should put an end to the king's "profound discouragement." They universalised Jehovah by revealing his will—that all men should liken themselves to him in holiness. "Jehovah asks nothing for Himself, but asks it as a religious duty that man should render to man what is right, that His will lies not in any unknown height,

[1] *Men and Women—Cleon*, Robert Browning, Works, vol. iv. pp. 280, 289, 290.

but in the moral sphere which is known and understood by all."[1]   But, seeing that Jehovah asks nothing for himself, he is withdrawn from man, and the conception of his holiness tends to render his person less concrete. Accordingly, the Jews, bereft of their wonder-working national deity, sought to possess themselves of the Holy One by methods of their own invention.[2]

But, while Jewish monotheism ran to extremes in its conception of God's transcendence, crushing out art, and even interest in nature—because the world and the heaven of heavens cannot contain Him—it at the same time had a more concrete side.   The intense God-consciousness, which was only developed in a higher form by the prophets, ever connected Jehovah with his people by special ties.   Malachi[3] might predict the re-cognition and knowledge of the Jewish God among the heathen, but Israel took no notice.   Their God Jehovah was, and theirs they intended him to remain.   Thus, even after the later view of Jehovah, with its predomi-nating quality of holiness, had been formulated, the tra-dition of national interest, as distinguished from individ-ual conduct, continued to assert itself.   God, although infinitely removed from the sins and imperfections of the world, is able to bring peace and prosperity to Israel " by the operation of his spirit."   It was this aspect of the Jewish ideal that constituted its per-sistence as a living force.   Had the sublime faith of Isaiah and the lesser prophets been confined to a belief in the attributes, to the exclusion of the action of God, the kernel of truth which it preserved would speedily

[1] Wellhausen, pp. 487, 488.
[2] Cf. ibid., p. 404 *sq.* ; Kuenen, Religion of Israel, vol. ii. p. 245 *sq.*
[3] I. ii.

have dried up. The interpretation put upon prophecy, and that with prophetical warrant, had more reference to God's dealings with his peculiar people than to the precise content of his character. Accordingly, monotheism continued a self-recuperating power among the Jews, until such time as the whole world stood in need of it, and this rather by its scope in practice than by its theoretical purity. Nor was this unnatural. God is the Holy One, and there is none other God beside him; such is the prophetical ideal. God is our God, and through his "anointed one" he pervades the entire national economy, social as well as religious; such was the interpretation which, to the people in general, supplied the practical aspect of the prophetic faith.

Belief like that of Amos or Hosea, of Micah or Isaiah, was not possible for the people as a whole. The ethical reflections which the holiness of God suggested may doubtless have been in conflict with actual manifestations of providence. But the writer of the Book of Job alone discussed such difficulties. For the nation at large the ideal of the prophets had need to be translated into a concrete fact, just as Job's reflections found their counterpart, not in popular moralisings, but in a people's physical sufferings caused by disastrous defeat.[1] Jehovah's presence in common life was the practical side of Jewish monotheism. The conviction that the Holy One condescends to regulate man's work-a-day world was the external husk which protected and kept alive the pure prophetic ideal through long years of nigh unparalleled misfortune. The strange contradiction

---

[1] Josiah defeated by Necho in the battle of Megiddo (B.C. 608); Jehoiachim defeated by the Babylonians (B.C. 597); sack of Jerusalem (B.C. 586).

between most exalted monotheism, with its transcendent view of deity, and the crudest belief in divine interference—this contradiction, which makes Judaism so hard to understand, was also at the root of its significance for the world. The Jews interested themselves in the pure Godhead of prophecy, because they saw God's hand favouring them in the most ordinary avocations of daily life. "The Hebrew saw God's hand and acknowledged His presence in his sowing and his reaping, in his sorrows and his joys. The rules of husbandry were Jehovah's teaching, the harvest gladness was Jehovah's feast, the thunderstorm was Jehovah's voice. It was the armies of Jehovah that went forth to battle, the Spirit of Jehovah that inspired the king, the oracle of Jehovah that gave forth law and judgment."[1] Later growth did not eliminate this patriarchal faith.

Now the acts of common life, taken as a whole, bore witness to some special connection between God and his people. And the entire history of the Hebrews, from the period of their great national disasters till the advent of Jesus, is a commentary upon this unusual relationship. The prophets had left the pure monotheistic ideal safely enwrapped in the curious doctrine of the messianic hope, and even although hidden by the later Law, it sprang to glorious life in Christ's impassioned teaching. The expectation of the "anointed one" is no more than the belief that the supernatural element in Hebrew history, which the successive heathen inroads upon the nation seemed to have extinguished, will again manifest itself. Its main interest for the present discussion relates to the power

[1] The Prophets of Israel, Robertson Smith, p. 312.

which it undoubtedly evinced of preserving the Jewish conception of the Supreme Being free from all base admixture.[1]

Ruled by foreign masters, living partly in a land "far from" Palestine, the Jews needed a hope wherewith to buttress their faith. To them the practical manifestation of monotheism must have been bereft of its chief power. God had now little, if any, opportunity to put forth his hand in common life as of old; for the place of that life now knew it no more. Had belief in Jehovah not found defence in some new tangible evidence, fitted to the altered circumstances, its object might very well have been forgotten. The messianic hope, or the expectation that Jehovah would again reveal himself by means of his "anointed," and thus rule once more over the people who were his peculiar care, supplied the place of that past evidence of overruling deity which the destruction of the temple had otherwise effaced from memory. His people might be broken, his service might be neglected, but Jehovah still lived in his far-off home, and would in his own good time reveal himself again to his own. The form of this expected revelation was determined by past experience. A united Israel, with a king anointed of God after the manner of David, was the only possible sphere of Jehovah's revelation, as a house at Jerusalem, guarded by "the anointed," was the sole place in which reparation could be made for the sins of the people. This marvellous persistence of belief in the power of Jehovah kept the ideal of God from being lost or debased. The providential aspect of the messianic expec-

[1] This is part of the "inspiration" of Jewish history. Compare Inspiration and the Bible, R. F. Horton, pp. 228, 229.

tation lies, not in what it is presumed by many to have foreshadowed, but in what it actually was and did. The preparation for Christianity in the development of Greek philosophy is one of the most impressive proofs that there is a divine order in human affairs. Another, also an integral part in the same preparation, is the preservation intact of the sublime Hebrew God-consciousness by a popular faith in the eternity of the Deity whom bygone generations had seen in every event of their national history.

Nay, more, this idea of deity itself underwent certain changes which foreshadowed the direction that religious evolution was afterwards to take. Deutero-Isaiah,[1] in some of the sublimest writings that the world possesses, points not only to the transcendence of God, but also to his care for the penitent. He promises the restoration of Jewish nationality in the traditional theocratic form, but he further develops the practical side of monotheism after a new and loftier manner. "Can a woman forget her sucking child, that she should not have compassion on the son of her womb? yea, these may forget, yet will not I forget thee. . . . Thus saith the Lord, Even the captives of the mighty shall be taken away, and the prey of the terrible shall be delivered: for I will contend with him that contendeth with thee, and I will save thy children."[2] This is as of old. But there is a higher view. "For thus saith the high and lofty One that inhabiteth eternity, whose name is Holy: I dwell in the high and holy place, with him also that is of a contrite and humble spirit, to revive the spirit of the humble, and to revive the heart

[1] Cf. Kuenen, Prophets and Prophecy in Israel, p. 180 *sq.*
[2] Isaiah xlix. 15, 25.

of the contrite ones."[1]   And again : "Arise, shine; for
thy light is come, and the glory of the Lord is risen
upon thee. . . .   And nations shall come to thy light,
and kings to the brightness of thy rising."[2]   And with
still greater definiteness : " I the Lord have called thee
in righteousness, and will hold thine hand, and will
keep thee, and give thee for a covenant of the people,
for a light of the Gentiles; to open the blind eyes, to
bring out the prisoners from the dungeon, and them
that sit in darkness out of the prison-house."[3]   Jehovah is to be restored to Israel not merely in the former
unity and prosperity of the nation, but in a veritable
revelation from the one living God, of whose manifestation the Hebrews are the depositaries—trustees for the
benefit of the whole human family.   Thus, the Babylonian Isaiah, in promising that restoration which,
during trying times, was the main preservative of the
Jewish ideal of deity, also forecast, unconsciously but
none the less truly, the final purpose for which that
ideal had been revealed to God's ancient people.   The
old order, which the Second Isaiah sought to recall, had
gone never to return.   But, with the instinct of religious
genius, the prophet knew of a surety that God's hand
still swayed the nations.   The restoration which he
anticipated for a contrite people in deliverance from
their oppressors, was to be realised in very different
form, in a renewed life of salvation from sin, obtainable
by any man who is truly repentant.[4]   The contrite
heart, in which God would take up his abode, had no
perfect exemplification before the suffering even unto
death on Calvary.   The Jews set forth for mankind the

---

[1] Isaiah lvii. 15.   [2] LX. 1, 3.   [3] XLII. 6, 7.
[4] Cf. Kuenen, The Prophets and Prophecy in Israel, p. 534 *sq.*

transcendent ideal of the Holy One. But the full application of holiness in the life of the individual was unknown, until exemplified in a perfect personality. In the former case a certain obligation was laid upon God—in the latter, duty is on man's side. Grace having been given, sanctification is thereafter within the power of the individual alone. The Jew could never reach a God whose holiness was transcendent, but the holiness of Christianity is adequate to the holiness of the Christian because it had embodiment on earth. Jehovah was the promise to a nation of what Christ alone was able to do for every individual apart.

Mosaism handed down to succeeding ages a doctrine from which the Jews were unable to shake themselves free. God's special interest in his own people had, as invariable corollary, divine obligation to vindicate Israel as a nation. This, as has been remarked, formed the tangible side of monotheism for the popular mind. When, during the Exile, the material supremacy of the peculiar people was beyond the bounds of possibility, an anticipation of a like domination, to be gained at some future period, provided the envelope in which the ideal of deity was providentially kept from contamination. But the remarkable course of Jewish history was a further phenomenon essential to the preparation for Christianity. The return to the Land of Promise, though at first marked by boundless hope, and by a religious enthusiasm which found expression in the rebuilding of the Holy Place, did not result in the vindication of Israel, to which Jeremiah and the Babylonian Isaiah looked forward. Thus, the prophets' transcendent God, being no longer brought near to the people in concrete form, might easily have passed into oblivion.

Jewish faith, however, had not yet performed its part in universal history, and the messianic expectation was supplemented, if not replaced, by another external embodiment of the religious ideal which, though strangely different from prophetism, preserved intact the divine conception formulated by the prophets.

As the Jews ever cherished the belief in Jehovah's Jewish predilections, so they always regarded the Lord as their own national property. He was the protector not so much of the individual Hebrew as of the nation. Accordingly, if he were under obligation to himself to vindicate his people, they, as a nation, must render God such service as would cause his exhibition of his power to be absolutely necessary. Thus the Law,[1] as representing Israel's debt to Jehovah, took the place of the messianic hope—the condition of the conclusion became paramount, instead of the conclusion itself—and formed the external manifestation of the transcendent God,[2] whose existence seemed in danger of being effaced from memory. Although there was much in the Law alien to the prophetic spirit, more especially in the tendency of the priesthood to come between the believer and his God, it is certain that, without it, the religion of Israel would have run grave danger of losing its distinctive conception of the divine nature.[3] God's covenant with his own people was impressed upon the popular mind[4] by innumerable rites and sacrifices. Thus the remembrance of its first author, no matter how far removed

[1] Cf. Wellhausen, chaps. viii., ix., and p. 495 *sq.* ; Kuenen, The Religion of Israel, vol. ii. ch. viii., vol. iii. ch. x.

[2] Cf. The Old Testament in the Jewish Church, Robertson Smith, p. 312 *sq.*

[3] Cf. Wellhausen, p. 491.

[4] Cf. Philosophy of Religion, Pfleiderer, vol. iii. p. 151 *sq.*

he might be, remained unweakened. The people whose
right it was to look for the fulfilment of the messianic
expectation, must needs perform the national duty of
purification. Till this, their part of the bargain, had
been carried out, they could not deem themselves a fit
instrument for Jehovah's self-vindication. The Law
was an epitome of the Lord's requirements, and in
proportion as it was faithfully observed, so was he
brought nearer and nearer to the nation. It had not
entered into the mind of the Hebrews to frame the
notion of a *personal* obligation. And naturally, a
purification, which was primarily the interest of the
nation, came to be in the end of secondary moment
to the individuals who composed it. The sublime
ideas of the prophets, having been long known to all,
gradually lost their living significance. But the conception of deity, to which they bore witness from the
first, remained as a potential force, even amid the
pseudo-religious religion of the Scribes and Pharisees.
The Law, as it has been said, performed the same
function for the Jews which Greek philosophy fulfilled
for the Gentiles. It was "the schoolmaster to bring
them to Christ." The Law of Moses, in the sense that
it kept alive Israel's knowledge of Jehovah, to whom
great debts were due, it was also the Law of God,
because it protected the pure Jewish conception of the
divine nature, which was to pass from under the Law
into the life of every man. For, as has been remarked
of the beginnings of legalism, "behind the legal aspect
of the movement of reformation, as it is expressed in the
Deuteronomic code, there lay a larger principle, which
no legal system could exhaust, and which never found
full embodiment till the religion of the Old Testament

passed into the religion of Christ. . . . The voice of spiritual faith rises high above all the limits of the dispensation that was to pass away, and sets forth the sum of true religion in words that can never die."[1] The Law did not destroy, but protected the prophetic ideal.

Nor was legalism itself entirely barren of results which tended in the direction of purer religion. If the idea of God had been proclaimed more directly and with greater sublimity in prophetic times, it had also been far removed from the comprehension of ordinary men. But later Judaism, though it did much to render this idea secondary to ceremonial observance, and to debar the worshipper from direct contact with deity, by the obtrusion of a priestly mediator, also aided not a little in the universalising and denationalising of religion by the institution of the synagogue. The habit of regularly assembling themselves together for worship, and for instruction in the Law, rendered the people personal partakers in religion far more effectually than the preaching of the inspired prophets had done. They were exceptional men called forth by the stress of unique circumstances. What they gave in the shape of idea, the Law diffused, after its manner, in observance. Few could become prophets, all might hear the Law, and, under the guidance of the priest, give due heed to its more rigorous requirements. In the Book of Psalms some instances of the best results of this popularisation of religion are preserved. The "Songs of Ascent,"[2] though differing widely from the earlier psalms in respect of their popular origin, represent a

---

[1] The Prophets of Israel, Robertson Smith, pp. 369, 370, 373.
[2] Cf. The Old Testament in the Jewish Church, p. 191 *sq.*

practical interest in matters of religion which has a distinct value of its own. The Law was not the vehicle of a new revelation, and so must be regarded as subsidiary to other creative periods in Jewish religion. But it served to arouse personal participation in acts of duty, and if it did not, at the same time, kindle new faith, it was valuable as the emblem of a religious intuition that could not be utterly destroyed.

CHAPTER X.

JUDAISM AND JESUS.

IN that progressive revelation which we call history, the office of Jewish religion and character was to evolve and to preserve in purity a fitting ideal of the divine being. By this, Judaism is once and for ever marked off from the other pre-Christian religions. Thus, the indisputable historical fact that Christianity arose from the midst of Judaism, may be further enforced by reference to an equally obvious spiritual continuity. Not only was Jesus a Jew "made under the law," but Judaism itself contained the elements necessary to nascent Christianity. The ideal of God which it possessed implicitly pointed to certain demands that the Old Testament dispensation could not supply. In other words, at its birth Christianity was not affected by Greek philosophy, but by the innate logic of the Jewish religion. Apart altogether from theological dogma, and as the result of a natural historical development, the person of its founder is unique. His character was moulded by a consciousness of God's nature and purposes, which Judaism, alone among the earlier religions, exhibited. The Old Testament literature does not present us with a series of systematised dogmas, but it tells of a nation's progress which was ever conditioned by relation to a specific ideal. The *theologia civilis* of "Deuteronomy" represents far more the means of natural approximation to this ideal here, than any scheme for securing individual bliss hereafter. Yet the God whose exaltation and holiness it attests, cannot but be a person who enters into personal relations with men. His exaltation, so overpowering to the Hebrews, was inseparable from the preservation in purity of man's conception of the transcendent being.

But another revelation was required to bring down to earth, as it were, God's power of imparting holiness to the individual sinner. The conception of deity is common to the Law and the Gospel alike. But in each case the manifestation of God's nature is different. Ezra, in the light of the Babylonian Isaiah's teaching, knew *that* God was; and the ceremonial law made this knowledge common property. But *what* God was, Ezra only comprehended in part. The rest of His nature was revealed by one who, as a matter of sober historical truth, stood in a relation to deity which no other ever occupied. No doubt Christianity was also determined by the desire of its founder to transcend or destroy the mechanical legalism into which religion, fenced by the law, had fallen. But, in order to accomplish this, a return to the nobler prophetic vision of Jehovah was necessary. In this return the monotheistic ideal was revivified, and the dignity of man as the friend, and not the mere slave, of God was vindicated. God remains, as with the Jews, but a new way of access to Him is opened up, and in this a hitherto unseen element in the divine nature is brought to light. "Think not that I am come to destroy the Law, or the Prophets : I am not come to destroy, but to fulfil."[1] The past is accepted as a necessary preparation for the present, of which, in turn, the better future will be but a further continuation.

Christianity could have sprung from Judaism only because the religion both of the prophets and of Moses was at its origin. The deity whose existence was to be hidden, and whose love was to be entirely obliterated by the Law, had been intimately known to the Prophets, and his close relation to human life had been understood so early as Moses. Nascent Christianity goes back to the older faith, exemplified but reduced to mechanism in the Law, and in the very act of fulfilling prophecy and legalism supersedes both. "To become a world-religion it was necessary that Judaism should not merely conceal or renounce its national character for a time, but should lay it aside in sober earnest. 'If a corn of wheat fall not into the ground and die, it abideth alone; but if it die, it bringeth forth much fruit.'[2] Would Israel prove herself capable even of this latter act of self-denial ? It is easy to explain and vindicate the answer which history itself has given to this question. If the historian of the Israelitish religion performs his task as he ought, he points to a number of lines which all start from the Old Testament and the later development of Judaism, and end at— *Jesus of Nazareth.*"[3] If the Law, as so many are prone to insist, killed the Judaism of the prophets, it also brought about a better resurrection. Its ceremonies may have obscured Jehovah, its customs may have

---

[1] Matt. v. 17.　　　　　[2] John xii. 24.
[3] Kuenen, Religion of Israel, vol. iii. pp. 276, 277.

afforded the soul a sheath of self-righteousness, but they performed an indispensable service in spreading abroad, formally if not materially, the notion of personal obligation in religious conduct. The prophetic ideal, of a God who was a nation's protector, still lived. And the new religion, which was to rehabilitate it, was also to transcend it, partly by the works of the Law. For Jesus, in calling man to a spiritualised faith, found it necessary to replace the accustomed ceremonies of legalism by an internal relationship of the individual with the God of Isaiah. By the Law He overcame the Law, and by reinterpretation of the holy life which the Law required according to the flesh, He at length brought the prophetic desire to consummation. It is still the God of the prophets who vindicates Himself, no longer, however, through a holy nation, but in a holy life, which, having been proved possible on earth once, remained possible always.

If, then, the origin of Christianity was not only historically, but also spiritually due to Judaism, some elements of the older religion must have entered into the consciousness of Jesus,[1] and by their presence have rendered Him such as no Greek philosopher ever could have been. For Jesus, apart altogether from His office as the Christ, was moulded by conditions to which Seneca and even Philo, and much more Socrates, were complete strangers.[2]

---

[1] Cf. Christ and the Jewish Law, Robert Macintosh, chap. x.

[2] The contrary is urged by Bruno Bauer in 'Christus und die Cæsaren.' Kuenen's judgment on this remarkable work may serve to dismiss it without further comment. " 'The origin of Christianity from Roman Griechenthum'—so runs the untranslatable second title of Bruno Bauer's 'Christ and the Cæsars.' Do not suppose that I am about to attempt, by way of an episode, a refutation of this singular book!

There was something in the very strength, not to say sternness, of Judaism, that altered the entire mental environment of religious conviction at Jerusalem, as contrasted with philosophical enlightenment at Athens or Rome. The divine attribute of righteousness, which had been distinctive of Jehovah from the prophetic age, imported an element of solemnity into life with which the Greeks were never acquainted. Had their civilisation been thus affected, they could never have rendered their own special service to human progress. The in-

When I tell you that Seneca and Philo of Alexandria appear in its pages as the founders of Christianity, probably but few of you will wish to hear anything more of it. And yet the eccentricities of this veteran writer deserved mention. A traditional opinion can only be safely followed when it has borne the test of a searching criticism. Now Bruno Bauer's book has demonstrated once for all that in order to make the denial of the Jewish origin of Christianity look, I will not say like the truth, but like a theory capable of discussion, we must set aside the whole of the New Testament, the well-known testimonies of Tacitus, Suetonius, Pliny the Younger, and—one might almost say everything else! Here we must deny and reverse all things, there we must ascribe conclusive evidential force to accidental or trivial details, before we can gain even the semblance of a right to come forward with such a denial. The Apocalypse alone, regarded as the work of Galba's contemporary, or even as written under Domitian, is enough to demolish Bauer's reconstruction of history. Any one of the Pauline Epistles annihilates it. Not only the Founder of Christianity, but Paul and Peter with him, must be banished to the realm of fiction. In a word, we must give full swing—no longer to criticism, but to pure caprice. Truly a tradition that can only be attacked across such ruins as these is for the present safe enough. Roman 'Griechenthum' must remain content with the secondary but by no means unimportant part which has long been assigned it in the spread and development of that Christianity which sprang up quite outside of it."—Hibbert Lectures, pp. 191, 192; cf. p. 329 *sq.* Cf. The Jewish and the Christian Messiah, V. H. Stanton, pp. 11, 12, 119; note 3, pp. 142, 143. Compare the interesting address on Roman Stoicism as a Religion, in the Rev. James M. Wilson's Essays and Addresses, p. 304 *sq.*

visibility of the Sinaitic deity, although it cut him off
from the earth in a way, found its counterpart in that
"religion of common life" which it was the glory of
Moses to have established.   The *naïve* supernaturalism
of the Socratic *Dæmon* was very far removed from the
ethical naturalism of a holy God, who communicated
with man through righteousness.   Judaism, at its best,
did not supply a deity who came forward on special
occasions to decide a difficulty.   But it recognised that
the moral law, which is innate in the natural man,
could only grow to fullest strength when fostered by
divine care.   The progressive disclosure of morality,
which has been and is still proceeding, acquired a
special significance for the Jews, who ever regarded
new ideas as manifestations of the divine being by
whom the "Ten Words" had long since been sanctioned.
For this reason alone, if for no other, it is true to
declare that "the morality of Jesus, considered as
morality, is founded, not on the theological theory
alone, but also on a peculiar insight that each man is
to have into the duty of returning the divine love."[1]

Now this constant reference of conduct to an indwelling universal principle is the result of the
characteristic nature of Judaism.   Christianity was
determined by it in that unrivalled consciousness of
communion with God, which is so conspicuous throughout Jesus' own teaching.   The amazing intensity and
tenacity of Judaism are almost entirely due to the fact
that it, and according to the Hebrew view, it alone,
possessed God.   What the "heathen" longed for, and
so skilfully sought, the Jew already had.   God who is
the Absolute, the Transcendent, the One, who mani-

---

[1] The Religious Aspect of Philosophy, J. Royce, p. 45.

fests His nature on earth in righteousness, and yet remains a being uplifted above the world, — this is the *proprium* of Judaism. It is the negation at once of the polytheism by which Socrates was surrounded, and of the pantheism to which, in dying Rome, Stoicism fled for consolation. To this conception even the most reflective Hebrew literature adhered.[1] The God "who layeth the beams of his chambers in the waters, and walketh upon the wings of the wind," ever remains, even amid this picturesque materialism, a transcendent person, who can cause the finite to subserve him thus only because he is infinite.[2] Nothing is more remarkable and instructive than the absolute confidence of the Jews in their consciousness of this God.[3] It was not a mere formal statement of faith, but an actual inner illumination. Controlling their social as well as their religious life, it was neither an abstract dogma nor a concrete dogmatism, but a principle which, springing from within, transformed the people of whom it had possession. This sublime God-consciousness, of which the Jews were the stewards for humanity,[4] entered into Jesus. In His personality it burst forth with new and unparalleled force, and that with a permanent application to common life, which the exigencies of its own preservation had previously denied direction.

If it be too strong to say that "there is one stream of revelation only—the Jewish,"[5] it is at least certain that the Jews alone had revelation after a special and

---

[1] Cf. Psalm civ.

[2] Compare the fine passage in Natural Religion, pp. 87-89.

[3] Cf. Christ and the Jewish Law, Macintosh, p. 9 *sq.*

[4] Cf. Mozley, On Miracles, Lect. iv. (quoted in Prof. Flint's Theism, pp. 308-310).

[5] St Paul's Epistles, Jowett, vol. ii. p. 395.

higher kind. What, with other peoples, was either a vague adumbration of deity, or an incentive to search after God if haply he might be found, was vouchsafed to them as a perception of the One God himself. Now this God-consciousness cannot but have given direction to the inspiration of Jesus, rendering Him absolutely different from and inimitable by any non-Jewish teacher. In strictly secular spheres, in art and literature for example, we know that even the greatest achievements have certain presuppositions. Phidias represents the artistic temper of an entire civilisation; Dante is the "voice of ten silent centuries"; and Goethe brings modern European literature to the promised land which, thanks to the French Revolution, it was able to seek. All alike are not mere individuals who chance upon certain unused and disorderly materials, they are rather the channels through which the struggling but dumb desire of an epoch finally formulates itself. In the same way, though on a higher plane, the conviction concerning deity, which was diffused among the Jewish people, must have affected the intensity of Jesus' communion with the Unseen. Through Him, the nation whose thought sprang to fuller expression in His life, at length gave to mankind a God whose whole nature was revealed by the holiness of love. No new deity was sought after the manner of Socratic speculation and doubt, but the divine was practically affirmed in the life and conduct of a human being. Philo's messianic hope[1] was fulfilled when the Logos, having become more than a mere attribute, gained a concrete personality, and was able to display its deepest meaning without severing its relationship with its Creator.

[1] Cf. Philosophy of Religion, Pfleiderer, vol. iii. p. 176.

Again, just as Socrates was determined by the weakness of sophistry, so Jesus found a clamant problem already set in the weakness of Judaism. This, too, rendered Him different from the Greek both in degree and in kind. Despite the service which the law rendered to Judaism, it steadily developed a deadening tendency in the course of its application. "It is but too clear that the teaching of the Scribes and the Pharisaism inseparable from it are smitten with internal contradiction. There is no real correlation between the dispositions and emotions which they rouse, and on which they desire to rest, and the practical goal to which they direct their efforts."[1] The law aimed at enabling the Jew to perform his part in the covenant with Jehovah, in order that certain benefits might accrue to the nation—in order that God might draw nigh. But the multiplication of rites and ceremonies only served to remove the deity further and further from his worshippers. For, the more complicated the law, the more difficult its observance, and the less likely the attainment of the purity which its performance in every jot and tittle was to assure. But, without this performance, what of divine nearness to the Jews? As the hope of fulfilling the law grew fainter, so, too, the aim of its institution grew difficult, and eventually impossible of realisation. As the *naïve* communion with God of Moses and the judges gave way to the exceptional intuitions of the prophets, so these in turn disappeared, to be replaced by a conditional manifestation of divine presence. Conditional—but with a condition which, growing harder and harder to observe, narrowed and finally closed the old channels of Jehovah's self-revela-

[1] Kuenen, Hibbert Lectures, p. 215.

O

tion. The need for communion with God was in no wise removed, yet the barrier between Jehovah and the Jew, formed by the sins of omission with respect to an unobservable law, had become impassable.

It was thus necessary that the law should be remitted. The exigencies of the case so far determined Jesus' teaching, that He found it advisable to use existent legalism as means to a higher end. He insisted upon its ethical character, and so came to be a moral reformer. Unlike Socrates, Jesus had to meet no scepticism, but rather a species of spiritual self-satisfaction. His it was to measure out true judgment to the Pharisee, no less than to reassure the publican. Here neither knowledge of self, nor minute acquaintance with ceremonial requirements, forms the mainspring of man's life, but "a quiet devotion to the sort of work which is permanently useful, and an infinite solicitude to do such work as well as possible."[1] The opposition is more than a Socratic reaction against speculative scepticism, for it is a constructive and concrete answer to practical cynicism—in comparison with which intellectual doubt must be deemed a good, if not an absolutely desirable state. The cynic, proud of experience contained in "knowledge" which is nothing if not pernicious, scoffs at all ideals; the sceptic merely doubts present attainment, and for him there is an ideal beyond. Socrates had to think down the latter on behalf of the Greek, Jesus had to live down the former on behalf of humanity. "Virtue is knowledge," but as such it is a luxury procurable only by the Greek. The best life is that which subserves the upbuilding of the highest type of character. This is free to all, and it has

[1] *Natural Religion*, p. 136.

in itself none of those limits which necessarily fence knowledge. Two and two make four; further than this man cannot go. But in the moral life knowledge cannot constrain him thus. It may indeed point to many acts which are specially good in themselves, but it can place no end to the growth of the good character which, as an organic creation, goes on ever approximating to an ideal that is to be realised only in perfect sinlessness.

As a further consequence of the inherent weakness of Judaism, the individuality of Jesus was distinguished from that of Socrates by a certain positive attitude. Socrates, so far necessarily sceptical, stood in negative relation to the faith of his generation. But Jesus accepted His ancestral religion, and by a positive addition removed its reproach. Judaism was not left behind like Greek polytheism,—outside of which philosophy, and indeed all higher ethical reflection, grew up,—but was taken up into and transcended by Christianity. "The Jewish religion," Gibbon has remarked, "was admirably fitted for defence, but it was not designed for conquest."[1] In post-exilian times the Law was essentially a defence of Jewish theistic purity, and not an instrument whereby the nations might be brought to a knowledge of God. Thus the religious attitude of the Hebrews as a people was almost entirely negative. The positive duty of doing good was conspicuous by its absence, but the apparatus for fending off the external evil of ceremonial impurity was everywhere remarkable for its intricacy. Now the tendency of a machine-made morality is to throw the major weight of responsibility upon the machine. We, in our modern rage for cheapness, encourage the

[1] Chap. xv.

mechanical production of commodities. Yet we use
"machine-made" as a term of reproach. Not the
material, but the machine is to blame for the comparative thriftlessness of the article. So with the
Jews, the machinery of the Law began to bear the
sins of the people. Responsibility was shifted from
the individual to the mechanism of his ready-made
morality. The relation between man, God, and holiness came to be forgotten, and the average Jew was
satisfied if regularity at prayers and purifications
enabled him to pass muster with his co-religionists.

To this inanimate round of posturings, in which
"the occupation of the hands and the desire of the
heart fall asunder," Jesus of necessity opposed a free
religion, based on the ancient prophetical ideal. God,
the Infinite One, requires of man no service regulated
as to duration and place. His demand, which is also
man's own demand, points to a dedication of the infinite element in human life. The desire of all nations,
of Jew and Gentile alike, when Jesus appeared, was
for communion with the one Holy God. In opposition
to the Law, and without any consciousness of the pressing speculative problem, Jesus proclaimed Himself as
the medium of that communion. And how ? By dedi-
cating the divine in Himself to the continuous service
of the deity. This, then, is a unique and positive
characteristic of His teaching, and it grew out from
the midst of the weakness of Judaism. Brushing
aside the Law, which, despite endless multiplication of
detail could never overstep its own essential finitude,
He reveals God once again. But this revelation is, at
the same time, a revelation of man. Man, made in
the image of God, is partly akin to God by nature.

Thus his best service to the deity is also his best service to himself. The kingdom of heaven upon earth will be realised only when all men have become as God—distinguishing absolutely between good and evil, yet raised above the power of the latter by the fully realised indwelling of the former. Jesus superseded the Law by referring man back to his own nature. It is in part divine, and the positive personal duty of each individual is to develop this higher portion, not here nor there, but always and in all places. This is neither a theory nor a speculative system, but a scheme of living which is so essentially practical that it is within every man's reach. Some may have ten talents, and others one alone, but to him who buries even this one, the final woe of a wasted life brings, as to the most gifted, the retribution which, in irrevocableness, is stamped eternal.

In addition to the native elements of Judaism there were, lastly, several circumstances peculiar to His time and country which exercised a formative influence upon the personality of Jesus. The superstition which, in the absence of living religion, was now rampant at Rome, found welcome in Palestine also. Hillel's "canons" represent it under one aspect, of which the "secret doctrine," originally imparted to the exiles by Chaldæan soothsayers, was but a particular example.[1] Out of the Law, as out of the Ineffable Name, the secret numerical theory brought many hidden "truths," truths believed to be effective in miracle-working, in exorcism, and in the various kinds of marvel-making now usually associated with the medieval "black art."[2]

[1] Cf. New Testament Times, Hausrath, vol. i. p. 113 *sq.*
[2] Cf. ibid., pp. 108-131.

Sufficient evidence of this may be readily gathered from the attribution of obscure maladies to the agency of demons, so conspicuously recounted in Gospel history. This, then, and many other facts, which might easily be cited, suffice to show that Juvenal's scoffing *credat Judæus* had a depth of meaning that he himself did not appreciate. The state of mind to which the prevalence of these delusions bears witness had various causes. Chief among them undoubtedly was the Roman domination, with its taxes, alien customs, and, above all, its arrogant ignorance of the Jewish faith. The cup of Israel's punishment seemed full, and the destruction of Rome, or the entire subversion of the contemporary mundane order, appeared the only means to the long-expected vindication of the nation. This diffused feeling of unrest, unrelieved save by the vague hope of some indefinite spiritual interposition, was particularly favourable to the spread of apocalyptic ideas. Indeed the spirit of the writer of Daniel never disappeared from Jewish literature until after the beginning of our era. "Enoch gives his hand to the writer of the Psalter of Solomon, this latter to the Targumists, Philo to the author of Jubilees, and he again to Josephus."[1] Nor should Second Esdras be forgotten, in which the visions of Daniel concerning Rome are repeated with rabbinical illustrations.

In Palestine, as throughout Western civilisation, the diffusion of "the wish to believe" attested the immediacy of the fulness of time. The Jews longed for that consummation of their religion which, since the return from exile, they had desired, but had in no way seen. With them, as with the "heathen," the seed-plot

---

[1] Hausrath, *New Testament Times*, vol. i. p. 199.

of a higher faith was now prepared. This readiness to turn in spirit from the old to a new order—readiness like that of the desperate to hope against hope—formulated itself in part round the prophetic doctrine of the messianic expectation. The movement, implicit in Judaism from the days of Amos and Isaiah, was now about to take explicit shape.[1] The anticipated final exhibition of Jehovah's power in behalf of the chosen people still remained as a traditional idea. But for its due fulfilment a new channel of communion with God, through which another potent revelation might flow, was needed. Only some such active display of Jehovah's presence could be adequate to the terrible condition in which the favoured nation found itself.

Now this general yearning for contact with God, more especially as it connected itself with the prophetic expectation of national deliverance, formed a most powerful factor in Jesus' self-consciousness. He did not come seeking self-knowledge, wherewith to refute scepticism, He rather brought a message of the inner spirit which should be sufficient for the infinite demand of a heart-broken world. His it was to be the organ of a new belief, which historical circumstances, ordered in the most marvellous manner, imperatively required. Here, even more than in the development of Greek philosophy, and in the evolution of Judaism, we cannot fail to see " the mystery of that unknown and miraculous element in nature, which is always escaping "[2] us, though we are unable to escape it. When the rulers of the world had given themselves up to despair, and were seeking to forget self-question-

[1] Cf. History of Israel, Ewald, vol. vi. p. 121 *sq.*
[2] Westminster Sermons, Kingsley, Preface, xxviii.

ing in the pursuit of pleasure, a people who occupied a
small corner of an eastern province was rekindling its
half-extinguished faith at the smouldering fires of
ancestral religion. The beacon-light that was to dispel
the universal darkness flared forth in a most unexpected quarter.

Jesus' conception of His mission was thus largely
determined by the religious necessities of the Jews, and
by the ancient form in which expression had been
given to these needs. But that form had to be broken
down. The spiritual starvation of the age, with its
accompanying wail for convenient food, deeply affected
Jew and Gentile alike. Satisfaction had need to be
given not only to the divine in Hebrew man, but also,
through Judaism, to the higher nature in all men. The
crisis, born of the ages, accordingly placed a problem
before Jesus such as no other had been called upon
to confront, and which, moreover, none but He could
have solved. He was a unique person because He came
to remove a unique difficulty. "He forms," it has
been admirably said, "the decisive crisis in the development of humanity, as Socrates was in the development
of the Greek consciousness."[1] The spiritual crisis of
Judaism was for Him formally what the crisis of
universal civilisation was materially. The elements
of the solution were set, their form lay in the Jewish
messianic expectation.[2] All that now failed was the
individual who, in his own person, might supply the
revelation for which the ages had wrought, and for
whom an expectant but trembling world waited. Was
not the man who had power to direct anew the universal

---

[1] Kuno Fischer, Gesch. d. Neuern Phil., vol. i. pp. 50, 51.
[2] Cf. Kuenen, Religion of Israel, vol. iii. p. 260 *sq.*

readiness to believe, a personality in whom elements of the most marvellously diverse character were to find organic unity ?

The messianic ideal was the magnetic centre round which all the formative factors of Christianity were grouped. An interpretation of the content of this ideal, as it found expression in the Prophet of Nazareth,[1] is quite beyond the limits which we have here assigned ourselves. But, for the purpose of further illustrating the Jewish origin of Christianity, and of emphasising the difference between Jesus and Socrates, some account must be taken of the influence which the environment of a revived messianic hope had upon the Founder of our religion.

Setting aside the various theories, many of them invented to buttress a preconceived theological opinion, which have been advanced with respect to Jesus' messiahship, it may be said at the outset, that the prevalent ideal of a better future for Israel was present to Jesus from His early days. And this implies that, by His own inner perception, he ceased to be Jesus, ceased even to be Messiah, and became, for all succeeding ages, *the* Christ. By His own intuition He assumed the office which, interpret the facts as one may, history had been preparing for some unique person. He felt Himself to be that person, and thereby became unique. " If any man shall say unto you, Lo, here is Christ, or there; believe it not. . . . For as the lightning cometh out of the east, and shineth even unto the west; so shall also the coming of the Son of man be. For wheresoever the carcass is, there will the eagles be gathered

---

[1] Cf. The Jewish Messiah, J. Drummond ; The Jewish and the Christian Messiah, V. H. Stanton.

together." [1] Jesus was divine by His clear vision of
His own divinity. There is little need to doubt this,
when each one of us, self-confessed, knows that he
would be diviner could he liken his life, even a little,
to that of the Master.

> " But the critic leaves no air to poison ;
> Pumps out by a ruthless ingenuity
> Atom by atom, and leaves you—vacuity.
> Thus much of Christ does he reject ?
> And what retain ? His intellect ?
> What is it I must reverence duly ?
> .Poor intellect for worship, truly,
> Which tells me simply what was told
>
>   .   .   .   .   .   .
>
> Elsewhere by voices manifold ;
> With this advantage, that the stater
> Made nowise the important stumble
> Of adding, *he*, the sage and humble,
> *Was also one with the Creator.*
>
>   .   .   .   .   .   .
>
> Why need *we* prove would avail no jot
> To make Him God, if God he were not ? " [2]

Like Socrates, Jesus spent His youth in retirement.
But, from the beginning of His public ministry, He was
conscious of His mission. Even Strauss and Renan
cannot gainsay His conviction that He was the Messiah
that should come.[3] The form in which the earlier
expressions of His conviction were cast might indeed
furnish material for sceptical comment.[4] But the ques-

[1] Matt. xxiv. 23, 27, 28.

[2] Christmas Eve and Easter Day, Robert Browning, Works, vol. v.
pp. 245, 246, 251. The italics are mine.

[3] Cf. Strauss, Critical Life of Jesus, vol. ii. p. 6 *sq.*; New Life of
Jesus, vol. i. pp. 302 *sq.*, 383 ; Renan, Vie de Jésus, p. 245 *sq.*

[4] Cf. Jesus of Nazara, Keim, vol. ii. pp. 292, 293.

tion has relation, not to the words concerning messiahship, but to Jesus' self-consciousness that He alone
could solve the problem which the ages had prepared.
And on this point dispute is impossible.[1] He was
aware that the power to fulfil and supersede the Old
Testament dispensation was His. Yet He recognised
the necessity of previous preparation, no less than the
inner rational certainty of present results. " For all
the prophets and the law prophesied until John. And if
ye will receive it, this is Elias, which was for to come." [2]

The effect, then, of the revived belief in a Messiah
which, under various guises,[3] was diffused throughout the
Jewish world, must be held among the special influences
formative of Jesus' personality. He did not realise any
of the ideals which were abroad, neither did He seek to
conform Himself to them. But in the needs to which
they pointed, and in the aspirations of which they were
the evidence, He found the reason for His own being.
" They that be whole need not a physician, but they
that are sick. But go ye and learn what that meaneth,
I will have mercy, and not sacrifice : for I am not come
to call the righteous, but sinners to repentance." There
was no call for a Christ, except in so far as the world
was already conscious of a disease which no power yet
known to man could cure. Jesus' perception of His
messiahship rendered Him different from all other lead-
ers past and to come. The world-crisis could not be
repeated, and Jesus, having grasped its significance,
undertook a task which had been prepared for Him
from the beginning. His messiahship was therefore

---

[1] Cf. Jesus of Nazara, Keim, vol. iv. pp. 62 *sq.*, 87 *sq.*
[2] Matt. xi. 13, 14.   [3] Cf. Stanton, *loc. cit.*, p. 133 *sq.*
[4] Matt. ix. 12, 13.

spiritual, not in the sense that it evaporated the semi-materialised ideal of Jewish prophecy,[1] but because He gave Himself to the solution of a problem which represented all the indispensably important elements of the age, and in His solution perpetuated them as essential parts of universal religious progress. In this way the character of His self-consciousness conditioned the lasting importance of His work. Being the Son of man, He knew man. His was a knowledge of the weakness of human nature. To this defect the world was already old enough to testify abundantly. Consequently, the messianic office was not assumed after the fashion of a national apotheosis, nor of a speculative theory, but was determined by a perception of the need which, from his very constitution, man must always experience. Jesus recognised Himself to be the Christ at the moment in which He saw that sin could not be removed, like a special impurity, by prescribed means, but only by the transforming power of a principle operative throughout the whole life.

The declaration of such a message was the pressing demand of historical conditions; the time of deepest searching after it had arrived; and Jesus' consciousness that He could declare it was the spiritual result of these circumstances, which found focus in the light of His own pure nature. When He had become convinced of the absolute value of His personality to mankind, then He was, in all essentials, the deliverer for whom the world waited. His inner recognition and certainty of Himself was the only final answer to His own question, "Whom say men that I am?" Was not humanity

---

[1] There was no need for spiritualisation and self-accommodation, as Colani appears to think. Cf. Jésus-Christ et les Croyances messianiques de son Temps, pp. 139, 140.

itself asking this very question, and what was to be the
fit reply but that life in which alone an answer could
be set forth? His messiahship was therefore an original possession of His own consciousness, which naturally formulated itself in the direction to which the
magnetic force of contemporary ideas pointed.[1] The
kingdom of heaven was at hand, for He was present as
the final, and from one point of view, the immanent,
cause of the ages; He was the Christ because He
alone fully appreciated the need for such an one, and
saw what He must be and do.

Men do not go about to question the authority of the
'Iliad,' of the 'Divine Comedy,' of 'Hamlet,' or of
'Faust.' These are taken on their own credentials as
contributions in which the service of the past to the
present, and to the future, is summed up. Surely the
same, if no higher acceptance, may be claimed for the
Gospel of Christ. If one dare so say, it is an outgrowth
of His genius. And this, in virtue of which He was
raised above His age, could be none other than His own
consciousness of what He could at that time perform,
and hand down to all eternity. This was the mark
of His Christhood — that He knew how to respond
to the universal appeal for a Saviour. His authority,
abstractly taken, may be made subject of dispute, as
can every fact of history or achievement of unique
power. Yet it must never be forgotten, even in criticism, that "man's rational nature affords the very possibility of history. He stands in the stream of development; the reason within him answers to the embodied
reason without him. His interest in the past, and his
power to interpret it, are due to his kinship."[2] But

---

[1] Cf. Jesus of Nazara, Keim, vol. v. pp. 122 and 163 *sq.*
[2] Christ and the Jewish Law, R. Mackintosh, p. 185.

this kinship may fail of its effect—it too often does. The blind cannot be expected to accept the authority of Raphael or Murillo as the trained artist can. Nor can the deaf appreciate the *schmerz* of Chopin, or the *stimmung* of Wagner. The authority of Jesus as Christ is only for those who, in the life of action and of speculation alike, find reason to realise the enormous significance of His personality and teaching. Criticism may —the probability is that it does—reduce direct accurate knowledge of Him to a minimum. But it can never explain away the transformation of classic culture, and the humanisation of Teutonic barbarism, by what is called Christianity. The idea of a dedicated life is comprehensible altogether apart from historical evidence. But the lesson which it bears as a personal message to each individual soul can appeal only to those who are in some measure able to grasp its content. What it may be Christ set forth; His messiahship lay in His consciousness of His ability to do so; His authority rests upon man's faculty of appreciating what such a consciousness, built into such a life, implies. It is universal, because it speaks to an element in every human being, and the limitations from which it suffers are the result, not of its weaknesses, historical or other, but of *our* individual inability to apprehend the universal and eternal in moral progress.

We too often forget that, as the best literary and artistic criticism is itself creative, and presupposes the ability indispensable to true creation, so the most Christ-like conduct has a newness of its own, and is consequent on the realisation of a moral faculty which, in turn, is the sole organ of real submission to Christ. His messianic inspiration enabled Him to grapple with the eternally prepared ethico-religious crisis, as no one else could. But, if the import of that crisis be hidden from us, we can neither be called upon to admit His messiahship, nor to submit ourselves to an incomprehensible authority. Yet, if this failure to fathom history exist, it must be recognised as failure. If Jesus be not the Christ to this or that man, the fault is the man's, not His. For it is one thing to question the Gospel narratives, another to be insensible to the lasting significance of the morally ideal personality round whom they cluster. The New Testament might indeed be swept away, and notwithstanding, it would be impossible to deny that such a deliverer as Jesus was the inevitable sequel to the development of Greek philosophy, to the doctrinal evolution of Judaism, and to the universal Roman polity, or to declare that His supreme realisation of ability to reduce the despair of the age was not the best, nay, the only possible, answer to the questionings in which the thought of the day found common expression. " Foolishness " and a " stumbling-block " Christ must ever remain to Greeks and Jews in all generations. But to such as can divest themselves of their Hellenism or their Hebraism, and who can bear the tale of man's necessity, so absolutely true to fact, He is "the power of God, and the wisdom of God." Not that any such light from on high as flashed upon and turned Paul to give this testimony, can now operate in the same degree. But its kind must be ever the same, for it exists " not as a kindled lamp only, but rather as a natural luminary shining by the gift of heaven ;—in whose radiance all souls feel that it is well with them."

¹ Carlyle On Heroes, p. 2.

Finally, it must be asked, within the limits set, what was the value of Christ's own personality in this development? The results of human progress, which history embodies, are presented to us and live for us more in general principles than in multifarious details. The Draconian legislation preceded the Periclean State, with its wealth of civilisation. The seed of the Christian Church was sown in Roman catacombs and amphitheatres. For the priceless gifts of the Reformation and of the French Revolution to humanity the world cannot tell to-day who died. "Plain is the story of the Sleeping Beauty; till the time is come she sleeps; . . . and the bones of lovers who have perished whiten the ground around; and when she is to wake it only happens that another comes, and does not care about the bones. . . . The question is not whether other men have perished; only whether she is prepared to wake."[1] What the unknown and irrecoverable past has been preparing, amidst slow individual efforts, with their suffering and self-denial, the present suddenly interprets. "These all . . . received not the promise; . . . that they without us should not be made perfect."[2] Some mighty individuality arises, who calls order from chaos, and, eliminating the temporal, presents the eternal. Now re-creation on such wise implies, not only the power of the moment, but also the power of the man.[3] Elements may be given, but their organic co-operation can only be effected by their passage through a unifying medium—through a medium in which they gain something. It thus remains to indicate this inter-

---

[1] The Lawbreaker, James Hinton, p. 164.
[2] Hebrews xi. 39, 40.
[3] Cf. Essays in Criticism, Matthew Arnold, p. 5 *sq.*

action here. What was the addition made by Christ, in virtue of His person, to the events of which He was the final interpreter?

It is a solecism to speak of 'Christianity before Christ.'[1] In a world of reason, such as this is, an ideal may implicitly pre-exist its revealer, but upon him its entire actuality depends. Christ rendered Christianity a historical fact, by setting forth in His own person that pattern humanity which, in earlier ages, had only such reality "as dreams are made of." His peculiar contribution to the circumstances of universal civilisation, into which He was born, lies most of all in the factual existence with which His pure life invested an ideal formerly unattainable. The selfhood of each individual consists far more in that by which he distinguishes himself from other self-conscious beings, than in his appreciation of the bare fact that he is as they are. The latter is experienced by all, save lunatics of a sort. The former in its fulness is reserved for the few, who become fewer as the intensity of man's self-consciousness reveals itself.[2] In Christ, nearness to a spiritual ideal, necessary for, yet unseen by humanity, formed the self-differentiating factor. His manner of life was His own distinctive peculiarity. He objectified an ideal career, or was Himself the medium in time of a principle which, in its truth, is eternal. The value of Christ's personality in the development of history is thus due to His double nature. Filled with a holiness which only Judaism could impart, and a Jew comprehend, He realised it in common life, thereby

---

[1] *E.g.*, Christianity before Christ, Charles J. Stone; or the treatment of Christianity prior to Christ in H. Lang's Dogmatik.

[2] They *are fewest* in the sphere of religion.

showing all men that a power capable of transforming evil into good was within Him, and might be reproduced by them. The practical character of His teaching, combined as it is with a boundless transcendentalism, was what rendered His personal revelation indispensable. This unaccustomed living of doctrine—not arguing nor speculating about it—is the formative factor which Christianity cannot want. " I must *work* . . . while it is day," said Jesus to His disciples, when they inquired, " Master, who did sin, this man, or his parents, that he was born blind ? " [1] This was a matter of no consequence, but it was very necessary to show in deed that sin might be avoided or removed. Christ knew that perception of holiness was the one means to righteousness ; but He was also convinced that even for man in this evil world, the realisation of holiness was no impossibility.

What Christ did, apart from all the preparation for Christianity, was to embody in a human life the ideal righteousness, capacity for which man possesses in common with God. One nature, matchless in its vision of the things unseen and eternal, yet unequalled in tenderness towards earthly suffering in sin, formed at once the medium through which the crisis of the ancient world found solution, and the Mediator through whom the divine element of goodness in humanity received proof in perfect exemplification. Christ's power of combining the ideal and the real in an ordinary human life is His personal contribution to the interpretation of universal history. If this life were lived, then Christianity is the absolute religion ; if it were not, then Christianity has no meaning, and we are still in gross

[1] John ix. 4, 2.

darkness regarding the possibility of a holy life for man. Nay, if Christ be a myth, Reason has for once contradicted herself. Never before, and never since, has the individual, for whom the ages had been preparing a way, failed her. But without the combination of ideal and actual, which Christ personified, the inner principle of ethico-religious development had been going through a long process of self-stultification. Unless the best life possible for man was revealed at the time when historical circumstances called for it, its possibility remains out of the question. For such a revelation the ages had conspired. Christ came; and despite that what He did is still "the most characteristic fact of modern times,"[1] we are foolish enough to deny His work. His unique personality, combining the possible for the race with the actual in the individual, forms as essential a part of historical progress as that of Luther, or Shakespeare, or Goethe.

All are human, if you so choose to say, but all are divine; for every character, although it has a history, defies analysis into its simplest elements. Affinity for what is good, with the real elimination of evil which it accomplishes, forms the revelation of Christ. Without Him goodness was doubtless known, but its power to cancel evil was deemed problematical, or at best, of occasional efficacy. He lived so that this partial conception of holiness was put away once and for ever. His personal work lay in His application of the highest standard of excellency in every commonest act of life. What we believe regarding His nature matters very little.[2] All his-

---

[1] Prolegomena to the Logic of Hegel, W. Wallace, p. xxvi.

[2] " It is a mistake attaching to nearly all preaching, that the utterance, 'He that believeth and is baptised shall be saved; but he that

tory goes to prove that man is possessed of a higher
ideal, which he is prone to judge too good for this world.
Christ's part in the progress of humanity was to overturn
this conception, and to show in His own person that the
perfect life is not only suited to this world, and possible
in it, but that man is man just in proportion as he
brings this better self to full stature. So far as knowledge alone is concerned, even the most acute must be
agnostic in a sense. From the very fact that man is a
finite intelligence, he cannot grasp the whole plan of
God's universal government. Finite theory can never
be absolute on every side, if on any. But in the moral
life, history has rendered agnosticism impossible. " If
I had not come and spoken unto them, they had not
had sin: but now they have no cloak for their sin." [1]
After elaborate preparation for a unique moral personality, that Personality, as was inevitable, appeared.
Our demonstrable knowledge of God must be very specially through the life of Christ. For that life, if man
be in any spiritual sense a moral creation, was a necessary revelation. Had Christ not come when He did,
the necessity for His coming would still remain; nay,
the "fulness of the time" must have been perpetuated
until the present moment. His personal *differentia*,
constituted by His combination of absolute ideal and
relative individuality, " is the necessary postulate which
gives our will and feelings their final end, their highest
good; not as if a moral consciousness which is based

believeth not shall be damned,' allowing it to be genuine, is preaching
the Gospel. It is not so. To say that he that believes the Gospel shall
be saved, is not preaching the Gospel that has to be believed ; nor is
condemnation any part of good news."—The Problem of Life Considered, Samuel Edger, p. 262.

[1] John xv. 22.

upon itself and might be sufficient for itself should need the thought of a transcendental supplement to eke out its partial insufficiency; on the contrary, all our willing would lack its highest and all-determining goal, our heart would lack rest and satisfaction, if the perfect ideal should be a mere subjective presentment of the mind without objective reality."[1] Man, in short, as an intelligent being, finds God a convenient postulate in metaphysics. But, as a moral being, God is necessary to him. The former idea can never be entirely grasped, the latter *is*—in Christ. Without His personal work, the *fact* that there is a divine state attainable by humanity, would be as unproved, and would remain as unprovable, as the other.

Christianity is not mysticism—no substance cut off from the thinker, no thought, human or divine, moving *in vacuo*, characterises it. A person, who showed what man can rise to be, is its centre; its principle is a work which every man, for the simple reason that he is human, can do. It is complete, both on the subjective and objective sides, with a completeness created at its origin by Christ's individual union of ideal and life.[2]

Nor does Christ's personal contribution to historical development end with this, its general aspect. His too were knowledge of the ideal, and power to apply it in practice. Under these two aspects His individuality may be viewed. One of them represents the universal, the other the particular, side of His life. Through His knowledge, then, Christianity was able to set before men His conception of life as it would be for a perfect

[1] Philosophy of Religion, Pfleiderer, vol. iv. pp. 301, 302.
[2] Cf. Ewald's four Mächte, in Revelation; its Nature and Record, p. 114, note 1.

being. Personality is the highest category known to
us, and the more we can expand its content, the less
hopeless does the search for absolute truth become.
Only in a spiritual person limited like ourselves, yet
uplifted as we are not, can we obtain any glimpse of
that infinity for which we yearn. Christ's knowledge
of the ideal, His clear conception of divine moral perfection, formed the medium through which His universal
nature dominated His particular individuality. Most
men, in whom a strong sense of right exists, control
the wrong within them more by special means than by
the right itself, just as orderly citizens interpose the
police between themselves and the ill-affected. But in
Christ contact with the ideal was so close as to determine the entire life. His knowledge of the perfect
nature is best attested by the influence which His conception of it exercised over Him. He does not seek
redemption from sin, for He is in possession of the
means whereby sin may be overcome. Goodness finds
embodiment in Him, because His is the secret of being
good. He sees the source of good, and is therefore
filled with conviction of the necessity for its revelation.
Its incomparable value has impressed Him. He must
needs impress it upon others.

Hence His knowledge of the ideal at once passes
over into real activity. What He Himself added to
historical development, then, was the universal principle implied in the conception that affinity for spiritual
good, as it exists in human nature, is not only the
sole channel of the highest revelation, but also the
one means to the completest service of Deity. He
brought down perfection from heaven to earth, and
this He was able to do because He knew God's nature

in the ideal, as well as man's possibilities in the real.
A deep intuition of the one germinated with Him into
fullest expansion of the other. "Monotheism used to
mean: 'God is one; there are no divine men.' And
Christ's reply was: 'Yes, there are men in whom you
see and hear God.'"[1] Christ's knowledge was thus
peculiar to Himself, and, withal, was universal. He was
acquainted with man's occasional inspiration, just as
we are aware of our own heart-beats. But it was His
to travel beyond this occasional contact with universality, by proclaiming, in deed no less than in word,
that man is the only medium through which the
divine personality, as such, can be revealed. By the
declaration of this knowledge He annihilated at a
stroke the distance of Deity. For He perceived that
God's constant activity is here, even although His personal essence, as infinite, may be elsewhere. Knowledge of God is eternal life—a life which is fashioned
after a perfect model, but which, if it is to be at all,
must begin now and here. God, as Paul teaches, is
above Christ, but only in Christ's personal knowledge has Deity a means of appealing directly to man,
showing in a common nature the essential necessity
for a common perfection.

If Christ were thus, in Schleiermacher's language,
a creative person, He was also capable of exemplifying
this creativeness in His life. He had the power to
practise what He knew. From creation of the knowledge of God for the human race—a universal moral
revelation,—He passed to the application of that
knowledge in His own life—a particular moral individuality. He was aware of his ability to develop,

[1] The Lawbreaker, James Hinton, p. 186.

as far as was humanly possible, the natural element
which differentiates man from the beasts.   But He
also possessed sufficient living energy to carry out this
marvellous work.   Divine, in that "divinity involves
humanity in its highest potence," He was also human
in that "humanity implies divinity to a minimum
degree."[1]   Nor is this a mere speculative faith, as
many would explain it.   It is the single conclusion
which historical circumstances, accurately interpreted,
permit.   It would be a mere assumption to declare
that man is as God, more foolish indeed than to hold
that "man is what he eats."[2]   But Christ, by His
power of applying ideal conviction in practical life,
has proved that there is an eternal part of humanity,
which is amenable to, and can only grow up under,
divine law.   "Man is not worthy of God," said Pascal,
"but he is not incapable of being rendered worthy."[3]
Christ's practical application in life of His intense
God-consciousness is our best witness of this.   His
nearness to God does not rest upon anthropomorphic
sonship, but on a conviction that the Eternal, nay,
Eternity itself, is unmeaning in relation to a life of
sin.   His personal power, which is a great portion of
His special contribution to religious development, consists in His practice of what is eternal and linked with
the eternal.   He knew the ultimate reality of life, and
so was able to live in the light which it shed.

Personal ability to pass beyond the grosser limits of
self belongs to every man.   It was Christ's in the same

[1] Journal of Speculative Philosophy, Art. on "The Personal Relation
of Christ to the Human Race," G. W. Abbott, vol. viii. p. 356.
[2] Feuerbach.
[3] Pensées.   K. Paul, p. 228.

kind, if not in the minor degree, vouchsafed to His brethren. The whole travail of the world had been for this special manifestation of divine, though never extranatural spirituality. Nor was the preparation balked of its result. At the head of all that takes place, it has been aptly said, stand individuals. Their power is to be measured by their treatment of the difficulties which, in the nature of things, they must overcome. Nor is progress ever disappointed by failure to remove obstacles which, but for the proper individuals, would bar its way. Christ's unparalleled triumph was relative to the mighty conflict of the time, which He was born to subdue. But His power, thus manifested, was only the reverse side of His knowledge. The world had been crying with a loud voice for a new revelation of God. This Christ supplied. Moreover, by His intuition of the ideal life as it must appear to a perfect being, He ended the universal question, not with a death, but with a life, which was steadfast even unto the cross for the truth which it alone could convey.

The final importance of Christ's person to the development of history lies in the addition which He Himself made to recorded events. He changed their entire course. Such, in short, was His consciousness of direct intercourse with the ideal world, and with the Supreme Being in whom it is contained, that He lifted Himself beyond that standard of greatness by which even the most exceptional of men may still be judged. Homer and Dante, Shakespeare and Goethe, can never be repeated, yet there is a relativity about them all. Christ lived in order to be repeated—that we might follow in His footsteps—yet He is absolute. Even the most naturalistic admit " that the exceptional goodness of

Christ was no figment of the gospels," [1] that " His moral superiority cannot be disputed," and that " the success of His system shows that He must have possessed unique personal power." [2]   No matter how profoundly we may differ in doctrine, or how acrimoniously we may bicker about ritual and vestments, one fact remains, which none who are willing to let history speak can gainsay, even if they would.   The genius of Christ is His person, and for that reason He stands alone among great men.   All these are mighty according to the flesh; but in Him the flesh, by the power of the Spirit, is compelled to a new illumination of the one certainty in human life.   So long as man is in this world, the struggle between good and evil within him must continue.   That it is neither hopeless nor unequal Jesus' life is the sole guarantee.   His clear vision of the ultimate in man's nature none other ever had.   But through His devotedness it was the immediate means of turning many an one terror-stricken by sin.   Moreover, it revealed a principle which cannot be taken away.   Man has but to fathom his ethical nature, as it now is, to find that salvation lies in the moralising of self.   In His own person Christ once proved the possibility of the transformation, and for this reason, He remains to all ages the one pledge that the eternal life of the Spirit is also the sole worthy existence for the flesh.   That He was man, and that He yet kept Himself unspotted from the world,—these constitute Christ's absoluteness for the realisation of man's highest humanity.   The great mystery of holy living is now a mystery no more.

---

[1] The Origin and Development of Christian Dogma, E. A. H. Tuthill, p. 66.
[2] Ibid., p. 70.

Goodness is not far from any one, nor is the perfect way barred. A human being is the more human, as, with increased clearness, he perceives his own divine possibilities. What these are, and to what they may lead, a truly human life has actually revealed. Omnipotence itself could not increase our moral capacity; the responsibility for its practical use, exemplified as it once has been, is with ourselves.

CHAPTER XI.

SOCRATES AND CHRIST.

THE "great solicitude" sometimes "shown by popular Christianity to establish a radical difference between Jesus and a teacher like Socrates,"[1] is a misapplication of effort. The contrast stands in need of no further emphasis than that which history has so plainly given it. Antecedents, problems, contemporary influences, were different for both, not in degree alone, but also in essential nature. Neither special pleading, nor introduction of supernatural attributes, is necessary in face of authentic occurrences, which must after all be largely self-explanatory. Every leader of men exists, "not for what he can accomplish, but for what can be accomplished in him."[2] But the "in him" has reference to a living organism, and not to dead matter. What can be accomplished depends very largely upon the co-operation with which the man is able to aid circumstances. Opportunity is the world's work, but no amount of external pressure will cause two rational beings to interpret opportunity in precisely the same

[1] St Paul and Protestantism, Matthew Arnold, pp. 78, 79.
[2] Representative Men, Emerson, p. 393 (Bell's edition).

manner. Each reacts upon it in his own way, and so the results are invariably diverse. Much more is this true when not only the opportunities, but also the individuals, are entirely different, at the beginning of the process. Action and reaction are not equal and opposite in the spiritual world, for in every given case the rule receives a new application. Abstract from Socrates and Christ everything, except the attributes "Athenian" and "Nazarene," and the "radical difference," which so many sincerely desiderate, but place on a wrong basis, remains unimpaired.

But no such narrow distinction needs to be adopted. The natural course of history, without any *tendenz* interpretation, has set a great gulf between Socrates and Christ. It could be shown, for example, that even if Greek philosophy and Christianity were traceable to a common source, the latter possessed elements which the former had not.[1] The factors of a complete revelation, which the Greeks had failed to derive from their Aryan ancestors, reappeared, by some inexplicable process, in Palestine, and that at the time of Christ. These, and like considerations, are, however, foreign to the present task. It is sufficient now to take Socrates and Christ as we find them, and to note, that totally different circumstances influenced them, that alien civilisations produced them, that self-consciousness found distinctive expression in each. The sense of defect which swayed Socrates had reference wholly to man's knowledge of himself. The power of the Sophists was both founded on, and productive of, misbelief. Socrates saw nothing to prevent individual wellbeing, if only self-knowledge could be obtained. Nor had the time

[1] La Science des Religions, Emil Burnouf, p. 220.

arrived at which to regard spiritual or mental research as hopeless. The external world, which the older Greek philosophers had studied so assiduously, seemed less important to Socrates than the inner sphere of mind. Of this view, and of the self-study which it implied, he was the Greek pioneer. The difficulties complicating such a search, and the possible illusoriness of the self-perfection in which it was to end, did not impress Socrates so much as the conviction, of which his *daimonion* was but an aspect, that there is a permanent principle in man. This, in his view, was far more worthy of attention than culture, than phenomena, material or political.

To one thus assured of the actual, the question of possible or impossible, probable or improbable, did not appeal with much force. Socrates had nothing to remove, he rather desired to arrive at something which certainly existed. He was thus able, as, for example, in 'Protagoras,' to deny the possibility of virtue through self-knowledge, and yet, by this very denial, to show that his negative is better than the Sophists' positive. Protagoras professed to teach virtue without a basis; Socrates was only seeking for it. Yet, his tentative efforts resulted in an assurance the bare possibility of which his contemporaries scouted. He set himself to discover a new realm of thought, but he was certain of its discoverableness ere he began to search. His it was to bring this reality home to the everyday life of the time, and to follow out his method of so doing, even though its conclusions were the prison and the poison-cup. He gave himself for the progress of rational inquiry at a crisis in its development, and on this account we enrol him with the greatest. Yet to mistake

his work, in this matter, were certainly a poor way to
do him reverence.

The circumstances into which Jesus was born were of
a totally different character.   Unacquainted with the
learning of the Greeks, and in all probability quite unaware of that peculiar Judaism[1] which Philo represented,
his work had little relation to the discovery of new
intellectual spheres.   Nay, it was brought about by
causes which were in strange contrast to any operative
in previous times.   The answer to the cry of a world in
pain, its inherent force proceeded in great part from its
very simplicity, as compared with systems which the
mental subtlety of a single people had previously produced.   Christ found it necessary not only to enunciate,
but also to prove the perfectibility of man.   And at the
time, such was the state of the nations, that the proposition was sufficiently improbable to be startling, the
practice unprecedented enough to be convincing.

The condition of the Roman Empire need not be
made subject of too complacent comparison.   "It is
a common remark, that very few lines need be altered
in Juvenal's Satires, beyond what is purely local, to make
them applicable to the London, or Paris, or Vienna of
to-day."[2]   But even thus, there is an irreducible difference.   The spirit—to take but one instance—which was
so greedy of blood, that the amusing slaughter of 20,000
men, slaves no doubt, could take place almost without
comment, has disappeared.   Superadd nigh inconceiv-
able brutality, rampant cynicism, and barefaced lust, to
all that is most devilish in our modern capitals; take
away shame from vice, cancel the sneaking admiration

---

[1] Cf. Is God Knowable? Prof. J. Iverach, p. 186.
[2] Catholic Doctrine of the Atonement, Oxenham, p. 202.

for goodness which even the worst will to-day accord,
and think of the absolute need, yet apparent folly, of a
doctrine of perfectibility. In Palestine itself, where a
larger remnant of moral effort still remained, goodness
was mainly misdirected. For, when morality takes the
form of special commands, it loses much of its cogency
in transmission. Conventional rules serve but to dry up
the springs of sympathy from which all that is most
valuable in life—all that is not of mere prescription—
flows. Christ gave Himself for the perfecting of humanity at a period when perfection either appeared an
absurdity, or was fenced round with regulations that
rendered its attainment impossible. To show Rome
that there was a life of the spirit, to tell Judæa that her
law was morally suicidal, this was His mission. Even
Pilate felt that his conduct had finished the former
work. As a cultivated Roman he might hopelessly
inquire "What is truth?" but as a responsible man, he
could declare, "I am innocent of the blood of this *just*
person." Christ's statement of perfectibility was proved
by His practice, but for the finality of the proof He
died. "We have a law, and by our law He ought
to die." The execution of this condemnation broke the
law in pieces, and issued in the possibility of perfection
for others everywhere.

But even here we cannot stop. Socrates and Christ
are separated, once more, by racial diversity. No
juggling with subjective presuppositions[1] can explain
away the fact that Christianity grew out of Judaism.
It did not come forth from a religious idea, but from a
religion. No law of abstract logical categories was the
cause of its birth. Had the stern intensity of the

[1] Cf. Hegel, *Werke*, xii. 166.

Hebrew spirit been absent, Christianity might have appeared, as did Philonism, in the guise of an intellectual system, it would never have been a religion. One might as well hope to Hebraise Socrates as to Hellenise Christ. Athens under Pericles brought forth men whose like has never been seen. Yet in a few short years others sprang up, in Greece and elsewhere, to inquire what might be the meaning and permanent value of all that had been achieved by their Periclean predecessors. Socrates was the first of such inquirers. A citizen of a unique city, he found it necessary to ask himself what were the presuppositions of his citizenship. Because he was a Greek, he had the means at his command to found the science which treats of man's relations with his fellows. Nevertheless, the subject-matter of his inquiry—a society based on rational principles—was known to the Israelites from early times. But they did not come together spontaneously like the Greeks, and thereafter proceed to reflect on the happy chance. They were members of an ordered community, whose relationships had been determined according to the dictates of a national conscience. (Socrates could demand justice between Greek and Greek; Christ could require purity of all men. Race distinction rendered their respective interpretations of life's realities radically different.

In several of its aspects Socrates' work overlaps that commonly considered peculiar to the religious teacher. His conviction, that "the penalty of unrighteousness is swifter than death,"[1] might be taken as the motto of his career. While others had been content thoughtlessly to assume the inner life, he was determined to know it, and, in the light of this know-

[1] Cf. Apology (Introduction), Jowett, vol. i. p. 326 (first edition).

ledge, to guide his action. Indeed, the formation of
character on a new basis, rather than the systematic
discussion of ethics, was his life-work. It was ethical
in its aim, rational in its method, practical in its
results. Without any dry body of doctrine to inculcate, Socrates was able, mainly by the force of example,
and by the application of new standards to things
wrongly held precious, to alter current conceptions
concerning conduct. By no means a metaphysician,
he yet made life subservient to ideas obtained and
tested in dialectic dispute. For he had already laid
hold on the principle that conduct consists in "the
application of ideas to life." Not to change his fellow-
citizens, but to show clearly the generally accepted
yet half-apprehended principles, on a tacit understanding of which the state found basis, was Socrates'
business. The just man has only to perceive the
"general definitions" underlying society, to become
straightway the good man. In wisdom he realises
what is highest. Thus, however little he may have
known what the good was, Socrates saw that social
wellbeing is dependent upon individual morality. The
Athenians had doubtless some vague notion of what
"morality" meant for themselves. But, like Euthy-
phro's piety, it stood in need of definition. Socrates,
by his conduct and conversation, indicated this need,
if he did not absolutely supply it.

Hence his personality was possessed of a semi-
religious influence, or rather, he exerted himself for
the conscious moralising of his fellows. The manner
in which the entire man Socrates pervades the work
of his greatest disciple, and is traceable neither here
nor there, neither with this limitation nor with that,

but is a constant living presence, may be taken as typical. In such a view Socrates' mission so far overlaps that of the religious teacher. The jailer in 'Phædo' felt the magnetism of the martyr's character. It was not the subtlety of metaphysics that caused him, on the bare enunciation of his errand, to burst into tears and go out.[1] He needed no more than Socrates' presence to convince him that this was a just man, for whose death he could assign no adequate reason. The possession of self, which true self-knowledge alone bestows, was in the highest degree distinctive of Socrates. He cannot but have impressed himself upon others more by his personality than by his doctrines. He could not tell Plato what "the good" was, but Plato knew that Socrates was good. Conviction was written upon his conduct, and this, far rather than set phrases, must have helped his friends to clearer notions of the "ought-to-be."

It is exceedingly difficult, if not altogether impossible now, to determine to what extent Socrates' ethico-rational work received from his living presence the "touch of emotion" inseparable from religious principle. Enthusiasm for the man could not, in any case, remove the limitations under which he necessarily laboured. Zeal for a more clearly defined political morality, and supreme confidence in the mental capacity to discover principles of social action, cannot but have been quickened to fullest life by Socrates' personal example. Yet, in the modern sense of the term, religious influences were but little formative of his career. His petition for "inward purity and for a lot that shall best agree with a right disposition of the

[1] Cf. Phædo, 116.

mind," is limited not only in its conception of deity, but also in its grasp of the possible relationships between divine and human. Concerned chiefly for self-knowledge,[1] he did not depart from this his way to overturn popular belief, and he was satisfied if he could see in the world a principle analogous to the self in individual life. Speculation, and nothing else, led him to entertain such doubts as he may have had respecting traditional polytheism. The unity of purpose, which characterised his whole career, was but the other, and the familiar side, of such well-grounded scepticism. Socrates was therefore a religious teacher in that he was true to what he understood. Strength to be himself was his, and, as a consequence, all the qualities of gentle manliness, which issued from conviction of personal superiority, linked, however, with hesitation in deep consciousness of ignorance, served to endow him with a sway sweeter as well as stronger from its artlessness.

Knowledge that the Athenian citizen lacked the inner sense which would have enabled him to act upon principle rather than from habit, and a presentiment that he could do something to fill this gap, stood to Socrates in place of the more spiritual religion only attainable by a later generation. Had he not been a "religious" man, after the manner in which it was then possible for him to be such, neither Xenophon nor Plato could have had such a testimony to bequeath. His religion consisted in his life, spent as it was in the exercise of his best social and intellectual powers for the discovery of a "good," which all Greeks might consciously pursue. He was "religious," because, realising the reason for his

---

[1] Cf. History of Greece, Thirlwall, vol. iv. p. 268 *sq.*

being, he used his life, regardless of consequences to self, in the true spirit of the moral artist.

Nevertheless, it remains true that Socrates was primarily a moralist. The genius of the Greeks produced a unique species of civilisation, which was mainly remarkable for the external presentation of an artistic ideal. Socrates applied this ideal to the life of the individual in the city state. He taught men, that by taking thought, they might put opportunity to better uses, or might be enabled, by the application of discoverable methods, to substitute dignity and beauty for the querulousness customary in common life. Laudable and indispensable as an aim of this sort is, one cannot but admit that it differs widely from the object of religion. Moral philosophy can furnish ideals, but it is unable to tell how far conduct, oppressed as it is by adverse conditions, may be brought into harmony with the universal " ought." " A man's religion is the chief fact with regard to him,"[1] not because he can put his signature below the Thirty-Nine Articles or the Westminster Confession, but rather because he has certain convictions with respect to the possibility of realising what is best, even in circumstances which might make the worse appear the more profitable act. Religion presents a concrete reality to man's consciousness, while morality witnesses to a mental ideal which is the *terminus ad quem* of an infinite being. The one is, the other may be. What Christianity has to tell is embodied in a life ; the teaching of Greek philosophy is, that happiness must be sought in wisdom, but what that wisdom contains for the bettering of men it never definitely declares.

[1] Carlyle, On Heroes, p. 2.

Moral life continually projects itself towards the best conceivable ideal. Formally, it may be entirely an extension of self for the sake of self-improvement. But the religious man cannot rest content with this. The mere growth of self is not sufficient. Nay, the direction which advancement takes, and the process in which it shapes itself, are both altered with him. Perception of goodness may assuredly be accompanied by a reaching forth to something like it. This is the highest form of the moral life. But religion implies, in addition, the possession of a goodness which, in the shape of a creative principle, transforms the entire man. It is so far easy to know and to discuss a speculative ideal, and it is well to conform to such an ideal, always granted that it is capable of partial realisation. Yet all this may be done, and thoroughly done, solely with reference to the self. In this sense personal morality is largely illusory, and so remains devoid of that ideal actuality which religion demands. It leaves something to be discovered, of which religion feels itself to be in possession. Morality testifies to the consciousness of a higher life, but it does not give man his kingdom *quâ* that life. Just as idolatry is a makeshift for the satisfaction of faith, so morality is a temporary salve to religious aspiration. It connects man with a supersensible sphere, through the inner conflict of his own nature, but it can affirm nothing with regard to the reality of that sphere. The truth is, that the ideal which morality sets forth mediately on rational principles, religion reveals immediately to the soul. The apparatus of proof that points to an unattainable "is" which "ought to be," finds substitute in a positive conviction of a real "is" which "has been." Self-sacrifice takes the place of mere self-projection towards the ideal, and this means, that the ideal is no longer beyond man, hid away perhaps in some impossible region, but is in him, and is attainable only through his willingness to actualise his own undoubted inner capacity for well-doing.

There are many who cannot see that morality finds any extension in religion, or who consider it derogatory to man's dignity, that reverence should be paid to a God—known or unknowable. But on the view just stated, religion is an advance upon morality, and its aim is not primarily the glory of God. "It is not for the benefit and honour of God, but for the benefit and ennoblement of Man. . . . God has nothing to gain by our devotion, but men have very much to gain by other men's righteousness."[1] But righteousness is not the result of precept, it is consequent upon the building up of character. And character is fully formed only when, by its own inner force, it brings forth the best that *is*, and does not merely abase itself before an external "ought-to-be." Righteousness, in other words, is a religious product. The moral greatness of Socrates, of Plato, and of many Stoics of antiquity, has rarely found equal in the Christian ages. Yet, in these last, the types of holy living have added something to moral greatness. The ideal has been brought down from an abstract heaven to earth. It *is* in man's own heart. Not the assertion of self, with its proud humility, but the real sacrifice of the whole man to that which is known to be good character — this is the Christian conception. Because the ideal is in man, self-sacrifice must be recognised

[1] *Christianity in its Cradle*, F. W. Newman, p. 127. I have taken the liberty of using the customary orthography.

as the sole self-realisation. The beauty of holiness transfigures him in whom others first bear witness to its presence. Socrates gave direction to life, but Christ revealed in His own person the very principle without which there would be no life. The ancient world, in the work of Socrates and of the few who were like him, sought to reconstruct man's life on the basis of a re-interpretation of his nature; and this must always remain the work of morality. But with the appearance of Christianity, God and man were shown to be co-essential, and the task of morality was superseded, if not eliminated, by the affirmative declaration of religion. Finally, within its sphere, the Socratic teaching had not fathomed reality fully. It is in no sense unfair to say, that the Greek sage knew almost nothing of the inner force by which men, as indeed all things, "fulfil the law of their being."

But on the other hand, it would be merest childishness to deny the influence of Socrates as a forerunner of Christ. The revelation of the one was preparatory to that of the other, just as morality is frequently the seed of religion. In the development of the religious consciousness, for example, the progress towards mono-theism, so conspicuous in Socrates and the other Greek philosophers, was but one of the many lines that ultimately converged towards Christianity. No doubt, such ideas were peculiar to thinkers who regarded superstition as spiritual food fit for the mob. Yet the confidence of Socrates in a supreme being was the foundation of Plato's affirmation, that man is like to God,[1] and this, in turn, is not very far removed from Christian doctrine. The Greeks had, in short, dis-

[1] Cf. Theætetus, 176.

covered a certain element in human nature, which demanded definite satisfaction. With this they were unable to supply it. God might be "single and one" for them, yet they could not conceive how, being such, he was able to enter into relationship with the many. They adumbrated one element in the religious conception, more than that they could not grasp. But Socrates, in that he tended to replace polytheism with a species of quietist monotheism, must not be denied his place as a forerunner of fuller religious development. Whatever may be said of the varied semi-religious conceptions of Greek philosophy, there can be no question that the light thrown back upon the past now enables one to estimate Socrates' value as a herald of Christianity. Here his true greatness must be sought, and that in well-authenticated facts. For "the ideal of Christian life is far more clearly distinguishable from the ideal of Greek and Roman, than the elements of opinion and belief which have come from a Christian source are from those which have come from a secular or heathen one."[1]

Now ethically, that is, in principles of rational action, Socrates and his followers were but one remove from Christianity. The investigation of self, begun by Socrates, although it ended for him in the identity of the knowledge of virtue with virtue itself, was the groundwork of the difference between goodness and counterfeit goodness, which Plato and Aristotle afterwards formulated. For these thinkers virtue is its own reward, and their praise is, that whatever be the form of man's religion, virtue must ever remain self-satisfying. This was the great principle which, by

[1] St Paul's Epistles, Jowett, vol. ii. p. 392.

means of rational investigation, Socrates was the first to bring to light. The common measure of all the virtues is the desire of virtue, which is excited by the knowledge that virtue can be obtained. Thus, Socrates represents in practical life the preparation for Christianity, which the Hebrew prophets supplied on the more strictly religious side. He taught that to be good is good because it is good, and thereby furnished the form in which true Christian morality has always presented itself.' In this respect Socrates was a real prophet, reaching forth to an end which he could not fully see. His life, no less than his teaching, pointed at once to an ideal, and to an acknowledged human need, which he could neither reach nor supply. When he thus gifted the Greeks with a perception of moral quality, he set the seal of insufficiency alike upon their exclusive citizenship,[1] and their polytheistic religion. But he could not tell what "the good" was, and his philosophy was powerless to stay the appetite which it had created. After him ancient thought occupied itself in the attempt to fathom human nature. Ethical need, infinite then as now, was man's to increase knowledge and sorrow. Religious aspiration was also his. But for the former no full satisfaction was obtainable, for the latter none at all. The Greek protomartyr merits, and surely none would grudge him, the homage due to his consistent life and glorious death. Yet he was separated from Christ both by attainment and by distance in time. He felt the yearning that Christ came to soothe. And whatever praise may be his, it must always be remembered that the end was not then. When, through what Socrates

[1] Cf. Prolegomena to Ethics, T. H. Green, pp. 264-308.

had *not* done, "philosophy had grown sad by thinking beyond its depth," there was necessity for a greater than he.

If the mission of Socrates had been mainly ethical, that of Christ was at once moral and religious. But the religion, of which he was the chief corner-stone, cannot be defined as "morality touched by emotion." Ethical and emotional elements it doubtless had, but these do not represent its entire content. So long as man is upon this earth his lot is to struggle with sin and misery. At no period in history did the issue of the conflict seem darker than when ancient philosophy, in the person of Seneca, became helpless to stay Nero's brutality.[1] Consciously or unconsciously, the Roman Empire was crying aloud for light upon the awful problem of evil. And the light burst forth in a life which, although moral and human, had itself a magnetic influence which all have agreed to recognise as unique. This is the point which, in the estimation of the properly equipped sceptic, even nineteenth-century blasphemy cannot blaspheme away. Christ taught man how to bear sorrow, and by the sacrifice of self, to eliminate sin from life. It was not possible that the cup of suffering should pass from Him, and as He drained it, He created righteousness, thereby proving that even for us the draught is not too terrible. Now the implication of this holy life is, that the moral philosophy of Socrates had been superseded. The ideal had been made actual, and that not as an abstraction, substantive or other, to which men could only progress. It had taken personal form—that is, it had been revealed as a principle organic to life.

[1] Cf. Essays and Addresses, J. M. Wilson, p. 107.

"If any man be in Christ, he is a new creature," not because something mysterious has been done for him, but because, by his own recognition of kinship with Christ, he is assured that he too can do what the Master did. Self-sacrifice is not only the character of Christ, it is also the one key to the movement of the entire spiritual universe.

> "Stirb und werde!
>   Denn so lang du das nicht hast,
>   Bist du nur ein trüber Gast
>   Auf der dunkeln Erde."

The deepest testimony to this truth is Jesus' growing conviction of it, which only found culmination on Calvary.

Nor is this self-sacrifice a mere piece of mechanism for the manufacture of happiness. It is rather a principle of moralisation which, in its long conflict with sin and selfishness, develops new faculties in the individual character. The width of the Christian conception, including as it does all men, imposes responsibilities upon us which the Greeks, even in their finest moods, could not have imagined. For it points to no small society cinctured with a holiness wrought out of the degradation of all beyond its own circle. It constitutes the pursuit of the good by self in sacrifice a means to the bettering of all men. Christ set forth, not the doctrine alone, but its application. He did not come unawares, but brought to an end the problem of evil, then ready for solution. Moreover, he proved the practical value of his solution as a working scheme. His self-sacrifice has nothing in common with asceticism. Renunciation of self is not sought for the mere sake of renunciation, but in order that, purified of all the self-seeking which shuts out true riches, man may become the instrument at once of his own and of his fellows' perfection. If any one apprehend perfectibility, as it stands revealed in Christ, he cannot but adopt Christian ethics. For only thus will he gain for himself a completeness, which is indissolubly bound up with an identical perfection in others. As Christ was the first to proclaim that God can only be served in man, so He was the first to tell that such service will never be absolutely worthy until wrought in humanity as a whole. In this, His true humanitarianism, Christ supersedes Socrates. He appeals to the whole man and to mankind, while the Greek sage speaks only to the freeborn citizen, and to him rather as a thinker than as an essentially moral agent. For this reason, Christ's work is eternal, and whatever one may think of His nature, Christianity cannot be separated from His person.

Eliminate the *theory* of Christ which was diffused among the Jews prior to His advent;[1] admit that nothing is directly known of Him, save what is told in the discourses collected by Matthew, and in Peter's reminiscences edited by Mark—who had never seen the Master;[2] allow that the "pedantic ingenuity of rationalism" is misdirected scarce at all,—and you do not detract one whit from the value of Christ's Christianity. His "application of ideas to life" still remains the one essential and commanding fact in His career. He not only promulgated but lived a principle, against which intellect cannot revolt, and for which conscience records its whole testimony. His religion is His, not

[1] Cf. La Science des Religions, E. Burnouf, p. 242.
[2] Cf. Through Nature to Christ, E. A. Abbott, p. 346 *sq.*; 373 note.

because He formulated any creed concerning Himself, but because He alone trod the only road to man's natural perfection.   Christianity is inseparable from His person in no dogmatic sense, but as a matter of everyday experience.   We cannot look back across the ages and fortify our faltering faith with "a tremulous *quasi*-knowledge of a whole globe of dogmas."[1]   Only if the Christ-life be reproducing itself here and now, can Christianity be regarded as in vital connection with the Person of its founder.   That it is thus connected His veritable creation of righteousness proves. He did good for the sake of so doing, and this His revelation may, nay, must go on reproducing itself.

> "So, each ray of thy will,
> Every flash of thy passion and prowess, long over, shall thrill
> Thy whole people, the countless, with ardour, till they too give
>   forth
> A little cheer to their sons: who in turn, fill the South and
>   the North
> With the radiance thy seed was the germ of."[2]

Reasonableness and naturalness are the chief characteristics of Christ's revelation.   *Non mors sed voluntas sponte morientis.*[3]   Only an unrivalled knowledge of the human heart in its origin and destiny could have effected the combination of material necessity and spiritual inevitableness by which it continues to sway the world.   The complete humanity of Christ's life is the cause of the permanence of His religion.

"To say that a man has genius is to say that all he effects is truly and entirely the result of others' labours

---

[1] The Kernel and the Husk, p. 257.
[2] Saul, Robert Browning, Works, vol. vi. p. 122.
[3] St Bernard.

and done by their power; that he is merely a stimulus, and owes his influence solely to his relation to an organisation built up, and a functional power accumulated, wholly by others. . . . Genius does things without force *because it does not do them,* as the fall of an uplifted body needs no force."[1] Of all the great this is true. But in relation to Christ, it receives an application *sui generis.* Theirs is the result of others' labours, and for Him too the whole course of civilisation had been preparing. But what he effected was not brought about once for all by the co-operation of prior and contemporary influences. His genius is not a mere expression of what others thought and urgently desired; it is a living force which still remains, and reproduces its own qualities in the lives of men now. "Heroes" and "Representative Men" are the quintessence of epochs; He is the germ which fructifies at all times. In this respect He is without parallel, and so we cannot separate His *Person* from His work.[2]

Nor does the contrast between Christ and the other masters cease here. He superseded Socrates, and it might very well seem, that after so many centuries, and in view of the "service of man," His time to depart had now also come. Notwithstanding, Christ's work cannot but remain so long as human nature retains its present constitution. Expansion is not without conditions. "Because our present house is too small for us, it is not to be inferred that we shall live henceforth in the

[1] Philosophy and Religion, James Hinton, pp. 113, 114.

[2] Lessing, in Die Religion Christi, and Herder in Ideen, like Goethe and others of the anti-eighteenth century school, seem to forget that the eternity of Christianity is not based, as they suppose, on a Person who is temporal, but on their own article of faith, that persons alone can transform a momentary act into an eternal principle.

open air. As a general rule of life and conduct, we see as yet no reason to believe that *liberty*, if this be its meaning, is better than service."[1] Christ revealed the source of virtue in His life of lowly obedience. The " service of man," of which we now boast ourselves, is a bare possibility only through Christ's subservience and humiliation. It is easy to take humanity as we find it, and convenient to ignore this fact, but then it is also easy to accept light without a scrupulous recognition of the sun's agency. The peculiarity of Positivism is that, apart from its distinctive philosophical tenets, it is virtually a reproduction of one portion of Christ's principle.[2] Why go about with a candle to see the sun ? Its altruism is His also, but without the integration which He deemed necessary to complete the character of an individual. His consciousness of God —which is but the more spiritualised expression of what has been rediscovered as " cosmic religion "—had its counterpart in His consciousness of mankind, which is to-day the *raison d'être* of that second faith so called, the " religion of humanity."

The supremacy of Christ is further enhanced by the strange circumstance that His revelation is not, like the work of Socrates, of Luther, or of Carlyle, representative only of a specific stage in the world's development. Like others, He came at a crisis which was for Him. It used to be supposed that in Him divine revelation culminated, and remained final thenceforward. After a sort it did, but progress has been continuous since. " God did not retire to rest after the well-known six days of creation ; but, on the contrary,

---

[1] Prose Remains of A. H. Clough, p. 409.
[2] Cf. The Service of Man, J. C. Morison, p. 177 (head fifth).

is constantly active as on the first. It would have been for Him a poor occupation to compose this heavy world out of simple elements, and to keep it rolling in the sunbeams from year to year, if He had not had the plan of founding a nursery for a world of spirits upon this material basis. So He is now constantly active in higher natures to attract the lower ones."[1] In this later advance the Christian revelation is continually renewing itself. Historically it appeared at the time which was prepared for it. But it is not only a stage like others, for it is perpetuated in a principle which is the motive force of human nature, and must remain operative, no matter how circumstances may change. In the other masters we see all that is, in Christ there was all that ought to be. Socrates was the forerunner of later ideals, Christ Himself was the exhibition of the ideal in history. Christianity, just on account of those elements which differentiate it from Greek philosophy, constantly stimulates the higher life, and that without laying any restrictions upon intellectual activity. For Christ's work is a spontaneous revelation of human nature—of a nature which has spiritual as well as mental and material needs. His kingdom is not of this world, and only in so far as this is true can it remain in the world. It makes little difference what dogmatic views recommend themselves to the individual mind. For there is religion without rites, and there may be churches without religion. But the power of a perfect life can never pass away. It is for humanity, because in man full expression was given to it.

The eternity of Christianity is based on human nature, the kaleidoscopic creeds are but accidental

[1] Conversations of Goethe, Eckermann, pp. 569, 570.

R

embodiments of the true reality.　What boots it for practical life that Christianity is often no better to its professors than was Islam to Mrs Skewton.[1]　Presented in such shape it is indeed useless, and the sooner that science completes its destruction the better.　But the answer given in Christ's life to the timeless question of man's relation to sin and misery, continues among the eternal verities.　And so long as man is

　　" Created half to rise and half to fall,"

it must remain.　Art may to-day revive Hellenism, in so far as that is possible, and baptise its find the " Religion of Beauty."　Physical science may go back to the abstract monotheism of Palestine, and call its setting of God over against man " Agnosticism."　But the interpretation of the great truths contained in each of these movements is already beforehand with them in Christianity.　There Hellenism and Hebraism met, not under the form of a doctrinal system, but in a nature which at once realised God's transcendence, yet continual presence, in the beauty of the world and in the human spirit.

The inner life which Christ illustrated and actualised is the highest revelation to man of the universal moral order.　But no seal is thus set upon the potentiality of things.　Men are Christians, not because they accept a few dogmas which outrage both intellect and conscience, but because they perceive in the man Christ Jesus a *kind* of being which is the one permanent index of a universal human " capacity of using and modifying any existing state of things," for the furtherance of well-

[1] "There is no What's-his-name but Thingummy, and What-you-may-call-it is his prophet."

being, intellectual and social, no less than moral and religious. Man's chief atheism is sin, and if the consecrated life of Jesus be without message to those who would live sin down, then, so far as revelation has gone, atheist man is doomed to remain. But there is a message which, whether willing or unwilling, human nature cannot shut out. The modernness of Christianity lies in this—that for sin we must even now " *suffer* with Christ whether we *believe* in Him or not." [1]

/While, then, there are points of external contact between Socrates and Christ, which render comparison by no means unreasonable, it must be remembered that in inner spirit they have little in common. Above all is it necessary to avoid the radical misconception of regarding Christianity as a species of sublimated Greek philosophy. The life of Christ could only have been lived when and where it was lived. No speculative system contemplating, like Greek philosophy, an explanation of being, could have produced that sense of sin which culminated in a life of grace. Socrates was able to consider his death an inevitable sacrifice, just as Christ did. Yet he died in the full assurance that punishment had already overtaken the evil men who composed the majority of the Dicastery. For this reason, were there none other, his fate does not appeal to us with the same power as Christ's. Both had strength given them to die in a just cause. But the occasions were not identical. The calmness of Socrates and the agony of Christ are separated by constituent elements which, if subtle, are none the less obvious. The Socratic philosophy represents the bringing to birth of what was highest in Greek

[1] John Inglesant, J. H. Shorthouse, p. 259.

thought. Its founder was able to die calmly, because he was persuaded that the world-order had universality. This universality he had tried to find in the life of each man. Yet even had he known the reign of law, and of liberty, as it is now understood, his revelation would still have been imperfect. Later thinkers, persuaded of this imperfection, sought to surmount it in various ways. But the conception of the moral governance of man was not to be completed from Greek civilisation. The wise man, so called, might think about it, and describe it, but unfortunately, the wise man himself never appeared, nor could he.

Only in the matrix of Judaism, surrounded by the consciousness of an ethical God, and determined by the idea of living to this deity, could the wise man appear. The Greek ideal of a mediator between the transcendent God and the world, the Græco-Roman conception of the sage's life, and the Jewish thought of a saviour, were all requisite to, as they were realised by, the Christ. He did not protest that He was such, but, by living as He did, He solved the universal problem. In a sense, He added nothing to the *knowledge* of Greek and Jewish thinkers,—Philo had all the elements,—but he brought thought about God and morality out of the theoretical region of discussion down to the practical sphere of the God-like and moralised life. And of this change the Jewish religion was the prime cause. Socrates and Christ are both revealers of principles, which they incarnated. For each the crisis of history called. The religious intensity of Jesus was impossible to Socrates, because utterly foreign to the entire mode of thought which he expressed. Yet without it, the lesson of the ages would have been proper only to the Greek man, not to humanity.

Socrates and Christ alike had faith in the ideal, but this was different for each. The artistically rounded life of the Greek citizen, set with nicest care into the united social fabric, could not, Socrates was persuaded, be produced on the Sophistic method. His work, therefore, was to find a new way to the ideal which his age contemplated. Like the other masters, he had to " fit to the finite his infinity." But the ideal, partial even as it was, still remained ideal, and no struggle of later thought availed, save as a process of development, to bring it nearer. Yet, although in Christ the moral possibilities of human nature found realisation, Christianity is no exceptionally supernatural phenomenon. It came in the fulness of time, when the passage of thought from the phenomenal to the real, as seen in Greek philosophy, had prepared a way for it. The spiritual discipline of the Jews was the determining factor in the life of Christ, but the problem, which He died to solve, was also set in the Gentile world. Judaism saw heaven from earth, Hellenism imagined earth heaven, and both at last felt that their conceptions were illusory. Christianity brought heaven to earth, and, by inculcating, as Christ lived, that this is the place of self-sacrifice for the moralisation of humanity and of the individual,

> " Goes changing what was wrought,
> From falsehood like the truth, to truth itself." [1]

The comprehensiveness of Christianity is the evi-

---

[1] A Death in the Desert, Robert Browning, Works, vol. vii. p. 145.

dence that it is no transfigured Hellenism. Christ breathed a new spirit into the world by living for the sake of righteousness. He put the existence of an ideal life beyond possibility of question. To-day His religion is not a mere recorded fact of intellectual history, but because His work is completed and human, Christianity goes on reproducing itself as a manner of life. In its essential eternity for man it depends ultimately, neither on historical occurrences, nor on theological dogmas, but on the constitution of human nature. Knowledge of Christ must be gleaned as is knowledge of Socrates. But, seeing that Socrates was a searcher after the ultimate in man and God, and Christ a verification of the divine in the human, knowledge of Him comes with power. The perfection which is possible for man He had. His life was the answer to every cry for deliverance from the burden of sin, because in it are to be seen certain spiritual experiences which, let knowledge be what it may, are continually repeating themselves in human nature as the sole means to moral perfection. What those experiences were, Socrates did not understand. But he was among the first to awaken that consciousness of defect, which went on deepening through the ancient world, until all spiritual functions were "smothered in surmise" of superstition. The appearance of Christ was eminently natural, and in the principle of His life all that the world desired was granted. His Personality, and the possibilities of human nature which it revealed, form His indestructible contribution to moral progress. As the great *Person*, who subdued the greatest crisis in man's history, He is, and, so long as the world is governed by Reason, must remain, the type, in assimilating themselves to which other persons may rise to further self-completeness.

"The true reality that is and ought to be, is not matter, and is still less Idea, but is the living personal Spirit of God and the world of personal spirits which He has created."[1] Before Christ the conception that self-conscious personality was common to God and man alike had been but dimly foreshadowed. The Christ-life elevated it into a certain fact. Here then is Christ's inalienable contribution to human progress. His religion cannot fail of endless application; for His perfect character is the sole guarantee that every man, though knowing the evil, can be true to himself only in being holy and in following after righteousness. But this righteousness is not an external thing upon which one can lay hold or towards which one can progress. In the self-conscious sphere the category of law, as usually conceived, has little or no application. Yet it must not be supposed, on this account, that personality develops aimlessly. True, present conditions are nought save as interpreted by it: but, wanting them, the interpretation could not be. Both are essential factors in a life which is constantly revealing and actualising an immanent cause—an inner principle. Socrates was the first to observe the importance of this *causa sui.* It was Christ's to realise the absolute value of personality as such, and to show how, by a full apprehension of all that self-mediation implies, each may, nay, cannot but escape the yoke of the law, by using it as a means to his own perfecting. And this perfecting is righteousness. The good man is truly free; for, by appreciation of the transforming power of char-

---

[1] Microcosmus, Lotze, vol. ii. p. 728.

acter, he finds himself capable of subduing all circumstances to his own growth in moral stature—a growth
inseparably bound up with a like advancement in his
fellows. Christ's life and teaching embody in full that
freedom which exists only amid limitation, and issues
the more triumphant the more it is circumscribed—
freedom which, for this very reason, can be attained,
in some measure, by all who, as partakers of His humanity, are able to make weakness the perfection of
strength.

INDEX.